A Picture of Kent

A Picture of Kent

PAT DAVIS

Illustrated by
NORMA FRYER

Text © Pat Davis 1989
Illustrations © Norma Fryer 1989
First published in Great Britain 1989

Robert Hale Limited
Clerkenwell House
Clerkenwell Green
London EC1R OHT

British Library Cataloguing in Publication Data
Davis, Pat
A picture of Kent.
1. Kent. Visitors' guides
I. Title   II. Fryer, Norma
914.22′ 304858
ISBN 0-7090-3822-4

Frontispiece: *Hilltop Goudhurst is*
set amid countryside rich in church
and farm, oast and hop garden

Photoset in Baskerville by
Rowland Phototypesetting Limited, Bury St Edmunds, Suffolk
Printed in Great Britain by
St Edmundsbury Press Limited, Bury St Edmunds, Suffolk
and bound by Hunter and Foulis Limited, Edinburgh

Contents

List of Illustrations 7
Foreword 13

1 Thames-side 15
2 The Hoo Peninsula 24
3 The Medway Towns 32
4 The Medway and Its Valley 40
5 The Quarry Hills 53
6 Wantsum and Swale 62
7 The Isle of Sheppey 72
8 The Isle of Thanet 77
9 Canterbury to the Coast 86
10 Romney Marsh 106
11 The North Downs 121
12 The Weald 143
13 The Vale of Eden 166
14 Green Hills – or Sevenoaks Ridge? 177
15 The Darent Valley 193

Index 201

Illustrations

Oasthouses at Goudhurst	*frontis.*
Map of Kent	10–11
Longhorn at Stone Lodge Park Farm	16
Cement kilns, Northfleet	20
Memorial to Pocahontas, Gravesend	21
Medway barges	22
Kingsnorth Power Station	26
Cooling churchyard	29
Cooling Castle	31
Rochester Cathedral	33
Rochester Castle	34
Monument to General Gordon	38
Kit's Coty House	41
Aylesford Bridge	42
Allington Castle	44
East Farleigh	47
A Stiltman in a hop field	50
Stoneacre	55
Balloons over Leeds Castle	56
Faversham Town Pump	66
Faversham Creek	68
Whitstable Harbour	70
The Gatehouse of Minster Abbey	74
Reculver Towers	78
Bembom's Amusement Park	81
Hugin, a modern facsimile of a Viking longboat	84
Ernulf's Crypt, Canterbury Cathedral	87
Tomb of the Black Prince, Canterbury Cathedral	88
The Norman staircase, Canterbury	90
Deal Castle	96
The south door of Barfreston church	98
Russell Gardens, Dover	100

The Pharos, Dover Castle   102
Locomotive on the Romney, Hythe & Dymchurch Railway   104
Brookland church   108
Old Romney church   109
Dungeness Lighthouse   111
Tenterden   117
Chilham   128
Throwley church boasts two richly coloured Sondes tombs   130
Eastwell Park   132
Meopham windmill   137
Headcorn Manor   144
The Maids of Biddenden   146
Sissinghurst Castle   148
The Union Mill at Cranbrook   150
The Pantiles, Royal Tunbridge Wells   157
Scotney Castle   163
Haxted Mill   169
Hever Castle   171
Chiddingstone   173
Penshurst Place   175
Squerryes Court   179
Deer at Knole   185
The Great Staircase, Knole   187
Ightham Mote   190
Mereworth Castle   191
Eynsford   195
The flotsam screen at Farningham   198
The mill at Farningham   199

All illustrations by Norma Fryer.

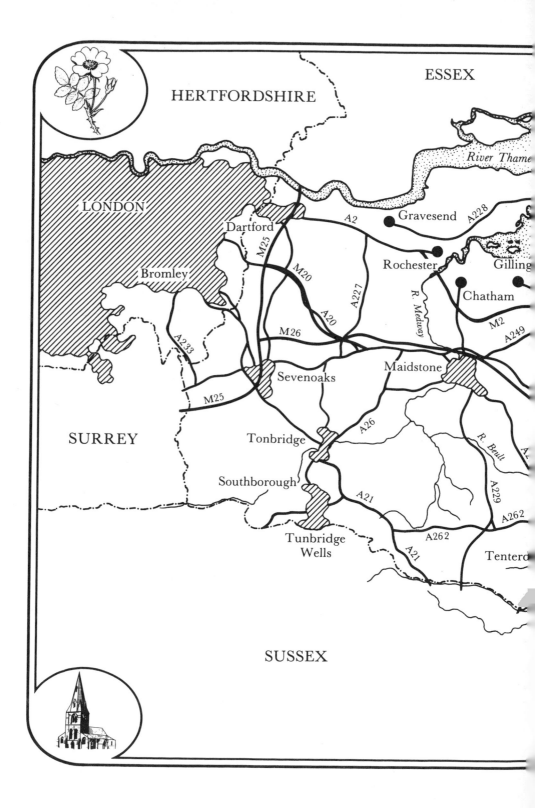

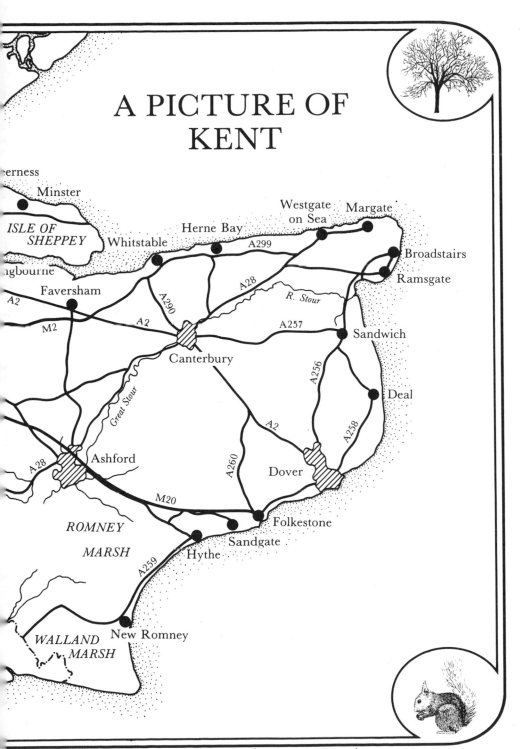

A PICTURE OF KENT

erness
Minster

*ISLE OF
SHEPPEY*
Whitstable
Herne Bay
Westgate on Sea
Margate
A299
Broadstairs
gbourne
Faversham
A28
Ramsgate
A2
A290
R. Stour
M2
A2
A257
Sandwich
Canterbury
A256
Deal
Great Stour
A258
A28
A2
Ashford
A260
Dover
M20
Folkestone
ROMNEY
Sandgate
MARSH
Hythe
A259
*WALLAND
MARSH*
New Romney

Foreword

A Picture of Kent has been a joy to write. May it be as pleasant to read.

It is no gazetteer or tourist guide or delineator of walks. Such books abound already. It is the distilled essence of Kent, and of a thirty-year-long love-affair with it. It is a sharing of those places where one man and his wife have found beauty, pleasure and interest, in the hope that others may also delight in them – and find their own special places. The only regret . . . that limitations of space have necessarily meant reluctant omissions.

This book describes people as well as places, for without them Kent would be like Marks without Spencer, strawberries without cream. Buildings and villages would lack character.

The county has been arbitrarily divided into geological areas which, on occasion, have been unblushingly overstepped for the sake of common sense and the reader's convenience. The book's route too is often a continuous one, a logical one, along highways *and* byways. Though Kentish lanes and villages are seldom respecters of strict logic . . . and worthwhile detours should never be shirked.

A book can be no hurried affair, so it is possible that during its span things have changed – especially at the hands of the 1987 hurricane, of which Kent bore the brunt.

It has known invasion and threat of invasion, from Julius Caesar to Adolf Hitler, for over 2,000 years. It has long been England's front-line.

And yet, in these days of peace, it is again under threat and Men of Kent and Kentish Men alike are fiercely up in arms. For all British Rail's side-stepping and pious pie-in-the-sky propaganda there is no doubt that its express Channel Tunnel line is going to irremediably scar some of Kent's loveliest countryside both audibly and visually.

Route 1 or 2 will shatter the peace of the North Downs (from Snodland via Hollingbourne and Charing to Ashford); Route 3 or 4, that of the Low Weald (from Borough Green via Marden and Pluckley to unenvied Ashford).

Gaunt overhead gantries will march across the Kentish countryside;

the 180 mph banshee scream of expresses will blast a mile wide swathe through its tranquillity. Not just half a dozen times each day but, by 2023, an estimated 130 times! Once every 12 minutes, day and night!

Why? So that we keep pace with the French . . . and save, not for overcrowded commuters but for the whole of Englands' Commerce, half an hour or so's travelling-time! It is a struggle that must be ceaselessly waged by *all* who love Kent, to salvage what they can of its heritage of beauty and tranquillity.

My sincere thanks are owed to:

The owners of private houses and lands who, without exception, offered me a friendly welcome.

The invaluable John Newman, to whom I'm indebted for a number of trenchant quotes. His books on East and West Kent in the Penguin 'Buildings of England' series are essential companions for all architecture 'buffs'.

Norma Fryer, for her willing co-operation and evocative illustrations.

And, of course, yet again to my wife, Patricia, who not only fuelled the inner man, walked and waited patiently throughout Kent but also deciphered, typed and typed again illegible manuscript, curbed over-exuberant spelling and punctuation, offered sound criticism . . . and unfailing encouragement.

Thames-side

London has brutally savaged Kent. It has swallowed a third of its population. From Thames-side alone, they have torn away Greenwich, and Wren's superb Royal Naval College, and Woolwich, with its memories of the launch of the 1,000-ton leviathan *Henry Grace à Dieu*, with its twenty-one huge bronze cannon, to say nothing of its modern miracle, the Thames Barrier, its four main gates each weighing 3,200 tons. And with the Thames itself, once a bustling highway to the Port of London before the dockers blindly committed *hara-kiri* and left it to the mercy of developers, now almost deserted, Thames-side might seem to have little to offer.

But even the industrial detritus of cement works and power-stations, oil storage-tanks and derelict wharves, skeletal pylons and towering chimneys has a certain fascination – that of another world in which there are still some small, half-hidden gems. Thames-side is a far cry from the beauty of Wealden orchards, but it offers another face of Kent, of a county of industry as well as of agriculture.

Dartford, just within the border, has a cheerful pedestrianized shopping centre, an excellent Carnegie museum-cum-library beside a still more excellent park ablaze with summer colour that leads to Darent and its quiet lakes, and the remains of a gunpowder mill.

The Royal Victoria & Bull is as resplendent as its title, with a black-and-white brick ground floor, a yellow-ochre upper one and tall windows cased in red brick. It bears *two* fine royal coats of arms and flaunts its name on an impressive sign bowed out over the pavement. The Bull's pillared carriageway below the upper storey leads into the coaching yard, glassed over, galleried on all four sides and bright with hanging baskets and modern murals. In pride of place, in swagger maroon, red and black livery, stands No. 7, the Dover Mail. Here, where Rotary dine now, so once did Richard III's father; Queen Victoria trod a modest measure in the Assembly Rooms; and Richard Trevithick, 'among the first inventors of the locomotive engine and of screw and paddle propulsion for steamships', died in poverty.

The cricket ground, successor to 'The Brent' on which, in 1707, Kent played Surrey in what is claimed as the first recorded county match, lies in Hesketh Gardens. As it was the gift of a total abstainer, it was inconveniently decreed that no liquor should be sold on the ground. But beer *is* served today – in that half of the pavilion which was cunningly built on private land purchased, ironically, from the Water Board. A small ground, it has given rise to mammoth scores and hurricane hitting. So much so that, when Lancashire's Clive Lloyd was at his most destructive, an ageing lady dialled 999 for police protection for her home!

Little of old Dartford remains. The priory virtually disappeared under an ironworks. But the Wat Tyler Inn, jettied, black and white, looks out still through bow windows onto the main street. A plaque in Bullace Lane reminds us that, 'Wat Tyler and the Commons of Kent came in great numbers to The Brent in 1381.' The poll tax (10 and 11 Downing Street, please note!) had incensed the common folk then as it does now. And a tax-gatherer's grossly personal investigations into his daughter's maturity led Wat to use his tiler's hammer in a very unprofessional manner. Kentish men, having demanded low rents and the end of serfdom, then 'called at this ancient tavern to quench their thirst with flagons of ale'.

A couple of miles on, in the unlikely setting of a busy main road, quarry-turned-rubbish-dump and looming chimneys, more recent history is re-enacted. Stone Lodge Park Farm is using the farming

The forerunners of this meditative Longhorn at Stone Lodge Park Farm acted as draught animals – and gave rich butter.

methods of 1887, when it was first created as a farm to the hospital still standing above it. Here, transport means horse-power. An ancient threshing-machine is worked by equally ancient steam-engine; and milking, of course, is by hand.

Animals are equally vintage, mostly disappearing breeds. Shires, 'the gentle giants', Clydesdales, even a pair of oxen are the draught animals. Wensleydales, Soay and Jacob's sheep feed in one pasture; Longhorn cattle, with horizontal horns and a 5,000-year lineage from *Bos primigenius*, and British White, introduced by the Romans and later hunted in medieval forests, graze in another. And in the sties you'll find Gloucester Old Spot losing his spots but still able to survive on orchard windfalls; and Saddlebacks, white-belted over the shoulders, massive and seraphic. Stone Lodge Park Farm has turned the agricultural clock back a century.

A mile further down the road, Stone-next-Dartford (to distinguish it from vastly different Stone-in-Oxney) springs another surprise. Just before the surely uniquely named Lads of the Village pub and British Rail's Stone Crossing halt, a lane swings to the right, to 'the Lantern of Kent': a title that makes you visualize a high-spired church on a cliff edge. Nothing of the sort. St Mary's has a lofty chancel but a squat tower, though, for all that, it was a returning sailor's welcome beacon. Nature with hawthorn, yew and elder has mercifully blotted out quarry and river banks from ground-level view.

'Lantern of Kent' is a not unfitting title for a church which has been described as 'the most architecturally magnificent in Kent' which 'should be preserved as a National monument'. Nor is it altogether surprising when you realize that the masons of Westminster Abbey in the reign of Henry III (so much better at architecture than kingship) may well have worked on it.

The delicacy of the lofty nave piers in which stone and gleaming Purbeck marble alternate are superbly accentuated by the massivity of the tower arches. In the rib-vaulted chancel are huge windows of rich colour, double arcading and spandrels filled with curling foliage. Hidden amid the latter, a single lizard nibbles succulent leaves – or is it its own tail? A symbol of immortality?

In the north aisle, three large wall-paintings: a dramatic martyrdom of Becket and, on each side, the contrasting gentleness of a young Virgin Mary giving her breast to the infant Jesus. All three are now shadowy figures long drained of their once brilliant colours, but unusual beauty still lurks in them. And in the north chapel is a hanging monument damned by Newman as: 'as uninspired as the doggerel beneath it'.

For all its beauty, St Mary's had its troubles. The main one undoubtedly was the rector who 'never came himself above once or twice in a twelve month and then only to reccon for tythe or pick quarrels'. Even the wretched curate was dismissed – and restored only when the good people of Stone petitioned Parliament itself. Shortly after, the church was damaged by a fire so fierce that it melted the bells. And it must, much later, have watched horrified when in Long Reach, fifty-three of the fifty-eight passengers in a tilt-boat were drowned due to the 'desperate obstinacy and rudeness' of a helmsman who turned deaf ears to his anxious passengers' warning of a fast-approaching storm.

Greenhithe, the real Greenhithe, 'at the XVIII milestone from London', lies peacefully at Thames-side, away from ever-spreading housing estates. In the eighteenth century, its wharves, boat-yards and slipways prospered noisily. Today, glimpsed through breaks in the high walls and fences that line its narrow riverside street, they look derelict and deserted. The clamour and clangour of men at work are spasmodic; the one small wharfside coaster, *Activity*, sadly belies its name. And yet among Georgian and twentieth-century cottages the old signs are still there: 'Ships Provisioned', 'Wharf and Repair Yard', while 'Ships Electronic Services' promises a shift to 'hi-tech'.

Tucked away beyond the Pier Hotel and Ingress Priory lies a tiny promenade: ideal for picnicking. On a grassy belvedere behind that, the Merchant Navy College, now more for computers than compasses, looks down onto a nearly shipless Thames. Its once familiar training-ship, the tall *Worcester*, really a peaceful merchantman behind its black-and-white war-paint, has gone to the breakers. And Ingress Abbey, built from the masonry of Old London Bridge, has had its rich panelling vandalized too.

Back on the A226, the Thames seems to loom dangerously straight ahead. Its Essex bank is forested with cranes. Swanscombe, cement-coated, lying between mess, marsh and quarry, is an unlovely place. But, for all that, its church, with part-Saxon tower, proves Swanscombe is no modern industrial wart. It has also a fine Jacobean tomb in coloured alabaster: of Sir Antony Weldon, James I's Clerk of the Kitchen. No serenity in death here. He looks perturbed. Is it caused by his pawkily punning epitaph: 'He hath well don – and so made good his name' or by memory of his ill-timed witticisms about Scotland that brought about his dismissal by an unappreciative Scots monarch?

Far more genuine is genuine Swanscombe Man – answer to fake Piltdown Man. Parts of his skull, together with the bones of woolly mammoth and rhino, were found, over a period of twenty years' active search, in a chalk quarry near Galley Hill. And proved to be some 200,000 years old.

Northfleet, equally cement-ridden, holds more tangible interest. Admittedly Rosherville Gardens, a nineteenth-century Margate, have disappeared. As today's Covent Garden finances show, culture seldom pays its way. A 'choragic temple' and 'terpsichorean lawns' were soon ousted by the hearty vulgarity of music hall, menagerie and bear-garden – money-spinners all. Tightrope-walker Blondin himself brought hearts into mouths as he swayed high across the quarry.

Northfleet's real interest, however, lies in St Botolph's. Partly in its rood screen and Kentish tracery. Partly in the recent tombstone of Emma Honeycombe whose hundred years have not spared it Youth's disrespectful spray-can daubing. Partly, a big partly this, in its tower: stone steps climb steeply high up one side, huge stepped buttresses support the other, to give it a splendid massivity.

But interest is largely in its site. Only a few yards behind the tower but a hundred feet and more below – a vast amphitheatre. Its chalk has long since turned cement. Its sheer white walls are green-splashed with creepers. Trees, like a rippling sea, fill its floor. And, to add scale to the scene, from time to time a pygmy locomotive hauling pygmy wagons tunnels through the far cliff face, clanks across the quarry and dis-appears amongst the trees as abruptly as it entered. A gently bouncing footbridge gives a spectacular bird's-eye view (as well as a Blondin-like sensation) as you cross the yawning gulf below.

Such scale does something to prepare you for the shock of Associated Portland Cement, the largest cement plant in Europe, possibly in the world and certainly in my limited acquaintance! As a gentle prelude, a mile-long drive circles back Thameswards through parkland, through two tunnels cut in towering chalk cliffs ('Use Headlights – Beware Pedestrians!') and finally into yet another vast disused quarry. One filled with towers, silos and sloping galleries, aerial conveyor-belts, pipe-lines and chimneys. All coated with a ghostly cement dust. A grey scene from a grey limbo.

The chimneys have metal rungs, neatly spaced up their 300-foot height. It is a means of ascent that makes any respectable stomach turn but one which each year was taken in his stride, or step, by a sixty-plus-year-old inspector. Up, up, up, hand and foot he climbed. Only the rungs immediately above him and below him for support. Steadily, without loss of breath, pinned like a fly to the chimney's very verticality, he climbed to the top and, with all Thames-side below him, first settled down comfortably for a smoke!

Such a giant grew from small beginnings. A century ago a thousand oddly shaped bottle-kilns dotted the banks of the Thames and Medway estuaries. In them, in a ratio of 3:1, Kent's limitless chalk was burned with alluvial clay to make cement. The oldest of them (1846) still stands

Thousands of these bottle-shaped kilns once made half England's cement on the banks of Thames and Medway. These are at Northfleet.

close to the six huge coal-fired kilns which today turn out 2 million tonnes of Blue Circle Portland Cement each year: 'Portland' because it has a resemblance to Portland stone. Nevertheless, Kent still has chalk enough, but clay – as slurry – has to be pumped from Essex under the Thames.

Enough of cement. Gravesend ahead offers a Thames ringside seat, the romance of the river, of 'Chinese' Gordon and of the American-Indian Princess Pocahontas. The latter successfully pleaded with her tribe for the life of an English adventurer, John Smith. But, duped with a fictitious story of the latter's death, she married the Secretary of the Recorder of newly founded Virginia. With him she returned to London in 1616 – to be fêted even at James I's Court. The English climate was much less kind. Pocahontas was forced to flee it for the sunshine of her own land. But, mortally ill, she had to be landed at Gravesend and, only twenty-two years old, died there.

Today, in the shadow of St George's heavily quoined brick tower, paid for, oddly, by a tax on coal, is her statue. She rests in Kent – but beneath the soil of Virginia. It was specially shipped across the Atlantic so that she might feel at home. On a nearby plaque, Falling Sky, Two Eagles and Little Bird on the Shoulder give the thanks of the Cherokee nation to that which 'graciously received her and treated her with great honour'.

In Riverside Gardens stands another statue, that of a bare-headed man, visionary as much as soldier. It bears only a single word: Gordon.

Soil from Virginia was brought to Gravesend so that a Cherokee princess might sleep beneath it more contentedly.

Medway barges with their huge russet sails were long the workhorses of both Thames and Medway.

No fulsome praise is lavished on the man who built nearby New Tavern Fort which effectively crossed fire with Tilbury to guard London; who spent much of his spare time and his money on his 'kings', the ragged Gravesend urchins whom he fed, clothed and taught; and who, in 1885, was to die at Khartoum at the hands of the Mahdi and his fanatical Dervishes.

Outside nearby Alexander Towing Company's new offices stands a splendid, swirling Poseidon of gun-metal and bronze. A cable's length down-river are moored *Sun Kent* and *Indomitable* and half-a-dozen other snub-nosed tugs, pocket-goliaths with big funnel, bigger heart and the ability to generate 3,500 hp. Seldom now are they needed to nudge and cajole, to pull and push big ships up-river to London Docks where dockers and lightermen so out-priced and over-restricted themselves as to make it cheaper to unload cargoes at modern Rotterdam and reship them in small craft to London.

Radar scans the river from the neighbouring Port of London Authority Headquarters that carries out river surveillance as far as Teddington. Royal Pier is a pilots' pier; Town Pier is closed. But you can still get a whiff of the sea on the Tilbury ferry. Its fare for the brief crossing is, *pro rata*, greater than the *QE2*'s! It is an act of desperation to try to end an uneconomic life sustained only by Act of Parliament.

All this and a twenty-mile stretch of the Thames can be viewed from the top of Windmill Hill – in company with, a helpful 'bobby' told us, CBS fanatics and courting couples who find its grassy summit equally well suited to their differing activities.

And so from the industrial wasteland of Thames-side, meanly hedging a splendid river, to Dickens' Land. The village of Chalk is incontrovertibly where Dickens honeymooned. And three different houses, with Manor House as the hot favourite, will lay claim to the honour of having housed a Dickens torn between completing the third instalment of *Pickwick* and enjoying his young wife. It is equally certain that Chalk church, isolated down a quiet side-lane, was where Dickens invariably paused to pay his respects to 'a comical old monk . . . carved in stone, cross-legged, with a jovial pot'.

A right turn from the main road will take you to an ever-growing Shorne and its churchyard. Dickens loved walking there; to him it was 'reading, writing, 'rithmetic – snuff, tobacker and sleep'. In its peace, 'where wild flowers mingle with the grass', he loved to pause for a while. And here his family would have buried him had not his fame decreed the overcrowded stone of Westminster Abbey.

A mile on, and there, glimpsed through trees, unmistakably, is Gads Hill Place – the house Dickens coveted as a boy and bought as a man. An 'old-fashioned, cheerful and comfortable' red-brick house with bold white bay windows on each side of a white portico; and, above a white frieze, a parapet half-hiding a mansard roof and wide dormers; and a delicate white cupola. It was originally built for an illiterate inn-ostler who nevertheless had learning enough to marry the landlord's widow. Still in use, as a kindergarten playground, is Dickens' bowling-green with 'hog-holes' in the surrounding low walls, perhaps to allow his dogs easy access. Still there too is a wooden cross commemorating a linnet: 'Dick, Best of Birds. Born at Broadstairs 1851. Died Gads Hill 1866.'

Beyond the house is a black-and-white pub dedicated to Shakespeare's Sir John Falstaff, who tried his hand as highwayman here on the Dover Road. Below it lie the Medway towns – and, to the north-east, the Hoo Peninsula.

2

The Hoo Peninsula

Few books on Kent give the Hoo Peninsula even a one-star rating. For them it is a dead-end to be escaped from as soon as decently possible. Its villages are down-to-earth, workaday places that have none of the charm of those of the Weald, which are tree-surrounded, rich in red tile and time-aged timbers. And their ancient tendency to sprawl is accentuated by the steady accretion of new and uninspired housing estates.

Its countryside is flat, a serious place where agriculture is taken seriously. Hedges are few, and trees are welcomed almost as long-lost friends. Even the magnet of technological marvels at BP's vast Isle of Grain refinery is no more. A million-pound appraisal of its viability gave it the thumbs down.

For all that, the Hoo Peninsula is different, refreshingly different. The old sneer that 'it leads nowhere' is a backhanded compliment, for there is therefore no need to speed unseeingly through a green landscape, one where a rise of a hundred feet or so is a miniature Everest rich in sweeping views; where green fields roll down to marsh and water. And surely no area bounded by the widening estuaries of great rivers such as Thames and Medway is one to be ignored.

That it is a land of power-stations and pylons as well as refineries is not damning evidence in the case against the Hundred of Hoo. There is something monolithic about them; they are the castles which, with the exception of Cooling, the peninsula lacks. They give point and scale to a flat landscape; they outdo Rochester and Dover in sheer bulk and power, if not in texture and profile. They spawn pylons. And pylons are not to everybody's taste. But they march with power and determination in double lines lending verticality to a horizontal landscape. And their distant cables are a giant spider's web.

For me the Hoo Peninsula is one of space. A place where the eye can roam at ease, without clutter of buildings, to horizons bounded by the glint of water, to great rivers growing greater as they wind seawards to complete their cycle. A place of solitude and quietness and towering skyscapes. A place where, expecting little, surprises are all the more pleasant.

Three Hoos in the one peninsula are confusing. Nearly as confusing as its roads that, doubling back on themselves, give a sense of 'I have been here before.'

Even the approach is tortuous. First you must cross the Rubicon of Rochester's hoop-arched bridge. Then thread your way through the narrow, bustling streets of the anonymity that is Strood. Fight your way out of Frindsbury, and then, before meeting Hoo St Werburgh, detour down to Upnor.

There is a lot to be said for this little village nestling under wooded slopes on Medway's banks opposite Chatham Dockyard. The latter was Upnor's *raison d'être*, for its now tree-shaded castle, dabbling its feet in the river behind a timber palisade, was Elizabeth I's belated and parsimonious deterrent. Its stone came from decaying Rochester Castle, its timber from Sir Thomas Wyatt's sequestered Allington Castle.

The fact that you will see there cannons from sunken English ships and cannon balls from Dutch guns says much of its later history. In 1667 de Ruyter, not holding to the popular Dutch belief that 'Holme's Bonfire' (the burning of almost the whole Dutch East Indies fleet at Vlie) had been divinely expiated by the Great Fire of London, added his broadside. With spectacular effrontery, he sailed up the Medway, unshackled the recently renewed fourteen-ton chain-boom, found little menace in Upnor's ill-sited and ill-supplied guns and wrought unprecedented havoc on the English fleet. Three English 'first rates' were vainly scuttled as block-ships. The *Royal Oak* was sunk, its captain, a Douglas, bravely if misguidedly going down with it in accord with family tradition. Cruellest blow of all, the *Royal Charles*, complacently left undermanned, was captured by a mere nine men and, '. . . heeling her on one side to make her draw less water, was carried away safe at a time, both for tide and wind, when the best pilot in Chatham would not have undertaken it'.

Hoo St Werburgh has an impressive ring. So too does its self-styled title of 'the Capital of the Hundred of Hoo'. But apart from a cluster of Dickensian cottages, the church's tall, shingled spire, once a welcomed landmark, and the rough-hewn nave roof, it has little to offer the tourist.

Kingsnorth power-station is vast. A latter-day ziggurat, an exporter of power and light. Despite all its architect's endeavours, by choice of colour and materials, to blend it into the landscape, and by its pygmy tree-scaping, its brown-and-white lower storey and its towering grey-and-white superstructure are as obtrusive as an elephant on your front lawn. Less obvious, almost welcome in a nearly treeless setting, are

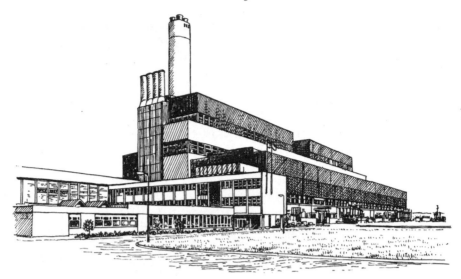

A modern ziggurat: Kingsnorth Power Station spews out its gases 600 feet above the Hoo Peninsula and Medway Estuary.

its pylons, massed like eager marathon-runners before they set off cross-county to carry power to Canterbury, Northfleet and Tilbury. Kingsnorth power also feeds the Supergrid, plunges underground to supply the Medway towns and finds its way unobtrusively to France via a 2 million kw cross-Channel cable line (which cost £600 million) from Folkestone to Sangatte.

Above all is the towering 'obelisk' of its single multi-flue chimney spewing out its gases over 600 feet above vulnerable Kentish lungs. Only skilful piling by a 2,000-strong workforce prevented Kingsnorth power-station's sinking into the reclaimed marshland of Damhead Fleet on the Medway's north bank.

And it is Medway's water that plays a large part in its success. 50,000 gallons of it are used each hour to cool the turbine condensers, so obviating need for unsightly cooling-towers. Boiler feed-water is another matter. Medway can lay no claim to it. Only town mains water is good enough, and that only after being de-ionized, de-mineralized, scrubbed, de-gassed and filtered several times . . .

Surprisingly, in such an environment, wildlife has thrived so well that the two ash lagoons and Oakham Island have been turned into a reserve for mallard, teal, widgeon and shelduck. These are joined in autumn and winter by dumpy, eager-feeding dunlin, handsome black-ringed plover, redshank whose harsh 'tenk! tenk!' of alarm has earned them a 'watchdog of the marshes' title, even the rarer, elegant green-shank and the boldly pied, gregarious oyster-catcher who find ideal building-sites among the Norfolk reeds.

Across the bleak saltings below the Stokes, Medway is seen at its widest; so too are Queenborough, Sheerness, Sheppey, even the hazy crest of the more distant North Downs.

The nag of black-and-white Nag's Head at Lower Stoke is rather a sorry-looking beast. But it is said that Hogarth and four roistering companions spent a night here before they were driven to Sheppey by damp beds and bloodthirsty gnats.

The very remoteness of the Isle of Grain, 'the dreary tip of a dreary peninsula', must have encouraged BP to open a huge oil-refinery of myriad gleaming storage-tanks, stacks and towers there in 1920. Its employees doubtless found solace in the neatly punning Cat & Cracker pub rather than in the tiny church. Today much of the refinery has been levelled to the ground – only for British Gas tanks to rise in their place.

In the early 1970s CEGB followed BP's lead. Grain power-station resulted. Another monolithic monster with a towering chimney squats over 143 otherwise unproductive acres to produce power enough for three cities the size of Birmingham, Liverpool and Manchester. Possibly the largest oil-fired power-station in the world!

Even Grain has had its moments of high life. At its jetty, the *Victoria and Albert* tied up alongside, conveniently to land or collect Queen Victoria on her royal journeyings. And it was there at Port Victoria, as the jetty was grandiloquently named, that Kaiser Wilhelm, *en route* to George V's coronation, stepped ashore onto a red carpet. Even a Royal Corinthian Yacht Club was founded there in an endeavour to take some of the wind out of Cowes' sails. And in 1912 it became a marine aircraft experimental base – a latter-day Farnborough.

To the north-west of Yantlet Creek, amid cornfields, lies All Hallows. From a rib of 'high' land (on Hoo the word is comparative), its church, with yews flanking its entrance, embattled aisles and a shingled cupola surmounted by a vainglorious and verdigrised weather-cock, looks down to the Thames estuary.

But All Hallows' real if transitory claim to fame is a mile north. Here, after 1930s Southern Railway ballyhoo, a new, nearer-to-London seaside, or rather riverside, resort was planned. Sea-wall, groynes and shingly sand are all there. So too is a view across the Thames' choppy waters to Canvey Island and Southend's tower-blocked coastline, a view to which distance does lend a certain enchantment. As at Port Victoria and the BP refinery, the boom did not last. But even today the comfortable British Pilot doubtless does a brisk summer trade with the occupants of the hundreds of neat, wooden chalets, well-spaced and flowerbed-surrounded, on Thames' grassy slopes, as well as with those of the nearby caravan site, no fly-by-night affair but solid and well-ordered.

The Hoo peninsula, it is said, once had more than its fair share of windmills – and gallows. All Hallows too boasts an unfair share – of summer sunshine, though wisely it makes no boast of bitter winter north-easters, the 'boneless wind' that cuts right through you.

Back south, towards civilization, the farms and houses of St Mary's Hoo are scattered like a handful of gravel. Even here, a mile inland, you can see not only two great power-stations but also the mingling of two great rivers, Medway and Thames. Its church, lonely save for a nearby farm, warrants few words, one of its eighteenth-century rectors rather more, for it was he who secretly 'married' the lovely (but Catholic) Mrs Fitzherbert and the Prince of Wales, before he hurriedly retired to the welcome anonymity of St Mary's . . . and death.

Further west and south, perched 150 feet up and almost in the centre of Hoo, High Halstow also has splendid views. Brick-buttressed and impressive, St Margaret's has as close neighbour the Red Dog Inn crouching beside it. The latter's roof is appropriately red-tiled with bow windows beneath. Opposite them is a postage-stamp village green on which the local WI raised an attractive wrought-iron sign to celebrate its twenty-fifth anniversary. It incorporates a heron – a tribute to the RSPB's nearby Northwood Hill Nature Reserve which boasts one of the largest heronries in Europe. From it can be heard the harsh 'krarnk! krarnk!' as herons fly marshwards, long yellow legs stretched behind tail, black-striped neck hunched back on shoulders.

New houses block the once splendid view through the lich-gate. But take a few steps down The Street, and there is a chequerboard of fields, yellow, brown and green, laced with a double row of striding pylons, as well as a hump-backed bridge and road stretching south towards welcome woods.

The road, 'one deep and miry', from Halstow to Cooling is a happy surprise in country so flat: a neat switchback that turns snake. Cooling itself has been succinctly damned as 'negligible' but St James's stands splendidly aloof in its spacious churchyard behind a screen of tall sycamores. Its fourteenth-century ragstone tower, characteristically and distinctively banded at the bottom with black flints, has a small slated spirelet within its parapet. Inside are an unusual thirteenth-century font and a tiny 'vestry' – decorated with thousands of little cockleshells, the symbol of a pilgrim to the shrine of Spain's famous St James of Compostela.

In winter, marsh mists give it that eerie atmosphere that Dickens (and David Lean) painted when, in *Great Expectations*, suddenly and

*Cooling churchyard may well have been where 'there loomed up a fearful man' to terrify Pip
in Dickens'* Great Expectations.

terrifyingly there loomed up '. . . a fearful man, all in coarse grey, with a great iron on his leg. A man who had been soaked in water, and smothered in mud, and lamed by stones, and cut by flints, and torn by briars, who limped and shivered, and glared and growled . . .'.

And, sadly, between sturdy church porch and pompous, plinthed chest-tomb lie Pip's 'little brothers' who '. . . gave up trying to get a living exceedingly early in that universal struggle'. The narrow, lozenge-shaped stones above them made him believe that, '. . . they had all been born on their backs with their hands in their pockets'. In reality you see not the fictional five small graves but a horrifying thirteen! A silent accusation of eighteenth-century man's insensitivity and medicine's insufficiency. To the west of the solitary tombstone that separates them lie three Baker children. They died at one, three and five *months* of age. To the east are the ten Comports, none of whom survived beyond seventeen months.

More cheerful but no less memorable and only a stone's-throw away, opposite the lane leading to chequered Cooling Court with its pond and willows, is Cooling Castle. In 1381 the French insolently sailed past Cooling to rape and ravage riverside villages as far upstream as Gravesend, to threaten London itself. Sir John de Cobham, patriotic and personally affronted, smartly slammed the stable door almost before the last French sail had swept down Channel, and stoutly fortified his manor.

The castle itself is still a romantic joy. Its squat gateway, almost top-heavy with massive rings of machicolations and battlements, is as forbidding now as four centuries ago. And yet behind it, and behind towering copper beech and flowering chestnut, a private house sits cheerfully secure and snug! For the rest, it is a joyous maze of dry moat and water-filled moat, of gate and drawbridge, of tall and jagged grey walls, turreted, highlighted with willow and lilac and a cascading froth of white flowers, enclosing smooth lawns and – of all things – a palm tree! As if all that were not enough, a huge brick and black-timbered barn lies between yet more moat and shattered walls. High on its tower, a plaque still proclaims:

> Knouwyth that beth and schul be
> That I am mad in help of the cuntre
> In knowyng of whyche thyng
> Thys is chartre and wytnessyng.

Almost reluctantly one heads for Cliffe. For worked-out quarries to the west, a main street of flaking weather-board and a decidedly 'We are not amused' Queen Victoria inn sign. But also for a lavish Early

Cooling Castle: a romantic picture-book castle that has escaped the over-zealous hand of the Department of the Environment.

English church, dedicated to St Helen (a reputed barmaid), with embattled porch, striking banding of knapped flints and a splendid interior. From its unkempt graveyard (where a tiny grave had, and needed, no other mark than the rich colours of massed pansies) are wide views across marshes to the Thames.

Thence south, through sparsely populated countryside to the Medway towns.

3

The Medway Towns

It is difficult to wax lyrical about the Medway towns as a whole: a still-growing octopus of largely drab urbanization, one in which it is almost as hard to define boundaries as character, to find gems as to avoid the commonplace. But gems – and history – there undoubtedly are.

Frindsbury's church is superbly sited on a bluff, man-made in quest for chalk. From it, there is a wide view across the Medway that includes Rochester's squat cathedral and its gaunt castle.

Neighbouring Strood's citizens were reputed to have been cursed with tails – for being rude to Thomas à Becket. Little sign of that today or, lost amid a desert of housing and industry, of the Knights Templars' manor house. But, flint patched with brick, the great hall over a vaulted undercroft has been saved from dereliction and sensitively restored by English Heritage.

And so across as ugly a latticed iron bridge as you will find, to the contrasting beauty of Rochester. Yes, beauty, for Rochester has too long played the poor relation to Canterbury. Second oldest see in England, it has 2,000 years of history in its bones; a widening Medway at its feet; a unique pairing of castle and cathedral; that monstrous bridge – redeemed by an intriguing history; buildings of charm and character, and everywhere the haunting touch of Charles Dickens.

Admittedly, its cathedral, short and stubby, lacks Canterbury's soaring grace – and that despite, the all-unwitting 'effort', in 1201, of a charitable and pious Scottish baker, William of Perth. Murdered nearby, his mutilated body gave rise to miracles – and sanctification. The flow of pilgrims and their alms down Watling Street to Canterbury and Becket's shrine was slowed – and Rochester's half-empty coffers were replenished.

Of it, Dickens wrote: 'It's like looking down the throat of Old Time.' And indeed it is said that from the Lady Chapel virtually every period of English architecture from the eleventh to the twentieth century can be seen. 'Dingy', 'cramped', 'small', 'lacking texture' are some of the

It's well worth the effort to climb Rochester Castle's 125-foot turrets for this spectacular view of the cathedral.

epithets heaped on it, but it does have superb Norman pillars, each pair different; a marble effigy of Dean Hole who grew 130 different varieties of roses; a finely carved fourteenth-century chapter house door; a roomy crypt, part Norman; an intriguing Wheel of Fortune wall-painting, part Early English, of striking simplicity; and an elaborate Romanesque west front that looks condescendingly down on a mere hundred-year-old catalpa tree, bright with its huge, vividly green leaves and almost lying on its side. All this, and more, arose from the ruins of the tiny Saxon cathedral left 'utterly miserable, forsaken and waste' by the Danes.

The castle keep, second only in majesty to the Tower of London, is slightly taller, at a towering 125 feet. So dizzy a height that even Mr Pepys's amorous advances to 'three young maids' were curbed. Mr Jingle with deft strokes painted an impressionist picture: 'Ah, fine place

'Ah, fine place – glorious pile – frowning walls – tottering arches – dark nooks – crumbling staircases' was how Mr Jingle saw Rochester Castle.

– glorious pile – frowning walls – tottering arches – dark nooks – crumbling staircases.' English Heritage has altered enough of that to make the long haul to the top less precarious than the one 'that did fright me mightily' (Pepys again!).

Rochester Bridge today, all lattice girders, rumbling trains and impatient traffic, makes a poor third to span the Medway. But its forerunners' history still shines through. The Roman bridge of masonry survived until AD 960 and was replaced by the Anglo-Saxons with a timber affair. Battered by floods, burned by Simon de Montfort's tallow- and timber-filled fireships in 1264, overburdened by marching troops, it was by 1382 'to be in such ruin as to be impossible'. Founded on 10,000 twenty-foot-long, iron-shod elm poles, designed by Henry Yevele himself, and endowed by Sir John de Cobham and Sir Robert de Knolles, rose a fine stone bridge that was to last 500 years – and even then put up a sturdy resistance to Royal Engineers' dynamite as they prepared the way for a new one, cast-iron and unlovely, to cope with increased road and river traffic and the coming of the 'iron horse'.

In its shadow is the original Bridge Chapel restored after centuries-long deterioration as store-room, ginger-beer and apple shop and roofless ruin. Upstream, beyond long lines of moored sailing craft, a new M2 bridge, of cantilevered, pre-stressed concrete, with a 145-foot main span airily bestrides the Medway.

The pedestrianized High Street and Eastgate, flavoured by Dickensian shops – Mr Tope's Restaurant, Fagin's Alley, Dodgers and even the delightfully alliterative Baggins Bargain Bookshop – put on a dazzling show. The Guildhall is magnificently surmounted by a gleaming, five-foot, fully rigged ship weather-vane. The Corn Exchange, with its jaunty bracketed clock, was built at the expense of orphan and powder-monkey-to-admiral Cloudesley Shovel; Eastgate House is all gabled and turreted red-brick flamboyance; behind it stands Dickens' famous chalet-workroom with heavily carved barge-boards and balcony. It was a gift of admiration from the actor Fechter and came to Gads Hill as a giant jigsaw puzzle of ninety-eight pieces packed in fifty-eight boxes.

Opposite it are the three dignified, gabled black-and-white houses with oriel windows in one of which lived Uncle Pumblechook . . . or was it Mr Sapsea? Three much more demure gables are those of Watts Charity, founded in 1579 for 'Six Poor Travellers who not being Rogues, or Proctors, may Receive Gratis for one Night, Lodging, Entertainment and Fourpence each'.

The once-galleried coaching inn, the Bull, Dickens' Blue Boar, has a 400-year-long history of hospitality. It became grandiloquent Royal Victoria & Bull when the young Princess lodged there overnight after being warned that the gale howling across Rochester Bridge might blow her, as well as her horses and coach, into the Medway.

There are, too, the Monks Vineyard, a deep-sunk memorial rose garden, Minor Canon Row and a row of staid old brick houses. Behind one of the latter's skewed doorways lived actress Sybil Thorndyke and her author brother Russell, and behind another, Dickens' Reverend Septimus Crispsparkle and six little Crispsparkles. But there is no trace now of the cherry orchard where Sam Pepys – as ever – found time for dalliance and a snatched kiss, despite the threatened Dutch invasion.

Merging Chatham, contrary to popular belief, is not *all* barracks and battleships. It has a proud and impressively towered town hall, which contains the commandant's sedan-chair and a mayoral chain containing glass once worn by a confrère – the Doge of Venice! Off the High Street is Sir John Hawkins Hospital, red-brick almshouses round a quadrangle, for, oh unhappy phrase, 'decayed mariners'. Surely an out-of-character penance for that smooth-spoken young seaman? He broke into Spain's monopoly of the rich slave trade by innovative and ruthless pillaging of the Guinea coast after he found that the natives of Central America ungratefully died when taken into the grinding, slow death of slavery.

Nearby, Army and Navy get together. The former to protect the latter in the Georgian fortress of Fort Amherst, fourteen acres of brick revetments and casemates, ditches and bastions, embankments, gun-emplacements and barracks. In the latter lived Wellington's 'scum of the earth'. And below ground is a mile-long labyrinth of brick-and-chalk tunnels and caves, bored through the North Downs by POW slave labour from Medway's infamous prison hulks.

Below the fort entrance, Kitchener, on horseback and for once a little ill at ease, gazes at St Mary's ornate tower. It too is redundant but, like many another church, is making a very good fist of its new role as a Heritage Centre, recalling Medway's fascinating story.

Dockyard Gate, massively towered and proudly carrying huge royal arms in coloured relief above the low central arch, is only a five-minute stroll up the road. But the docks beyond it are also out of a job: brutally axed by the Admiralty in 1984. Now, like so much of Britain's industrial heritage, it is in transition from bustling dockyard to museum and executive housing, a living museum of functional, clean-cut Georgian architecture. A time-jump from Elizabeth I to Elizabeth II; from the building in 1586 of the fifty-six-ton pinnace *Sunne*, carrying five guns against the Armada, to the launching in 1966 of the submarine *Okanagan* for the Royal Canadian Navy – and the 400 ships between.

On the dock slipways lie HM Submarine *XE8* – a mere thirty tons but it hounded *Tirpitz*, marked Juno beach on D-Day and cut the Saigon–

Singapore undersea cable; *CMB103*, a 37-knot drop-it-and-run mine-layer; and HMS *Gannet*, with two layers of teak on an iron frame and a horizontal compound steam-engine, epitomizing the 'high tech' of her day. All to be given new life!

Victory too was built here. Into it went 2,500 oak trees, twenty miles of rope, four acres of sail. And on the floor of the mould loft the marks that decreed her shape when she was first 'laid off' can still be seen.

Though Mr Pickwick and Tracy Tupman found more than enough excitement when they became embroiled there with manoeuvres – and a testy colonel, Chatham Great Lines, for all their Sally Port and King's Bastion, may sound dull. Far from it! For, magnificently sited on the hilltop, with the Medway and its towns spread wide at its feet, there stands the Royal Naval War Memorial – impressive and moving. Curving white walls surround it: outside, aglow with pyracantha; inside, deep etched in endless rows with the names of the thousands who died at Dunkirk, Crete, the Solomons . . . on suicidal convoys to Russia and to Malta . . . In the centre, amid lawns and roses, stands a towering column flanked by four austere lions. Below is a sweeping view from the broad silver ribbon of the Medway to the green haze of Hoo peninsula.

In nearby Brompton, the Army, not to be outshone, has its Ravelin Building, splendidly towered and turreted, in brick and Portland stone. Today it houses the skilfully displayed story of the Royal Engineers. It ranges worldwide from Bishop Gundulf, King's Engineer and architect of London's White Tower and Rochester's curtain wall, to Irish-Australian Louis Brennan's late nineteenth-century land-to-sea guided missile and mono-rail car; and from a sapper commando raid which brought back a heavy-water cell from Rjukan (Norway) to desert-raider Glubb Pasha's gleaming medals and orders. Gordon, of course, shares pride of place with Kitchener, the sapper who avenged his fellow-sapper's murder in Khartoum.

Near neighbour is the Royal Engineers' School of Military Engineering. It boasts a fine trio of monuments to the east of the vast tree-lined parade-ground. The triple-arched Crimea Gate bears impressive battle honours. Behind it, a tiny plaque recalls 'Snob', 11th Company Royal Sappers & Miners canine mascot. 'Annexed' at Sevastopol, he served in India, retired to Brompton and was buried nearby. Today, thanks to the taxidermist's skill, he lives on in the museum.

A towering obelisk remembers the dead of two World Wars. On the Boer War Triumphal Arch are plaques depicting the sappers' work: pontoon bridges, fortified blockhouses, rebuilt railway lines . . . Close to it, Gordon, stern and unbending, one hand on the reins, one on his

General 'Chinese' Gordon sits aloof on his richly caparisoned camel but Gravesend's ragged urchins, 'his kings', were very much his concern.

goad, rides side-saddle on a gorgeously tasselled and caparisoned camel.

Up on the A2, the glaring yellow brick and staring eyes of the New and Latter House of Israel's half-finished Jezreel's Tower, nineteenth century's religious fanaticism's stepping-stone to Heaven in down-to-earth Gillingham, has gone the way of many such idiosyncratic follies. Further east, amid spring daffodils and crocuses, a modest clock-tower (1934) celebrates Will Adams, Richard Clavell's 'Shogun', a Gillingham man who, by breaching Japan's centuries long barrier of secrecy, changed world history.

Rainham and Wigmore's vast new estates round off the Medway towns in a flurry of curiosities. European Award supermarket; ice-rink; Bowater paper-works with a sky-blue balloon of a water-tower; punning Long Hop inn; Rainham's St Margaret's, with battlements and turrets towering up like a modern Gulliver; Wigmore's twentieth-century riposte with cruciform sixty-six-foot-tower – and inside, a waterfall from font to baptismal pool.

And, as the final word, Twydall's Holy Trinity, with soaring pyramidal roofs. Uplifting as taut spinnakers? Or Newman's 'craziest display of modish Brutalism'?

4

The Medway and Its Valley

Sussex-born but Kentish through and through, the Medway cuts through Quarry Hills and North Downs to split Kent neatly into two, with 'Kentish Men' to the west and 'Men of Kent' to the east. Flowing through some of Kent's loveliest scenery, it adds character to Tonbridge, Maidstone and Rochester; waters the Garden of England, together with its tributaries, Beult and Teise; braves the grey cement country around Snodland; makes naval history at Chatham, and through marshes and saltings joins the waters of the Thames, no less, beyond Sheerness' Garrison Point.

It has known cruiser and red-sailed Medway barge, 45,000-ton tanker and rowing eight, paddle-steamers and *Victory* itself. It has carried Kentish iron and timber, cement, gunpowder and paper pulp. It has flowed through fourteen locks made of Kentish oak floated downstream. And it has seen its sometimes turbulent waters controlled by the touch of a switch at Allington sluice gates. Tidal Medway's saga has largely been covered in other chapters. This is its gentler story upriver from Rochester.

The Medway, it must be admitted, is not at its best as it cuts through the Downs between Rochester's sinewy M2 bridge and Aylesford's medieval one. On its western bank it runs the gauntlet of the tall chimneys and the grey smoke and dust of Halling's and Snodland's cement works gouging out the chalk flanks of the Downs far below the secluded peace of Whitehorse Wood and Holly Hill; and the sprawling agglomeration of Reed's vast paper-making empire at New Hythe.

On its eastern bank, some atonement is made. Borstal, magnificently sited on a spur of the Downs above Rochester, cannot live on stocky Fort Borstal's part in deterring Napoleonic invasion or on yellow-brick HM Borstal Institution's failure to deter today's ill-disciplined Youth from further forays into the widening underworld of crime. It can, however, congratulate itself on the Foord Almshouses, gracious as an Oxford college.

And in Borstal's church hang seven unique lamps of beaten brass.

Just before World War I cut off the Middle East, Kentophile author Donald Maxwell lovingly commissioned them in Damascus in the Street Called Strait. Six years later a far from sanguine Maxwell returned – to find the old Turkish craftsman still alive and the lamps, each uniquely hand-crafted, safely hidden in the cellar.

Between Downland scarp and broad Medway lie Wouldham and Burham, drab villages that quarried yesterday's chalk. Below, on the edge of Horseshoe Reach, stands the latter's deserted church. Above, Burham's new St Mary's, battlemented and turreted like a toy fort, boasts the grave of Walter Burke, in whose arms Nelson died at Trafalgar. Opposite, symbolically perhaps, a sea of corn sways in wind-ruffled waves – stained red with poppies.

Almost directly above New Hythe's riverside 'high tech' industry stands a 4,000-year-old long barrow – Kit's Coty House. On the edge of a wood three huge stones drunkenly support a fourth, the ten-ton capstone. They are behind bars – to protect them from the spray-cans of this century's vandals.

A bare mile away, the remarkable industrial sprawl of huge warehouses, ranging from Safeways to Danish Bacon Producers, should not

Four thousand years old, Kits Coty's burial-chamber stones still stand; southwards, Little Kits Coty has long collapsed and become the Countless Stones.

deter you from exploring Aylesford. Sited for over 4,000 years at Medway's lowest crossing-place, it was the scene in AD 455 of bloody battle between Vortigern and the Jutish leaders Hengist and Horsa.

It has much to offer. Holy Trinity Almshouses with their half-dormers in irregularly spaced gables stand picturesquely above garden and stream. In the village itself, The Little Gem, with its tiny bay window and lichened, tiled roof, offers cheerful hospitality. (England's smallest pub it may be but, judging from high-stacked barrels in front of it, certainly not with the smallest consumption of beer.) So too does the long, bow-fronted, black-and-white sixteenth-century coaching-inn, The Chequers. Overhanging on both upper storeys, it looks out of oriel and gabled windows.

Above it, steps lead up to St Peter's, which gazes down on a splendid jumble of tiled roofs. In it, close to the altar, hands serenely clasped in prayer, lie Sir Thomas Culpeper, handsome in black and gold-lined armour, and his wife. Three sons kneel below on one side; three daughters on the other. With the colours almost as fresh as 300 years ago, it has a quiet dignity and beauty. Unfortunately, it is overwhelmed by the sheer weight of marble and the brazen and baroque effrontery of the tomb of late eighteenth-century *nouveau riche* Sir John Banks beside it. Its garlanded cartouche of arms towers – some eighteen feet – to the very ceiling. Sir John himself, full wigged and cravatted, yet in semi-Roman dress, poses, oozing self-satisfaction. Opposite, his wife, nearly bare-breasted, plays the Roman matron. Below lies son Caleb, indolently lounging on one elbow; above, plump cherubs playfully flutter the rich backcloth. Ostentation at its most massively odious!

Aylesford's medieval bridge, gabled houses and church make a peerless view – best seen at high tide.

Further along the road, past the distant pale blue-green waters filling a huge sandpit and past the thinning thatch of Court Lodge's immense black barn, lies the Carmelite priory, a modern miracle.

In 1242 Richard de Grey brought back to Aylesford from the Holy Land, from Mount Carmel, hermits threatened by the Saracens. There they built a gatehouse, church and priory. At the Dissolution, it passed to the hot-headed Sir Thomas Wyatt who, poet and sonneteer though he was, vandalized both church and chapter house for their lead. The centuries took their toll until, in 1930, a disastrous fire, destroying also much Venetian glass, brought it to its knees. Billeted World War II soldiers, as was their wont, added their quota of damage and left it a gaunt skeleton.

A common enough story. Where then the miracle? On 31 October 1949 a small band of brown-habited, white-cloaked Carmelite friars, chanting the Litany, walked in solemn procession from Aylesford's medieval bridge to start an epic – the restoration to its former glory of the shell of the priory from which their order had been driven 400 years before. It was a miracle witnessed by Pope Paul VI when he visited the priory in Holy Year to celebrate its Silver Jubilee and found a building where modern and medieval blend into a harmonious whole.

Almost as if to remind us that this is no ivory-towered escape from today's world, beyond its lawns, its high conifer-hedged Rosary Way and its lakelet, willow-islanded and home of belligerent geese and snowy Aylesbury ducks, there rears up the contrasting unlovely bulk of Reed's New Hythe paper-mill.

On the site of the old church, Adrian Gilbert Scott designed a spacious piazza which fills on occasions with 5,000 modern pilgrims. Facing it is a high arched shrine in which stands a statue of the Virgin Mary, 'the moon at her feet and crowned with stars' – so finely carved that in 1960 it gained the Royal Society of British Sculptors' Otto Beit Medal. The shrine is linked by loggias to other chapels, unapologetically modern, with striking ceramics by the Pole Otto Kossowski, an ex-soldier, who, after achieving the impossible (escape from a Siberian prison camp) dedicated his life to God – and the priory. Today, Aylesford Priory, once again, has the mellow timelessness of a medieval abbey. Without proselytizing, it welcomes all creeds.

Another medieval miracle, one that has withstood time and tide for over 600 years, is Aylesford's famous bridge. The centre and longest of its five spans has all the graceful strength and flight of a long-jumper. The two refuges, jutting out over its piers like pulpits, on each side of the narrow roadway, are refuges indeed as cars and lorries impatiently flood across it.

A mile or so east but out of M2 earshot is Cobtree Hall on which

*In peaceful Allington Castle lived Sir Thomas Wyatt, musician, linguist, jouster, poet –
and Clerk of the King's Jewels.*

Dickens based Dingley Dell's Manor Farm: 'There ain't a better spot o'
ground in all Kent.' Here the Club were welcomed with cherry brandy;
Mr Winkle shot Mr Tupman – and not the elm-tree rooks; and Mr
Pickwick himself, 'feet about a yard and a quarter apart', braved the
slide, to the 'gratified shouts of the spectators'.

Poplar-veiled Allington Castle, dramatically medieval right down to
its austerely furnished great hall, stands on a strategic curve of the river.
For all its thick, embattled, ragstone walls, arrow-slits, stepped buttresses, half-round bastions, machicolated gatehouse and moat, its very
asymmetry, its lawns and trees, its dovecotes and oriel windows make it
a house of gentle strength rather than a grimly defiant castle.

It has housed the great. Here Cardinal Wolsey met his sovereign in
equal splendour. And here lived the Wyatts: the 'cat-succoured' (see
p. 135) Sir Henry and his son and grandson, Thomases both. It was the
former who first employed poetry's strait-jacket, the sonnet, and fell
under the spell of Anne Boleyn's eloquent black eyes, and nearly paid
for it with his life; the latter, equally rashly, rebelled against Mary's
Spanish marriage – and lost his estates as well as his head.

A derelict ruin in 1905, it was, over thirty years, lovingly restored by
the mountaineer Lord Conway before, in 1951, he passed it on to
Aylesford's Carmelites as a Christian Retreat.

Upstream lies Kent's county town – Maidstone. Its crest silently speaks volumes. One of its supporters is a golden lion 'passant'; the other, one of Maidstone's oldest inhabitants, an iguanadon 'proper collared gules' which may have roamed the district, then a vast Wealden lake, a hundred million years ago. And, surmounting all, the white horse's head is 'gorged with a chaplet of hops fructed proper', a tribute to local farmers and brewers.

Maidstone's splendid grouping of medieval buildings stands beside the Medway itself. They are, however, a little too near the bus station for the taste of a Richard Church driven to a peak of withering disgust: 'That noisy, greasy, stinking terminus where petrol fumes creep like gas.'

Archbishop Islip, in 1350, built the Old Palace with stone torn from his Wrotham home – but not the nearby dungeons, which are of still earlier date. Archbishop Morton, 'greatly augmented and beautified it'. So too did Jacob Astley, who gave it its graceful E-shaped façade, steeply roofed blind central porch and two smaller flanking ones above flights of steps. It was he who prayed before the Battle of Edgehill: 'Lord, I shall be very busy this day; I may forget thee but do not Thou forget me.' The less felicitous but equally practical 'Up boys and at 'em!' was also of his coining!

Along one side are pleasant gardens through which runs the River Len. It pops up like a minor pantomime demon from beneath a tiny but sturdily buttressed medieval bridge hidden in its turn beneath a far less charming or durable modern one.

Across the road, a thirteenth-century mill masquerades, rather unconvincingly, as a gatehouse. Beyond that again are the archbishop's stables, strictly utilitarian but impressive, with outside staircase, arched doorways between powerful buttresses, and a welcome splash of chestnut-red brick-nogging in the timber-framed upper storey of the stone porch.

Within, they are still more interesting. The days of their stable glory are retained in a collection of gleaming carriages under a crown-post roof. Barouche and phaeton, gig with carved dragons, and four-in-hand drag are all there. So too is the Duke of Connaught's landau (given to Maidstone's mayors but in which they are a trifle reluctant to travel – whether for reasons of modesty or road safety is not known); Count Walewski's chariot; a Lonsdale wagonette, yellow and black, of course; and the truly splendid travelling-coach of the twelfth earl of Moray. The latter was lovingly built in 1840 to ensure a high-society honeymoon worthy of the charms of his bride-to-be. Sadly her beauty was only skin-deep. She jilted him! Heartbroken and distraught, the earl ordered that the coach be locked away and never used again – and that its team of six high-stepping greys be shot.

Nearby again is All Saints Collegiate Church (1395). A splendid Perpendicular building, it is the largest and probably the finest parish church in Kent. Its eighty-foot tower, which has been condemned as unworthy of the rest of the church, is surely redeemed by the fact that in 1730 lightning robbed it of a soaring hundred-foot spire. Pepys climbed it: 'Up to the top of the steeple and had a noble view, then down again.'

All Saints lays claim to an impressive lineage: built, in 1395, by Henry Yevele, as master mason, for Archbishop Courtenay, with the blessing of Pope Boniface IX! Its first master, John Wotton, is splendidly honoured with a canopied tomb-chest behind which he is depicted as being presented to the Virgin Mary by 'tall and boneless' saints. Tribute too is far-sightedly paid on one of the misericords to an equally indispensable man – the cheery college cook, meat hook in one hand, ladle in the other.

The nave, ninety-three feet wide, one of the largest in England, was specifically designed as a 'preaching chamber' to accommodate huge congregations up to 2,000 strong, and for the chancel to seat all twenty-four chaplains. There, sumptuous, pinnacled sedilia are rivalled by the towering reredos. Among its many monuments are the unique Beale brass depicting six generations, a tablet to one of George Washington's forebears and another to Sir John Astley, with life-size figures standing gaunt and grim in their shrouds.

Away from the Medway, Maidstone has yet more to offer. Chillington Manor, an E-shaped Elizabethan house of deep red brick with stone dressings, is delightfully set in Brenchley Gardens. But its wide-ranging museum exhibits extolled by the ever-enthusiastic Arthur Mee were not at all to Richard Church's more fastidious taste. And its art gallery pictures were scathingly dismissed as: 'Beneath contempt.' Newman was equally critical of the pargeted royal plumes and arms in Bank Street: 'In vulgar pink, yellow and green, vulgarly shaded – an excellent match for the vulgarity of the plasterwork.' Damning, to say the least?

Mote Hall, despite its Portland stone, is a little forbidding, as might perhaps be expected from the drawing-board of prison architect D. A. Alexander, who, under the influence of Piranesi's futuristic fantasies, designed not only Maidstone Prison but also Dartmoor. For all that, it does sterling work as a Cheshire Home. The lake in its 450-acre park gives relaxation and excitement to anglers and yachtsmen. And Kent County Cricket Club have long held Maidstone Week there. It was here in 1976 that Kent supporters waited in anguished suspense to know whether a hovering helicopter would bring them the John Player League Cup or whisk it away again westward to a still-battling

East Farleigh with kinked bridge and oast-houses personifies the Medway Valley.

Glamorgan. Land it did! On the 'sacred square' itself. And was fined £5,000 for other aeronautical offences!

Past Tovil, once famed for its Royal Paper Mills, the Medway finally throws off industry's shackles in a peaceful, wooded reach. Second only to Aylesford's is East Farleigh's bridge. From Barming, the road drops sharply across the railway line, past the Apple Pie Joinery Works and over a narrow fourteenth-century bridge. Jervoise, a leading authority on bridges, claims it is 'the finest in Southern England'. Built of ragstone, with five arches, springing almost from river-level, and powerful cutwaters, it is slightly kinked, a fault not without charm, doubtless due to a slight miscalculation when building out from each side simultaneously. Orchards, oasts and spire rise beyond it.

East Farleigh's church has a chapel 'newly built' in 1411, and a memorial cross to forty-three hop-pickers whose squalid hovels in 1849 bred fatal cholera. Fifty years later, probationer Edith Cavell (who was to be shot as a spy by the Germans in 1915) nursed typhoid victims here.

Teston, not to be outdone, has an equally fine medieval bridge, of ragstone, and recessed, of course. Don't be fooled by its two outer arches – they are nineteenth-century. Nearby are an admirable car-park-cum-picnic site and riverside path. It is a blamelessly idle stroll to admire the bridge or, equally idly, to watch the play of sunlight on water at the weir and sluice above it. Or admire the ease with which amateur mariners swing closed the massive lock gates as they pursue a tranquil course up or down stream through a smiling countryside. The derelict building opposite was a linseed oil-mill until fire left it scorched and black-eyed.

Teston's other claim to fame rests with Alfred Reader's cricket ball factory, whose workers formed their own trade union, the Teston Independent Society of Cricket Ball Makers, the smallest union in England. More to the point, perhaps, are these statistics: in twelve months 13 million hand stitches and 15 million machine stitches are put into ninety tons of cricket and hockey balls. Since Alfred Reader began making cricket balls, they have used enough thread to stretch halfway to the moon!

Neighbouring Wateringbury is equally popular at weekends. Georgian houses look down wide-eyed at the stream of traffic, and shops retire into a discreet arcade supported on slender cast-iron pillars. The picturesque Old Mill now produces pottery rather than flour. Georgian Wateringbury Place, long owned by the Style family and almost rivalling Bradbourne for the beauty of its subtly hued bricks, has both delightful formal and water-gardens.

In the church, unusually sombre with its slate roof, Oliver Style's aldermanic robes still glow scarlet; Life and Death, angel and shrouded skeleton, confront each other across him. In the graveyard lies another Oliver Style – one of the few survivors of the Smyrna earthquake.

Parish clerk Edward Greensted vividly recorded the dramatic hail-storm of 1763: 'Our houses flooding with water . . . scarcely a pane of glass to be seen . . . roofs and walks shattered . . . corn, fruit and hops destroyed, scarcely any saved.'

From the towpath half a mile below Wateringbury, a track, steep and overgrown, leads to one of Kent's finest pairings, Nettlestead Place and church, not forgetting Nettlestead cricket ground where a harassed long-on can find shade under gnarled apple trees.

It is a church with a difference. One that owes its striking nave to Agincourt, for during that campaign Reginald de Pympe saw the majesty of French stained glass. Here, at Nettlestead, was a chance to build to the glory of Reginald de Pympe as well as of God. The squat west tower, built on Saxon foundations, was left untouched, the nave torn down and rebuilt with three great windows almost completely filling each side. And each glowing with English stained glass at its finest. A veritable Sainte Chapelle full of the swirling colour of the Twelve Apostles' robes. Sadly, 'impious hands' and the storm of 1763 have left only a patchwork of the original glass, but the church is still full of rich colour.

Beyond the lofty gatehouse, yew and box hedges lead to the L-shaped Tudor house. Its tiny thirteenth-century undercroft of beautifully proportioned piers and simple vaulting is a silvern miniature – perfect in both dimension and delicacy of lighting.

Along the south front, below a charming informality of windows, magnolias shelter between tile-capped buttresses and *garderobes*. Below, a sunken fish-pond, with descending double steps, is surrounded by low walls white with arabis, their corners softened with juniper, willow and yew. Its water is dappled yellow-green by artistic but indestructible algae which demand weekly, wadered dredging. On terraces above, slender lavender and trim rose-garden, gnarled lime and sleek yew hedge, smooth lawns and yet more magnolias . . . A dream garden for a dream house!

If Nettlestead is all church and house, Yalding, on Medway's left bank, scores its winners with *two* bridges and a splendid Georgian High Street. Insects, however, subject to summary death from ICI's Yalding Plant Protection Works, may well think less kindly of the village. For me, unimperilled, Yalding is much more than Leland's 'praty townelet'.

Twyford Bridge, with its sharp cutwaters and deep refuges, is a splendid opening chord, one well sustained by the grassy riverside Lees which sprawl up to the Town Bridge over the Beult on its last lap to join the Medway. 'Causeway' might be a better word, for its seven wide arches span marsh as well as divided river.

The church stands on a knoll beside the bridge. Red-brick-framed windows and a flat-topped tower flanked by a strangely bulbous lead cupola on the circular south-east turret are just visible above the trees. Church House has a primly hipped roof; Randell Cottages have gleaming white weather-board with striking black doors and railings. Court Lodge, with adjacent hop-barn and a background battery of oasts, is characterized by Newman as 'striving after grandeur'. It achieves it with bludgeoning white quoins and delicacy of red-and-blue chequered brickwork.

All these lead the eye pleasantly to the war memorial's backcloth of towering, white-candled chestnuts. Behind the former, almost veiled, is

An all too rarely glimpsed stiltman harks back to the heyday of the hop.

red-tiled Cleaves, built as a free school in 1665. Here lived the headmaster's son, Edmund Blunden, Kentophile and cricket-lover, author and poet:

> . . . their steepling hollyhocks,
> Bees' balsams, feathery southernwood, and stocks,
> Fiery dragons'-mouths, great mallow leaves
> For salves, and lemon plants in bushy sheaves.

Set randomly below it – or was it by pointed choice? – is a tiny lock-up of inviting vermilion brick but with uninviting studded door, enormous padlock and a judas-grating peep-hole that still swings easily open to the enquiring touch.

South lie Beltring's serried oasts (see p. 158). West is East Peckham's Norman church, lonely and redundant on a beech-crowned hill two miles from the village. Its nearest neighbour, Roydon Hall, has crow-stepped gables, striking chimney-breasts, rich brickwork in walls and terraced gardens, and memories of the remarkable Twisdens: Sir William, MP and buccaneer; Sir Roger, author of a 1,650-page treatise; Sir Thomas, a judge of the regicides.

North of Hammer Dyke, the Medway's loneliest stretch, frequented only by Wealdway walkers, is Hadlow. Its soaring 170-foot octagonal tower with slender pinnacles is a magnificently useless folly. In 1820, it was optimistically built either to give wealthy Walter May a distant sea-view or perhaps to cock a snook at Beckford's Wiltshire Fonthill – where the virtually foundationless tower toppled in ruins almost as it was completed.

Above its southern bank is Tudely. In its farm-surrounded church is Marc Chagall's only stained-glass window in England. Blue, yellow and red, it shows Sarah d'Avigdor-Goldsmith floating on the waves which drowned her.

'North of Medway, old and beautiful; south, young and ugly' is a not unjust criticism of modern Tonbridge, which owed its early prosperity to barge, coach, market and railway. And it may well rankle with its citizens that the Archbishop of Canterbury was prepared with no hesitation to swap its castle and its encircling league of land with Fitz Gilbert for his castle in Normandy.

Of Tonbridge Castle there now remain only its steep sixty-foot, tree-covered motte and an impressive thirteenth-century gatehouse of mellow golden sandstone. A veritable one-castle Maginot Line, with *two* portcullises, *two* sets of oaken double doors, *three* rows of machicolations, a battery of well-angled arrow-slits, a drawbridge and a moat. Only when slighted (rendered indefensible) after the Civil War by

Cromwell's Ironsides did it know defeat. Today, not unhappily wedded to a Georgian house, it slumbers peacefully, with gardens, river and rowing-boats at its feet.

Past hugely gabled, black-and-white Cobleys and Chequers; the patterned brickwork of Rose & Crown; Portreeve's House, half-timbered and with oriel windows; Bordyke, and Georgian Judd and Ferox Halls, lies Tonbridge School. It was founded, in 1553, as a 'stately Free School' by local boy-made-good, Andrew Judd:

> To Russia and Mussova
> To Spayne, Gynny without Fable
> Traveled he by land and sea
> Both Mayre of London and Staple.

Most of it is drab if worthy Victorian Gothic. Its showpiece, loved or hated, was the rich, orange-red brick of the modern chapel set in a rose-garden and overlooking the playing-fields where Kent's three cricketing Cowdreys learnt their trade. Inside was a wealth of sumptuous decoration: barrel vault and hammer beam; rich stained glass; a Luini *Last Supper* fresco; and a war memorial gateway with bronze St George and angels, patterned alabaster, gentle Virgin and Child, and a youthful Christ. All tragically ravaged by fire in 1988. All, thankfully, to be replaced.

Beyond Tonbridge, the Medway sportively encircles the town's fifty-acre sports ground. Westwards, just beyond Lucifer Bridge and below the A21 viaduct, are the massive sluices built in 1979–81 as a barrier to prevent a recurrence of the floods which inundated the low-lying town in 1968. Effectively they put an end to the one-time dream of navigation as far as Penshurst. Beyond, Medway has meandered through a rolling countryside and fittingly acted, near Ashurst, as county boundary for two miles.

The Quarry Hills

A line of modest hills weaves its way across the width of Kent between Downs and Weald. At their highest and most splendid in the west round Sevenoaks, they steadily diminish in stature to a final and gentle fling at Aldington and Lympne in the east.

Never properly christened, they are variously and confusingly known as Green, Stone, Quarry or even Lower Greensand Hills, though they are neither green, low nor sand. They are seen and described at their best in Chapter 14, but the 'tail' wags pleasantly and merits a brief chapter of its own for those who delight in 'off the beaten track' exploration and relish unravelling a tangled skein of minor roads.

NB: 'Fine views' should be taken as read.

South of Maidstone on the A229 is Loose. Fortunately, at least as far as the Women's Institute is concerned, it is pronounced 'Luze'; unfortunately, derived from *leose*, a pig-sty. Its houses perch precariously on the slopes of a little combe alive with the murmuring of burrowing rivulets. Near the gabled Chequers Inn they join forces in the main stream which for centuries powered mills and watered cress-beds. Here a low causeway – in winter spate, too low – runs its length between upright water-iris and aubretia tumbling, as do still smaller rivulets, over the walls of gardens attainable only by tiny flagstone bridges. For eager barefoot youngsters brandishing shrimping-nets, it is a watery heaven.

The National Trust's splendidly tall, close-timbered Wool House turns an unfriendly back. But its story of years of dawn-to-dusk restoration by its devoted owner, Colonel Statham, is heart-warming, one that overcame 'leaning walls . . . undermined chimneys . . . beams gone to powder . . . ivy clambering onto the roof through attic windows . . . a stream running *through* the house . . .'.

There is, however, nothing decayed about Telford's fine viaduct, a Gulliver to Loose's Lilliput, with its fifty-foot spans between tall piers, that sweep away Maidstone-bound traffic as easily as it was planned to hurry troops to any Kentish beach attacked by Napoleon.

Back on the B2163 westwards, the standardized suburbia of Cox Heath rests on a site that once throbbed with excitement when the militia gathered there to bar Napoleon's possible advance on London.

To the south-east lies showpiece Boughton Monchelsea Place, a fine L-shaped, Elizabethan ragstone mansion in landscaped gardens and with parkland below, where fallow deer graze with one *white* doe – for luck. Beside it stretches – for sixty yards or more – a barn made the more impressive by being pierced by a wide, covered carriage-way. And across the road, veteran apple trees surround white-cowled oasts.

But it's the low-towered church that steals the show. From the fine medieval lich-gate, one of the oldest in England, with its six stout supporting pillars, a path winds round to the porch between standard roses. Roses and still more roses, standard and rambler alike, continue down the sloping churchyard to give a riot of midsummer colour.

A mile north, across the main road, is modern Boughton. And beyond it, a little triangular green, with proud village sign, that lies beneath three flowering chestnuts. And beyond that again is a unique dell, site of old ragstone quarries: 'unique' in that it enfolds three equally enchanting half-timbered, garden-enriched houses – and throws in a converted maltings for good measure. Rock Cottage, once a derelict gardener-cum-chauffeur's cottage of the 'Big House' above, has been flawlessly restored and its garden re-born from a wilderness by the green fingers and dedication of the Murrays. Its centrepiece – two towering cupressus, bought from Woolworth's for 1s. 6d. each.

Nearby Quarry Cottages speak of the generations who worked the ragstone of which so many Kentish and London Victorian churches have been built. Brittle, yet in places soft, it is difficult to work into square or dressed blocks. Less disciplined, its coarse-textured, palest grey-brown surface is seen, uncoursed, in two of Kent's finest buildings, Rochester Castle and the incomparable Knole. Today the stone the Romans used to create Londinium is largely relegated to use as base road-metal.

Further north, Boughton Mount is a school for the handicapped. Its owners have ranged widely from John Braddick, a West Indian trader, legendarily keeping slaves in his cellar, to George Foster-Clark who put Maidstone on the custard map.

At Five Wents, Otham and Leeds lie north, Sutton Valence south. Otham, set among orchards, hop fields and old quarries boasts no fewer than *four* handsome Wealden houses: National Trust Stoneacre, Synyards, Gore Court and Wardes, the latter the scene of a horrific murder in 1985. And in the churchyard, English idiosyncrasy at its best: a tombstone erected to Nobody by Friends of Nobody! Downland views for good measure and a change.

Stoneacre, one of Otham's sixteenth-century gems, was lovingly restored, enlarged, and given to the National Trust by antiquarian Aymer Vallance.

'Loveliest castle in the world', lovelier than Azay-le-Rideau or Chenonceaux or even Château Gaillard, is a difficult tag to live up to. But Leeds Castle does just that.

Devise ruined barbican and mill, aloof Maidens' Tower and a nineteenth-century castle turreted and battlemented that blends imperceptibly into thirteenth-century Pons Glorietta and Gloriette itself. Build them of Kentish ragstone. Place them on two tiny islands to rise sheer out of the widest of moats. Set them among Kentish woods and meadows. And there you have Leeds Castle. See it best in a daffodil-dappled spring or over golden bracken wraithed in the pale blue evening mists of autumn. Magical from across the moat; magnificent from the air!

Queens' Castle indeed. Known and loved by Philippa of Hainault, Anne of Bohemia, Joan of Navarre, Catherine de Valois . . . But also one which knew siege – when the castellan's haughty wife rashly refused admittance to Isabella, 'the she-wolf of France', and Edward II, with 30,000 Kentish levies, exacted swift revenge.

Leeds' beauty is not just skin deep. Inside, superbly furnished, are apartments equally magical. The walls of '*Les Chambres de la Reine*' are covered by green damask and golden lovers' knots 'H & C' (Henry V and Catherine de Valois): a background foil for the status symbol of an enormous state bed; the lofty state chair that set her above her nobles; crowned day bed; and simple cooper's tub, linen-lined and curtained, in which the queen bathed. Oaken Gothic staircase; twelfth-century vaulted cellars; chapel with Kentish tracery windows; Fountain Court,

Ancient Leeds Castle moves with the times: Hot Air Balloon Festivals, Gold-diggers'
Balls, Easter Egg Treasure Hunts and Medieval Banquets.

half-timbered; and Henry VIII banqueting hall where ebony floor and
oaken rafters fuse with silver-grey walls adorned with Flemish tapestry,
Cranach's *Adam and Eve* . . . each adds its own beauty.

To bring you back to earth, there are grotto and aviary, dog-collar
museum and duckery, vineyard and tithe barn, Culpeper walled
garden . . .

Back on the A274, or mercifully just off it, Sutton Valence sprawls
sleepily along the slopes of the Quarry Hills – compactly too, for it lies
in four tiers, one above the other. Its famous public school's neo-
Georgian buildings crown them. They look down on their austere
ragstone predecessors which in turn have at their feet six-single-
storeyed almshouses shaded by towering lime trees, and unassuming
save for their sky-blue doors. Both were founded by London clothmaker
William Lambe in the 1570s.

High Street widens out into Broad Street, which curvets round a
Plain Jane Congregational chapel with all the assured charm of a street
that knows its own good looks: tile-hung, brick and timber. Beyond the

White Swan, living up to its name with long and elegant white weather-board and plaster, the road swoops down to a tiny triangular green and more Lambe's Almshouses, this time a solid Victorian rebuild in ragstone.

Follow the raised cobbled pavement east for a glimpse of the few remaining eight-foot-thick walls of the unassailably sited castle now under siege only by a growing army of hazels. Retracing leisurely steps along High Street – one feels there should be no other pace in Sutton Valence – gives time to admire Valence House and Old Place . . .

The church lies across the main road – a little more aloof than its rather prim 1828 modernity warrants. But with such a view as that, framed by its golden cupressus, it may perhaps be forgiven. It is the view glimpsed through High Street's fine trees, but here it is unobstructed, as wide as the Weald itself that lies at its feet: pasture and arable, copse and wood and hedge, its greens and browns roll away into an indistinguishable blue infinity.

Pause, as you retrace your steps, by the last tombstone. It is that of John Willes, 'patron of all manly sports and the first to introduce round-arm bowling in cricket'. Without his sporting sister's hooped skirts, which precluded conventional underarm bowling, and his own shrewd observation, we might never have known the power and glory of Lillee and Larwood, of Hall and Griffiths, of Malcolm Marshall and a score of other great fast bowlers powering up to the wicket, body straightening, arm high, left leg thumping down.

In Ulcombe you pass – or don't pass, as thirst or hunger dictates – the unusual Provender and the two powerful pictorial horses of The Harrow. On the hill above, All Saints stands behind two thousand-year-old yews of Falstaffian girth. In 1985, during a lightning-lit storm, restoration work unearthed hundreds of human bones and relics of a far greater age, probably from a pre-Christian burial site.

Inside, the church has been restored with sensitivity to leave it spacious and uncluttered. A painted demon snatches at the soul of a feasting Dives; upturned misericords reveal double dragons; and a tattered mat covers a flamboyant brass of mightily armoured Roger St Leger who lies, unmoved, beside his wife, trim-waisted and in a revealing off-the-shoulder dress.

Grafty Green, irresistible name, also shows originality in pub signs, Who'd A Thought It and a jaunty porker at the Pig & Whistle, as well as in garden paths, 'hedged' with decorative cabbages, red, yellow and white-veined.

Boughton Malherbe ('Bortun Mallerby' to locals) can be seen at a glance: a plain but prepossessing farm of warm brick with two oasts; a village school, with bell-cote to speed the dawdlers (now home of Tom

Baker, once a flamboyant Dr Who), a hunched church set behind a low, ivy-draped wall and closely surrounded by yew and ash; and the seemingly prosaic, rendered south walls and gables of Izaak Walton's 'ancient and goodly structure', Boughton Place, long the home of the Wottons.

Greatest of them all was Sir Henry, though Katherine, Countess of Chesterfield, deserves mention for jilting a much-smitten Van Dyck – but not so smitten as to reduce the price of her portrait! Sir Henry was scholar and poet; it was his hand and heart that wrote the epitaph:

> He first deceased; she for a little tried
> To live without him, liked it not, and died.

He fought bravely too – at Essex's side on his ill-fated Cadiz expedition.

From the road, the Place (private) shows little of its magic. Fortunately, hospitable James Clark showed me the varied charm of its three other very different faces. East, a delightful *mélange* of long, sloping roofs, tile and ragstone; north, brick laid upon brick in huge chimney-breasts and towering chimney-stacks; and west, from the walled garden, a grey mist of ragstone, of lovely oriel windows, of tiny lower ones, honeysuckle, wistaria and creeper curtained, all below a dormered red roof.

Inside, its once famous 350 superbly carved wall-panels have long crossed the Atlantic, and the magnificent domed plasterwork of its ceiling, under which Elizabeth I herself danced, has disappeared. But above you there is still the same forest of stout oak beams – and about you, generations-old warmth and beauty.

The neighbouring church is dark but full of unusual interest. A brass under the carpet; three lions, curly maned and heavily clawed in deep-throated laughter; two enormous brass tablets in the lofty chancel commemorating Thomas and Mary Wotton; and an alabaster one for Dr Leonell Sharp, who preached for forty years and was 'by her own choyce' chaplain to Queen Elizabeth, despite his association with the Earl of Essex. 'Briefly he preached, fruitfully he lived, and dyed joyfully.' What better epitaph for a clergyman?

Just south-west of the church, Nature adds its quota. Below stretches the rich Beult valley. The Weald, too. From Tenterden spire to Fairlight, they say. Hedgerow trees, coppices, woods and fields slowly merge in a misty blue blur. Only rarely is there a dab of red-tiled farm roof or a streak of white weather-boarding.

It was through wraiths of distance-diminishing, shape-smudging, colour-cooling mist that we came to Pluckley. It is a lively village always ready to plunge downhill to a mile-or-more-distant, sleepy railway station and a dead brickworks. Church and Black Horse public house stand shoulder to shoulder on the top of this thrust of the Quarry Hills. The Black Horse is all Dering windows; even its dormers are round-arched – and it has a beer-garden, cool under green and white sunshades.

The church (where we met a giant Canadian with a friendly, thunderous whisper), orchard to one side and the blue of the Weald below, is, as one might expect, largely a Dering chapel. But of the eight Dering brasses in front of the lectern and under the chapel's blue carpet, seven, Newman sadly admits, are frauds: ingenious forgeries by Sir Edward Dering, an archaeologist, whose passionate love of family overcame the nobler scruples of truth. At least the nine-sided font displaying the three left hands of the Malmains is genuine enough.

Only the least curious can be uninterested as to what lies behind the endless, too-tall-to-be-peeped-over roadside wall south of Pluckley. It hides the surviving north wing and turreted stables of an H-shaped, red-brick mansion burned down in 1952 – and an overgrown garden where roses riot over shattered walls and gables. The home of *thirty* generations of Surrenden-Derings.

One Dering held the title from the age of three – for eighty-five years! Another just squeezed through a round-arched window with Ironsides in hot pursuit – and made such 'lucky' windows obligatory in all his estate cottages. Yet another, 'the greatest learned man in England', denounced Elizabeth I to her face for her acquiescence in 'the whore-doms of hawkers and hunters, dicers and carders, and morrow-mass priests' – and kept his head!

Shattered walls and tower of aloof Little Chart church make a spectacular modern ruin. Literally out of the blue, in 1944, a buzz-bomb ended 500 years of worship there. Today an impressively large, if pale, modern church with an uninspiring tower and empty graveyard stands in the village itself almost opposite the regally signed Swan Inn. In its light cream-washed interior lies a survivor of the bomb – sixteenth-century Sir Robert Darrel of Calehill.

Most of the village lies round a pleasant green alongside the mill. With the help of two shady reservoirs above it, paper has been made there for centuries.

Hothfield calls, but *en route* a rather faded finger-post ('Little Chart Forstal ½ m') offers a far more inviting interlude than seems likely. Here is a secluded oasis near the stripling Stour. On one side, towering oaks guard it jealously; on the other, Forstal Farm, brick and half-timbered, with gables, bargeboards and tall chimneys, dates back to the fifteenth century. It is not surprising therefore that its door is drunkenly skewed and its thatched barn balding.

Beyond them lies the wide sweep of Little Chart cricket ground. The pondlet behind the pavilion must be a nagging spur to village Jessups and Bothams. On one side, a doll's house of a black-and-white weather-boarded cottage. On the other, the old barn and wilderness trans-formed into a home by a then-penniless short-story writer, the future creator of the larger-than-life Kentish Larkins, H. E. Bates. By the ceaseless skill of his pen (he wrote early and late 'until spots danced before his eyes') and the strength of his shoulders, the wilderness was turned into one of the loveliest small gardens in Kent.

Hothfield Common, once a source of grazing, peat and firewood for villagers, was fire-ravaged in 1949, and myxomatosis lingeringly slew the rabbits which kept down the steadily encroaching trees. Today the Kent Trust for Nature Conservation have the same task of stemming the smothering advance of graceful silver birch and shoulder-high bracken, of high hawthorn and spreading sycamore. A web of paths, a Nature Trail, criss-crosses open heathland and valley bog. A causeway over the biggest of the latter gives glimpses of cotton-grass, bog asphodel, spotted orchid and even carnivorous sundew. Here you can clear your lungs of exhaust fumes and stretch car-cramped legs.

Nearby is Hothfield church, low and stubby-towered. Inside, a tall tomb chest bears fine alabaster effigies of Sir John Tufton and his family. 'He re-edified the aisles of this church after it was burnt' (1603). And here, nearly three centuries later, Arthur Sullivan first played 'The Lost Chord'!

It is to Captain Nicholas Toke that we owe the rambling, russet hall at nearby Godinton, rich in stepped gables and, with its massive clipped hedges and topiary, a veritable Kentish Compton Wynyates. To him also is owed a sumptuously carved staircase with heraldic beasts on the newels; the oak panelling of the Great Chamber with its striking frieze of soldiers at pike and musket drill; an overmantel in the library giving 'a lively display of naked females symbolizing Faith and Hope'; and a lintel along which dolphins swim boisterously.

Great Chart, burnt down by the Danes in AD 893, is pleasantly unremarkable except for its many distinctively shaped gables, which give it a certain harmony, and for a tiny, single-storeyed timber-framed house with eaves deep enough to shelter the entire congregation of the nearby church. It is set amongst blue-green waves of periwinkles along a cobbled path. Controversy still rages: pest house or priest house? Inside, two brasses render the church unique. Each recalls a man who had *five* wives. And yet, nearby at Godinton, Nicholas Toke, a sheriff of Kent, slashed even this record. Aged ninety-three, he died while journeying to London to marry *a sixth*.

Birthplace of that headstrong man of Kent, Jack Cade; market town

for Romney Marsh livestock, Southern Railway engineering centre –
and now Channel Tunnel boom town. Such is prosperous Ashford.
Crowded and congested, and with the Chunnel likely to bore beneath
it, it nevertheless still has a central oasis of calm beauty.

St Mary the Virgin's imposing 120-foot tower, turreted, pinnacled
and embattled, is best seen soaring above the red roofs and half-
timbering of Middle Row, a seventeenth-century rabbit-warren of
narrow alleys, rich in gables and overhangs. It is surrounded by an
unpretentious close of cottages of weather-board, rosy brick and white
plaster; cinema turned Bingo hall; and an ancient, 'disconsolate'
grammar school.

Inside, massive tower piers block lines of view – but not of regal
Charles II arms or four magnificent tombs. Although his massive tomb
chest was rudely despoiled by Puritans, staunch Yorkist Sir John
Fagge, in pride of place by the altar, still reclines on it – peacefully
reading his book. And in the south transept, in the warmth of a glowing
heraldic window and in Jacobean flamboyance, lies 'Customer'
Smythe, Controller of the Customs of the Port of London to Queen
Elizabeth (to whom he paid £30,000 per annum for the privilege). Near
him, equally splendid, are his two sons; one of son Richard's four
kneeling daughters is a dwarf; to her went a double portion of the estate.

6

Wantsum and Swale

Rochester, Chatham and Gillingham are now things of the immediate past. Ahead lies the second leg of Kent's 140 varied miles of coast. Wantsum and Swale have a melancholy ring, in keeping with the melancholy of the Medway's gleaming mud-flats and lonely bays and islets, and of the nearby treeless pastures and marshes bordering the narrow sea channel of the Swale which makes Sheppey an island.

Chalets and caravans of Seasalter and Swalecliffe, and Victorian propriety of Whitstable and Herne Bay, break the lonely spell only for it to be resumed on the marsh pastures west of the Wantsum. The latter, is now no more than a sluggish stream. In medieval days, it was a three-furlongs-wide channel for London-bound shipping. Roman Watling Street and the modern M2 rule decisive lines between coast and Downs – but cherry orchards are still the jewel in the crown. It is varied landscape – of varied moods.

North of the A2, Upchurch lies on the slopes of a peninsula jutting into the Medway, a pleasant enough jumble of houses amid cornfields and orchards but today it lacks the real tang of the sea. And yet from it the Romans exported locally made pottery all over Europe.

Hasted, something of a health Jeremiah, trumpeted that, 'The noxious vapours arising from the marshes subject the inhabitants to constant intermittents and shorten their lives at a very early period.' The modern generation looks healthy enough. St Mary's shingled steeple is an eccentric double candle-snuffer, an octagonal cone spitted on a pyramid.

Upchurch's greater claim to a place in these pages is that the vicar in Tudor times was also Chaplain of the Hulks, redundant and laid-up warships, often turned into noisome prisons. And in 1560 its living was given to a man who had fled religious dissent in Devon. His name? Edmund Drake. And one of his twelve children was Francis! For all Millais's pictures of 'Westward Ho', it was on the Medway's treacherous waters that Drake learnt the seamanship that was to take him round the world, in a 100-ton cockleshell, the *Pelican*, which only became the more familiar *Golden Hind* in a bid to assuage the wrath of his patron, Sir Christopher Hatton, whose crest it was – and whose mutineering secretary Drake had just been forced to behead.

Nearby, Lower Halstow disentangles itself from orchards to assert its maritime quality. Its willow-sheltered church is red-flecked with Roman tiles. Inside is a small twelfth-century font, decorated with kings and angels, that long hid its light under – if not a bushel, then a plaster cast. During World War I, after a night of heavy firing, the parson's wife was horrified to find the font in pieces on the floor – or at least the plaster which had been put about it, to save it perhaps from Cromwell's men, eager for lead for their bullets.

In the swiftly widening creek itself, the blackened bones of old-time barges lie amid the sleek hulls of modern sailing-craft. At low tide, it is a grey-brown sheen of glistening mud reaching out to Sheppey and Slaughterhouse Point. To the east, orchards slope down to it; to the west, jagged timber piling lines the quays where rusty chains still lie embedded, quays where Romans loaded their pottery and where, until World War I, more modern methods produced 17 million bricks annually.

Milton Regis, a little overwhelmed by Sittingbourne, outstripping it, rests quietly on its laurels: the title of 'Regis' was bestowed on it by King Alfred when it was in the front-line of his battles with marauding Danes, and its oyster-beds flourished. Green-encircled, its fifteenth-century Court Hall, with low cells on the ground floor and council chamber on the upper, stands at the head of a street where good houses mingle with bad. The Three Hats Inn has, for this inelegantly hatless age, a novel hanging sign of three golden top hats that now replace the original shako, billycock and naval hat. The church, with its squat but massive tower of dark flint, stands sombrely aloof from the town. The black-and-white post office could well stand alongside Ludlow's Feathers.

Sittingbourne's long and rather dreary High Street is one to hurry through – as far as still-heavy traffic allows. In doing so, the passer-through is unaware of the bulk of Bowater's Paper Mill or the extent of its modern industrial estate, clean and spruce in its broad roads. Admittedly they are hardly enough to entice tourists to linger, but Sittingbourne does have a couple of aces tucked up its sleeve. The Sittingbourne & Kemsley Light Railway runs on one side of the creek; the Dolphin Barge Museum lies on the other. The S&K L R, 2 feet 6 inches gauge, worked hard for its living hauling paper and raw materials between Bowater's factory and Ridham Dock, two miles away. Today it has been put out to grass, and the green-gleaming tank-engine *Triumph* pulls its maroon carriage-loads of the young-at-heart in the enthusiastic care of volunteer steam fanatics. The first part of the journey offers wide-ranging if unromantic views over marsh and factory from the concrete viaduct on which it runs – one of the first ever to be built.

The Dolphin Yard Sailing Barge Museum lies at the end of a rutted track flanked with rose-bay willow herb. In the creek are no tarted-up barges-turned-houseboat. *Cambria* and *Celtic* lie thwart to thwart in working rig of peeling paint; on their decks, faded green hatch-covers, rusty chains and rustier anchors, frayed cables, bleached planks and oil-thick gear castings . . . And beside them is a contrastingly trim, black weather-boarded museum with its own sail-loft, carpenter's shop and forge, as well as eye-catching display boards.

Despite some timber-framed houses, Teynham (pronounced 'Tann-am'), sprawling along the A2, doesn't get the justice it deserves on two important counts. Indeed, local rhymesters went so far as,

> He that will not live for long
> Let him dwell at Murston, Teynham or Tong.

Certainly part of the parish is low-lying, but for me Teynham is the gateway to the magic of Lynsted and the Downs (Chapter 11). Even more than that, it is the English birthplace of the cherry – and other fruit, for here, in 1533, Richard Harrys (pandering perhaps to Henry VIII's taste for 'ripeness that is all' in fruit as well as in women). '. . . with great care, good choice, and no small labour, brought from beyond the seas the sweet cherry, the temperate pippen and the golden reinette'. Thus the cherry, first brought to Britain by the Romans, came back to Kent again. It spread, so Hasted, Kent's prolific eighteenth-century historian, tells us, 'into 30 other parishes on each side of the great road from Rainham to Blean Wood'. There is no official plaque to Harrys' memory but, in Spring Newington and Teynham, churches, rearing up like great ships in a wind-frothed sea of blossom, are far more unforgettable.

Back on the A2, Ospringe heralds Faversham with a fine fifteenth-century Maison Dieu, of seemingly unshakeable plaster, timber and flint, with lattice windows tucked under its eaves. In 1234, thanks to Henry III's piety, it housed the poor and needy – princes and lepers too; today it is an admirable local museum.

To the north lies Oare. Its name derives from the Old English *wàr*, seaweed, which was burned on the beach to make fertilizer. It also made so noisome a stench that Queen Elizabeth, fearful for her subjects' health, banned the practice. Despite that, Oare is another creek village of distinction – though huge modern warehouses and transit sheds (opposite a derelict windmill) detract from its essential isolation and character. The Three Mariners greets you; the Castle Inn, richly strawberry-coloured, points you, amid a tumble of houses, down to the creek. There in the thick, grey ooze squat *Joy*, *Fiona* and a score of other sailing-craft awaiting the first ripple of incoming tides; on the quayside, above two mouldering barges, stand *Grey Heron*, *Dazzler* and *Limbo*. A seven-ton crane will dandle them, light as a feather, down to the water when tide, time and wind are right – for a trip to the Friesian Islands.

From the heavily buttressed church on the hill, where even the tombstones seem to lean against the wind, are fine views down the widening creek – to yet another crowded anchorage. The road winds past it on to the former Harty Ferry. No houses here. Not even a ferry boat. That has long since gone, despite fruitless attempts to use modern amphibians. Only tall poles outlining the mud-thick causeway add a vertical line to the horizontal ones of sea wall, Swale and Sheppey.

Faversham is quietly splendid. Too often to Canterburians like myself it has meant little more than the draughty station platform where one waited impatiently to be speeded on to the far, far better sights of Canterbury. In fact, it has much to offer, and only recently have its modesty and good breeding allowed the once quiet market town to become a sophisticated tourist-trap – not by any gaudy display of finery, for Abbey Street is a triumph of a controlled and subtle colour-scheme, the joint work of amenity society and local council. It probably boasts a wider variety of charming houses, which seldom put a gable, roof or window wrong, than any other town in Kent (which is saying quite a lot).

Prime favourite is the finely timbered sixteenth-century house of Richard Arden, Mayor of Faversham. Mean and covetous, in 1551, he was murdered while playing draughts by his young wife, Alice, 'well favoured of shape and countenance', and her lover Thomas Mosbie. Beauty not brains was Alice's forte; it was a sadly bungled job that led Mosbie to the gallows at Smithfield, and Alice to the far crueller stake at Canterbury.

And where else, other than Faversham, would you find a brewery high stacked with aluminium barrels wafting its heady, hop-laden miasma over its next-door neighbour, the church of St Mary of Charity? In it King Stephen lay after his body had been pillaged from the nearby abbey for the sake of its lead coffin and then thrown into the creek. Cut off from the main street, the church claims attention, with its dark flint tower and the delicate tracery of its lantern steeple. A copy of Wren's St Dunstan's-in-the-East, it replaced in 1799 one that had collapsed.

The old grammar school, with its white weather-boarded upper

Outside Faversham's arcaded Guildhall stands the majestic Town Pump, splendid in scarlet, black and white.

storey supported on black arches, and eighteen-inch-high latticed windows hiding under the eaves, is almost opposite its modern successor, all glass and light. The guildhall has a nineteenth-century top-hamper of cream and gold. It is set on unusual octagonal timber pillars to make a covered market-hall. From one side of it rises an impressive cupola-ed clock-tower. And standing in front of it, like some gorgeous beadle, is the town pump.

The abbey grew to vast proportions, but with magnificence came worldliness: meat was eaten; silence broken; discontent rampant; and porters admitted 'dishonourable women'. Dissolution in 1538 was inevitable. Today all that remains is a single arch in Arden's House.

Nearly two centuries later Faversham fishermen apprehended a panicky James II as he fled the country. They searched him crudely and were simple enough to mistake his diamonds for glass but shrewd enough to hand him over for interrogation at the Queen's Arms. It was a slight that, even in his magnanimous memoirs, he never forgave.

Not that Faversham is all *ancient* history. From the thirteenth century to the sixteenth, it was a port with a thriving Baltic trade. Even though the creek is a working waterway, old barges, *Oxygen* out of Rochester, *Mirosa* from Maldon, *Lux Aeterna*, spruced up in green and gold, and sailing-craft tie up alongside grass-grown quays. In a side creek, heavy with the smell of watery decay, are two still older barges, sunk deep in glutinous grey mud. Behind them, like half-submerged hippos, are a score of old timber jetties.

Faversham was to know far worse disasters than a king's displeasure. Gunpowder had been made here in Elizabeth I's day. Nelson and Wellington owed some of their success to Faversham. So too did World War I offensives, for four factories with wide-spaced buildings stood on Uplees Marshes – defended by ack-ack guns. Unfortunately they couldn't defend it from human error. In 1916 an explosion was triggered off that, for all the scattered, sand-bagged hutments, killed over a hundred men and women. The women were known, from the nitric oxide they handled in making TNT, as 'the Yellow Hands Girls'. Allan Sillitoe, in his graphic 'Saxon Shore Way', immortalized them:

> At Uplees Mills
> And Guncotton Folly
> Sing Alice and Alma
> And Ivy and Dolly –
>
> Our wages are good
> And the work isn't harsh
> But our hands go yellow
> On Gunpowder Marsh.

Faversham Creek with its old coasters and barges is as fascinating as nearby Abbey Street's listed houses.

It was perhaps a carbon copy of 1781, when 7,000 pounds of gunpowder, in a pillar of flame and smoke seen in the Isle of Thanet and with a roar heard in Canterbury, were, 'of some unknown accident', detonated. 'Trees were charred . . . buildings unroofed . . . chimneys thrown down . . . glass universally shivered to pieces . . . still flaming timbers blasted across Faversham . . .' Yet only three men were killed.

Enough of harsh destruction. There are pleasant oasts and orchards about Graveney church, where light floods in on canopied brass and box pews. And in the marsh meadows below, in 1971, the blackened timbers of the 'Gravy Boat' saw their first light for a thousand years. For Roy Bolting it was perhaps to be another day of humdrum drainage clearance when his mechanical excavator struck solid timber. Investigation proved it to be the massive rib of a clinker-built Anglo-Saxon merchantman. Forty-six feet long, with a thirteen-foot beam, it contained cooking-pottery from France, millstones from the Rhine – and hops. And still attached to the stem-post was the original hawser of three twisted osier branches! In a fortnight's race against time, before the ditch was flooded again, volunteers and experts wallowed in the thick mud. Delicately they dug out, dismantled and numbered its timbers, one by one, before all were dispatched to the conservation tank at Greenwich National Maritime Museum.

If you park at Seasalter's Sportsman Inn for a drink, take a glance at the mark, barely discernible now, near the front door, where in 1953 the sea lapped four feet high. Glance too at nearby Shellness, where the beach is as much of millions of crushed shells as of sand.

Better still, follow the curving grass embankment that could take you almost back to Graveney. It is cared for by the Kent Trust for Nature Conservation: a resting-place for birds of passage, a summer breeding-ground and winter quarters. During the year you can see snow-bunting and godwit, curlew and grey plover, dunlin and wheatears, and Brent geese . . . The latter roost and graze on the pasture behind the sea-wall, where in summer male lapwings tumble acrobatically about the sky before suitably impressed females. They plunder the forbidden fruits of winter corn, and they probe the mud-flats for tasty marine life.

These grey-brown flats stretch out beyond Sheppey's green coast-line until they merge into a blue-grey haze where sea and sky are one. Their endless wrinkles are the work of tide and sand-devouring lug-worms. For all their thousands (thirteen to an acre), the latter are protected, save in limited areas. Here predator anglers, equally aware of their gourmet quality, quest with bucket and fork far out to sea. Yellow horned poppies and Dragon's Teeth thrive near Castle Coote; lavender and golden samphire on the salt marsh. It is a splendid walk for those who love silence and space, a fortifier against the crowding caravans, chalets and bungalows of the Seasalter coastal ribbon below the sea-wall.

Whitstable eventually emerges. It makes few claims to seaside holiday status. Its best face is seen in Middle Wall and Island Wall, where fishermen's weather-boarded cottages and cramped workshops crowd together in narrow streets and alleys behind the beach. They were dropped, it is said, by the Devil when, licensed by the cessation of prayers at Becket's tomb, he plundered Canterbury.

It has had its moments of glory. On 3 May 1830 it proudly welcomed a panting locomotive, the *Invicta*, carrying the world's first fare-paying steam-transported passengers. And it was to carry coal, off-loaded at its docks from Newcastle colliers, to keep Canterbury chimneys smoking. In 1832 the walls of the enlarged docks were lined with 10,000 excited spectators as *Phoenix*, chartered by the directors, steamed in with colours flying to the strains of a vigorous 7th Dragoon Guards band.

Today, after being down on its luck, the little port is enjoying something of a revival. Container-ships lie on the mud far below the tall quays where red and green nets, bleached ropes and coloured floats are

The day of the Royal Native oyster may be over but Whitstable Harbour still shelters fishing boats and small coasters.

heaped in piles. In another arm of the harbour, workaday fishing-boats jostle each other below the quay on which weekend sailing-craft are being spruced up. Two-storey black weather-boarded sheds, balconied, are limned tall and sharp against the sky.

The oyster was Whitstable. Seasalter's oysters may have had 'benefit of clergy' in belonging to the Dean and Chapter of Canterbury Cathedral. But with George III's Charter in 1793, Whitstable's became *Royal* Natives. The oyster, delicacy of Pliny and Juvenal, favourite seafood of Pepys, staple food of the poor, became the luxury of the rich, and throve. In 1912 19 million were 'dredged' from Whitstable's 5,000 acres of foreshore.

Two miles and more out, it was an oyster paradise. It offered rocky debris, 'culch', to which the stay-at-home oyster could anchor himself for life; protective sandbanks; enough tidal water to foil normal frosts; and fresh water from the Medway to dilute the salt. Oysters were zealously cultivated. Sea-bed, like seed-bed, had to be weed-free. The oyster's shell was protected from the boring whelk and the prising starfish alike. When the oyster spawned, its filmy 'spat' was collected and carefully sown in pole-marked beds. In due course, the oyster was harvested, 'dredged' by four-man crews in Whitstable's famous yawls before being trans-shipped into speedy hoys for the London market. In the oyster's heyday, sixty or more of the former could be seen off Whitstable waiting turn of tide or wind.

Now there is only *Gamecock*, for over-fishing, killing frosts, pollution and disease have virtually wiped out the oyster-beds. Today, spat is scientifically bred at Reculver, but the halcyon days of the Royal Native are over. Its epitaph is surely Richard Church's: 'It wipes away the taint of the world. It prepares the way for the most superlative of vintages. It keeps us sober – but makes us susceptible.'

Whitstable itself was as vividly painted – from hard personal experience – by Somerset Maugham in *Cakes and Ale*. He spent an unhappy boyhood there in the care of an unbending uncle, the vicar.

Herne Bay's Brighton aspirations were never fulfilled and its mile-long pier has been lost. But it does have miles of bracing promenade – 'North Pole 2,675 miles' warns a finger-post. And part of it is past bow-fronted Regency houses, a bandstand and a Victorian clock-tower whose columns are Doric-based and Corinthian-capitalled. From it are glimpses of fiery sunsets over Sheppey and long views of Reculver's dramatic twin towers.

Herne, three miles south, has a splendidly restored smock-mill on Beacon Hill, smuggling associations and a church tower which it doubtfully hopes Ruskin claimed as 'One of three perfect things'. Here the *Te Deum* was first sung in English, an innovation which, together with other 'corrupt and naughty practices', brought Bishop Ridley to the stake in 1555.

7

The Isle of Sheppey

The Isle of Sheppey comes almost as a relief to the writer who knows that later his superlatives are going to be taxed to their uttermost. Indeed, it has been said that to praise Sheppey would be as difficult as for Betjeman to go into raptures over a strict Baptist chapel in Hoxton.

Admittedly Sheppey, unlike Oxney, Grain and Thanet, is a *real* island bounded on the north by the Thames Estuary's last fling, on the south by a tidal watercourse, the Swale. There, for me, is the snag. Swale is neither wide enough nor wild enough to give that essential element of island isolation. Nor can Sheppey's modest 250-foot whale-back elevation, try as it will, give mountain grandeur. Its mud and marsh merely make for melancholy.

But, that said, Sheppey has its modest attributes. To the north there are sweeping sea views, enlivened with a stream of passing shipping and of a distant Essex shore; to the south, the gentle fall of green fields to marshland unpeopled save for cattle and the sheep which gave the island its name.

Sheppey has its pleasures, too, as Sheerness's fine Leisure Centre and Leysdown's crowding caravans testify, and it offers them with less brash ballyhoo than Margate. Nor can many small islands claim two smaller 'islands', those of Harty and Elmley; an 'islanded' island town such as Sheerness; the birthplace of British aviation; and two churches in one.

Kingsferry Bridge, a modern megalith, promises much but might be accused of misrepresentation under the Trades Description Act. It has four impressive towers. Needs them. For by their concerted cabled efforts they must lift the centre section vertically to allow passage for coasters bringing raw materials to Ridham Dock for the insatiable mainland Kemsley Paper Mills. It is a splendid opening act. But it is one that Queenborough signally fails to maintain.

If you are not in a hurry to reach Queenborough – and why should you be? – a track on the right a mile beyond the bridge leads to King Hill Farm. And from there to the 3,300 acres of the RSPB Reserve on

Elmley Marshes: wild-fowl thousands-strong, myriad waders from long-beaked curlew to pink-legged oyster-catcher, and even vocal marsh frogs find refuge and home there. An excellent school for even the least bird-minded; a paradise for the true ornithologist.

One shouldn't kick a town that's been down on its luck, one that Defoe pilloried as 'a miserable, dirty, decayed, poor, pitiable fishing town'. Oddly named Bynnee was lovingly renamed Queenborough by Edward III for his consort, Philippa of Hainault. Over sixteen years, he built there a vast castle-cum-palace, the latest in the technology of its day, probably designed by Winchester's William Wykeham and supervised by master mason John Box. With circular towers surrounding circular keep within circular walls within circular moat, it was a piece of consummate concentricity. Today the glories of the castle are reduced to an indistinguishable mound by the railway line.

Not to put too fine a point on it, Queenborough, to the visitor at least, is drab and drear. True it has a yellow-brick eighteenth-century guildhall, with a Tuscan pillared colonnade, pyramidal roof and bell turret; and in it, I'm told, a glittering civic regalia. Hogarth lived it up at the Ship Inn; Lady Hamilton, doubtless more discreetly, at Church House. But it seems a lost town, one without clear purpose. Its main street peters out rather messily in the Creek.

Brimstone was made here by a Brabant merchant, but Queenborough, for all I – and Defoe – have said, is no hell, though across the Swale there is Deadman's Island, grim burial-ground of those who died in the squalor of the hulks or in quarantine. Queenborough's penance for sins of architectural omission and commission has perhaps been a head-on view of the Isle of Grain's jumbled retorts, tanks and cylinders. Harsh, but not unfitting.

Sheerness, on Sheppey's deep-water north-west tip, also has little to commend it architecturally – unless you prize bleak dockyard walls, Victorian terraces, cast-iron clock-towers, late Georgian hotels or a vast, D-shaped granite fort. But commendation it must have for its recovery as a car-ferry and container port when, after 300 years sterling service as a naval dockyard (known as 'Blue Town' for the prodigality with which everything, moving and static, was painted), it was brutally axed. And commendation too for its fine 1½-mile-long sea-wall (forced on it by the equally savage attack of the sea in 1978), gardens, Leisure Centre, swimming-pool, bracing air and a ship-dotted, catamaran-bright prospect ranging from the Essex coast at Shoeburyness eastwards to the Nore Lightship.

On Samuel Pepys' advice, Charles II, who had a penchant for closing the stable door only when the horse was distinctly restive, built the dockyard and fort in 1669. Already the Dutch were sabre-rattling,

The impressive twelfth-century Gatehouse of Minster Abbey founded in AD 664 by widowed Queen Sexburgha – destroyed by Danes two centuries later.

and Commissioner Pitt at Chatham was 'in a fearful stink'. With only seven of its sixteen guns serviceable, the garrison, save for seven laggards, hastily decamped when de Ruyter's men landed. The seaway to Chatham was open!

Trouble brewed again, in 1797, with the Nore Mutiny. England's jolly Jack Tar, press-ganged, ill-paid, abominably fed, harshly disciplined, had all too little to be jolly about. Inevitably it fizzled out and its leaders were hanged or, possibly worse, 'flogged round the fleet'. But under pressure from Nelson, a disciplinarian with a heart, the stone-faced Admiralty belatedly took the hint.

Should you be travelling by car, it may voice the gentlest of protests at the unaccustomed labour of a Sheppey hill-climb. At 235 feet it would be of little account save for the minster that once crowned it, and the two churches, indissoluble, wedded like Siamese twins, that still do. Flanked by a fine ilex grown from a Crusader's Levant acorn, only the rock-solid minster gateway, battlemented, with unusual chequered parapet and almost as broad as high, has survived 'heathen devastation', neglect and Nature's onslaughts. There Sexburgha, widow of a Saxon king, took seventy-seven nuns in *c*.674 to devote their lives to the 'sick, needy and oppressed'.

The church consists of the rebuilt nunnery church and, literally as one with it, the added parish church. Together they provide a lofty and impressively high building, dark and rich in atmosphere. Equally impressive is the angle-buttressed west tower, echoing the minster gateway, save for a squat timber belfry whose peal includes a bell rescued from Old Warden church when the sea claimed it.

Its monuments are equally fascinating – a world away from workaday Queenborough and Sheerness. The big de Northwoode brasses bring dress of the day (1335) to life. A recessed tomb bears an unusually tall knight in armour, wearing a Yorkist collar of alternate sunbursts and roses. He is reputed (though Tewkesbury Abbey has other ideas) to be the Duke of Clarence who, it is said, *chose* to be done to death, for high treason, in a butt of malmsey wine!

Sir Robert de Shurland is there too, under a broken canopy, his head uncomfortably resting on his helmet – his horse's head rising from the waves beside him. Symbolic perhaps of his manorial right to all the flotsam he could reach with his spear on horseback at ebb tide, or of the Barham *Ingoldsby Legends'* witches' prophecy that 'the horse which saved your life will be your death'? Worth reading.

From Pigtail Corner, a lane winds down to the scant remaining walls and turreted gatehouse of once vast Shurland Court. Here Sir Thomas Cheyne, Henry VIII's Lord Treasurer, royally entertained his master and one Anne Boleyn, 'of swarthy complexion and with bosom not much raised'. But within forty years its splendour was in decay, due to Sir Thomas's son's wild prodigality elsewhere.

Eastchurch, where the B2008 joins the A250, teeters along the same ridge and does not overly advertise its Open Prison. Sheppey is no Alcatraz but, with just a single bridge connecting it to the mainland, the only other route open to time-servers hankering for the bright lights and anonymity of 'The Smoke' is a dangerous one of mud and water.

Eastchurch's real claim to fame lives on on those same acres, for at Stonepitts Farm the Aero Club of Great Britain was formed – and J. T. C. Moore-Brabazon of Tara became the first man to fly a one-mile circuit. The Short brothers, Horace, Eustace and Oswald, designed and built *Twin* and *Seaplane*; the Royal Naval Air Service saw first light of air; and the Honourable Charles Rolls made the first return cross-Channel flight before crashing – and leaving the world to Royce.

Opposite Eastchurch's good-looking church of ragstone, but with flint battlements, all this is fittingly recalled by a splendid monument. On it are recorded those pioneer planes, aviators, designers and 'Craftsmen of Sheppey', all too easily forgotten in this touch-button, Concorde age.

Below Eastchurch, lush pastures, nearly treeless, slope gently down to the rougher grazing and ploughland of reclaimed marshes. To the north and east, a minor road makes a beeline for Warden Point, a rewarding belvedere for viewing inshore coastal shipping. Its brown clay cliffs, some 150 feet high, are steadily surrendering to the sea's relentless nagging. Fissured and cracked, they have slithered down into the sea, taking with them half a village – and a church built from the stones of old London Bridge. Yet, almost indifferently, it has left intact coastal defence pillboxes sprawling across the most recent ochreous mud-slip thirty feet below.

Beside the unobtrusive post office, once the Snack Inn, a smugglers' haunt, paths inch their way precariously alongside yet more crumbling cliff. A worthwhile stroll, if vertigo holds no terrors. Below: a grassy, well-ordered caravan site; cliffs slithering to a sandy, groyned beach; Leysdown and its serried ranks of caravans; marshland to Shell Ness and the Isle of Harty; the grey ribbon of the Swale; the blur of the North Downs with, matchstick high, Dunkirk's sole remaining radar mast. And to the east, the Kent coast disappears into hazy infinity.

Leysdown is caravan country with a vengeance. So if you have no liking for cheek-by-jowl gregariousness, Shell Ness and the Isle of Harty are both for you. The former can be reached by footpath from Leysdown or Harty. Another reserve, it is rich in bird life – and on occasions authorized nudists.

Not even Sayes Court, the Ferry Inn and the Church of the Apostle St Thomas can make Harty rank as a village, but for lovers of the near-desolate it is full of atmosphere. The oil-lit church, one of the loneliest in Britain, outdoes even Romney Marsh's Fairfield. It contains George II's royal arms, a miniature hand-organ and, dredged from the Swale itself, the beautifully wrought 'Flanders Kist' with its vividly depicted tilting-match carved on the front. Recently stolen – and recovered.

A boat from the Ferry Inn, if there were one, could row you back to North Kent shores in a mere ten minutes – as it is, you have nearly that number of road miles to cover before you re-cross Kingsferry Bridge to the mainland.

8

The Isle of Thanet

Few of even the most fervent Kent addicts can claim love of Thanet for her beauty. Unless you are one that loves vast and endless spaces where hedges are few and trees comparative rarities, it has all too little appeal inland. Skyscapes, yes; landscapes, no! Even the main roads seem to hurry to be done with it all, to reach its *raison d'être*, the encircling sea.

In summer there is airy spaciousness, a lack of constraint, but in winter north-easters cut to the bone and mist often draws a grey veil across sodden fields. Small wonder that few of the gentry, save the eccentric Lord Holland, built mansions there.

Inland, much is emptiness. Villages, lacking becoming slopes, are flat rarities in a flat landscape. Birchington sprawls into Westgate, Westgate into Margate. Margate and Cliftonville have become Siamese twins, performing a Brighton-and-Hove act. North Foreland, almost England's most easterly point, has lost its lonely dignity. A lemming-like urge for the sea has spawned a bungalow-builder's paradise, long avenues of featureless 'desirable residences' far from sight or sound of the sea, to bloat Broadstairs and Ramsgate.

Thanet's coastal profile is quite another thing. Its cliffs, though hardly Dover giants, have height enough. And at their feet are bays of fine sand or broad sea-walls, ideal for brisk and breezy walking.

Fortunately Thanet doesn't fashion all its towns in one mould. Its 'Big Three' have characters as different as those in any family. Margate, though it may not have sold its soul to Mammon, makes unashamed overtures to the Good-time Charlies and Charlenes. Broadstairs is richly redolent of Dickens and old-time family holidays. Ramsgate, with Torremolinos snapping at its heels, adds to its slightly faded Georgian elegance both a marina and a bustling maritime future.

For me, if not for the meticulous geographer, Thanet begins when I have skirted the massive cliff-slip at Beltinge. It left houses teetering on the brink and gently lowered an almost undamaged tennis court some thirty feet. Now they are sturdily and expensively defended with graded slope, herring-bone pattern of drains, massive concrete sea-wall-cum-promenade and skirmishing groynes.

Then, past the tiny ravine of Bishopstone Glen and with close-cropped grass underfoot, down to Reculver, to its twin towers sharp etched against the sky. The Romans built a flint fort (Regulbium) here to guard the northern entrance to the Wantsum Channel, to complement Richborough (Rutupiae) at the southern end.

Although the ever-hungry sea has gnawed its way inland and swallowed half its area, and Time has levelled its walls, traces of it still remain. Within its walls, King Egbert, in 670, in atonement for the murder of his two nephews, built palace and monastery. The latter, rebuilt in the twelfth century, had imposing twin towers, erected, it is said, by the abbess of Davington in thanksgiving for her miraculous escape from shipwreck on a nearby sandbank. Almost equally miraculous perhaps was the 'bouncing bomb' that Barnes Wallis successfully tested here before it breached the heavily defended Moehne dam – and inundated the Ruhr.

Reculver Towers: once 'a quarter of a myle . . . of the se syde'; today stoutly protected from further depredation.

The towers – and their spires – served as warning to shipping for centuries, but by 1809 the still-hungry sea had undermined the church that had once been 'a quarter of a myle . . . of the se syde'. Crowds flocked to see it; fallen stonework was sold to the Margate Pier Company. Scandalized, the young vicar's mother sent him post-haste to the bishop to demand the church's demolition before it became 'a poppet [*sic*] show'. So, as the heartbroken parish clerk wrote: 'And down came the church and what was his thoats [*sic*] about his flock that day no one knows.'

Trinity House, however, intervened to have the towers restored as a landmark for shipping.

Reculver could have rested happy but for another invasion – of tatterdemalion caravans,, 'caff', bingo hall and vicarage-turned-pub. Fortunately now the former, in their turn, are under threat of eviction.

It is possible to skirt the low marshland pasture along the sea-wall to Minnis Bay and Birchington. Hard by the door of the latter's church, and beneath a cross sculpted by Ford Madox Brown, lies the drug-taking eccentric Dante Gabriel Rossetti: 'Honoured among painters as a painter, and among poets as a poet', leader of the Pre-Raphaelite Brotherhood.

In the richly ornamented chapel lies Sir Henry Crispe – nicknamed '*Bonjour*' Crispe because, after being abducted from nearby Quex House and held to ransom for eight months in the Low Countries, it was, in typical English insularity, the only word he'd learnt! Or ever used!

Today Regency Quex House has spawned the Powell-Cotton Museum. It is set in a spacious walled garden, and in its grounds are two unusual follies. After Birchington church council had vacillated too long over campanologist John Powell's offer of a ring of twelve bells – one from a Burmese temple – he swiftly built his own Waterloo Tower in 1819 and on top of it he placed a gleaming miniature Eiffel Tower way ahead of its time in technology. He also built a second tower, and from it he logged the time of the first sighting of his Thames-bound East Indiamen and sent it post-haste by mounted courier to his London wharf. Few of his skippers dared delay *en route* in surreptitious trading of the owner's merchandise!

Major Percy Horace Gordon-Powell-Cotton was a man of uncompromising mould. Explorer, ethnographer, big-game hunter, he made twenty-eight major expeditions to Africa and Asia – including, in 1905 a Congo honeymoon! Thus came into being a fascinating collection of animal dioramas and native artefacts. The first curator-taxidermist died scalpel in hand; the second rose from boot-black boy; and currently widely travelled Derek Howlett, with his wife, maintains the high standing of a museum in a Kentish backwater with a national reputation.

The Thanet pattern of low chalk cliffs protected by massive concrete sea-walls with gaps leading down to sandy beaches continues through decorous Westgate, once ideal prep-school territory, Westbrook with its sunken garden – and into Margate, first of Thanet's great triumvirate.

It gained a flying start thanks to Dr Wittie and Dr Russell, and to Benjamin Beale, a Margate Quaker glove-maker. The first in 1660 advocated sea-water bathing as a cure for not a few illnesses. Dr Russell in 1750 ranged far wider, from gout to glands, and advocated internal as well as external application, half-a-pint at a time – laced with port to taste. Beale, in an era when gentlemen bathed 'wholly exposed' and when most ladies, wholly unexposed, refused to bathe at all, in 1753 invented the covered bathing-machine. The modesty-conscious entered it fully dressed; changed in 'utmost privacy'; were pulled out to sea by the old horse; shivering, descended the steps; and, as often as not, were swiftly ducked by brawny 'dippers'.

Charles Lamb, having travelled queasily here from London on one of the famous Margate hoys, had 'the most agreeable holyday of my life'. Doubtless he would have enjoyed a modern 'knees-up'!

From the crinkle-edged seventeen-storey Arlington Flats to the inevitable Victorian clock-tower it is all 'go': candy-floss and French fries, Space City and Mr B's Amusements; Dinkum Dog and a host of other attractions all there to give you a good time. So too are Winter Gardens and aquarium, stilted casino, with the tide swirling beneath it, and Georgian Theatre Royal, modelled on Covent Garden but now prostituted to the great god Bingo. Even English hockey is ousted from Jacky Baker's sprawling recreational acres when Thanet Vikings play Chingford Crusaders at American-style rugby.

Above all, literally and metaphorically, there is old-time Dreamland, present Bembom's Amusement Park. Pay once and ride all day! Defy whirling centrifugal force or plummeting gravity in giant swing boats, 140-foot-high big wheel or looping-the-loop cyclotron. It is twenty-five acres of non-stop white-knuckle thrills. It's eager Youth's 'You ride till you're sick'.

But you can just as well plunge underground for thrills in Margate. The caves, in Northdown Road, optimistically regarded as 'Minoan in origin' but certainly cavernous, smack of medieval torture and smugglers. The shell grotto, discovered by accident in 1835, is not some wee garden affair but 2,000 square feet of winding passages patiently and artistically mosaiced with millions of sea-shells.

A silver Tudor House, not surprisingly, is wide-eyed in amazement

Looping the loop on the roller-coaster at Bembom's Amusement Park.

to find itself sandwiched between gasometer and supermarket. And at the end of Bingodom stands the harbour master's house on the mole built in 1810 to 1815 by Sir John Rennie. The latter had a hand in other trifles, such as London Docks and Waterloo Bridge – to say nothing of helping to drain the Fens.

The house, delicately light blue and white, is a replica of the 1830 original, destroyed by enemy action in 1942. Plaques on it remind you that 46,772 exhausted troops were welcomed here from Dunkirk, a short fifty years ago. From the beacon at the end of the mole, there is a clear view across choppy water of the famous pier – or what is left of it. The great storm of 1957 crippled it but, despite twelve attempts to blow it up, its head is still above water!

The change from Margate, 'superficial and brazen', to 'restrained Cliftonville' is wrought felicitously enough by the terraced and balconed houses of Fort Crescent and Fort Paragon. Here, round its oval gardens and bandstand, spruced-up hotels are fighting the lure of sun-drenched Málaga and Marbella with 'sauna' and 'solarium'. And further on, the cliff-top verges become ever wider so that in some peace you can air yourself and your dog(s), meditate, luxuriate in the sunsets beloved of Turner or pitch-and-putt on a modestly bunkered course.

From the bellicosely battlemented but hospitable Captain Digby public house can be seen the long flint façade of Kingsgate Castle. It was built in 1760 – probably with Government money – by venal Henry Fox as an impressive but impractical folly. One more recently summed up as 'a sad, meretricious conceit of foolish extravagance'! Nearby, in stark contrast, stands the North Foreland Light in Trinity House livery of gleaming white-and-green footings. In 1505 its light was blazing coals in a suspended brazier. Today, remotely controlled, its beam ranges over twenty miles of busy seaway.

Broadstairs. Prep schools. And more bays. Seven of them! Here the accent is on family holidays, sandcastles and sun, paddling and pop-corn, trampolines and Punch and Judy. It is leisured but never sleepy. How could it be, with 'Charlie' bounding down from grimly battlemented Fort House (now Bleak House), where he wrote 'in a room about the size of a warm bath' parts of *Pickwick* and much of *Copperfield*, to yarn with sailors on the sixteenth-century quay. A quay big enough for Dickens' friends to dance quadrilles on it, as he played on the comb. Big enough to accommodate the office of the harbour master (Mr S. P. M. Whisper), lopsided, black-and-white, with a kilted figure-head Highlander at the top of its steps. Boards on its side record the 275 lives saved between 1869 and 1912 by its lifeboat from all manner of craft from ketch to barquentine. It is more than big enough to shelter today's handful of fishing-boats sprouting a forest of red marker-flags on tall poles.

For fourteen years Dickens holidayed at 'Our Little Watering Place', enjoying its trim Georgian and Regency houses, its steep, cobbled lanes, Hollands and gin at the convivial Albion, walking and bathing, 'salmon coloured as a porpoise', on the 'rare good sands'.

And doubtless he enjoyed protective York Gate, set across Harbour Street in 1540 to hold back the marauding Frenchies – who never came, the flint cottages in Serene Place and the ruins of 'Our Lady of Bradstowe' chapel so venerated by sailors that passing ships lowered their topsails in respect. And, of course, he knew the house in Victoria Parade from which Mary Strong, Betsy Trotwood's prototype, sallied forth to rout the donkeys. Today, like Bleak House, it is a museum, with its front parlour refurnished exactly as Dickens – and 'Phiz' – had described it.

Sadly it all came to an end in 1851. Dickens was driven away, not by the modern scourge of wailing transistors but by 'vagrant music of the most excruciating kind, organs, fiddles, bells, and glee singers'. For all that, his heroes and heroines – villains too – are back each year in period costume for the Dickens Festival.

Broadstairs merges into Ramsgate – a town of intriguing contrasts. It has risen from down-at-heels fishing village to bustling modern port where glossy yachts give its marina a Continental tang, *Sally Line* heads for Dunkirk, and freighters disgorge endless regiments of Volkswagens in swift turn-round. Near the Customs House, brash amusement arcade and funfair jostle sophisticated casino. Karl Marx visited Ramsgate; Van Gogh taught English there. Regency bucks, Queen Victoria-to-be (in one of her two gingham dresses) and London East-Enders have enjoyed its fine beaches. So did the artist W. P. Frith whose brilliantly detailed *Ramsgate Sands* was snapped up by the nostalgic Queen for Buckingham Palace.

From either side of John Smeaton's harbour (two breezy piers and forty-six acres of it!), Ramsgate sweeps up to its elegant legacy of Regency crescents. Near Royal Parade and Paragon stands unobtrusive St Augustine's Church. It was built by A. W. N. Pugin, creator of the Palace of Westminster's rich decoration; champion of Gothic; fierce denigrator of Renaissance, that 'embodiment of sin'; financially prodigal but architecturally narrow. Built to his own taste – at his own expense.

Flint and Whitby stone banded, it has a tower sturdy and solid enough for the spire Pugin had planned before his money ran out. Inside it is 'rich, dark and exquisitely over-decorated'. And amid its splendour, in his own chantry, lies Pugin himself, swathed in a long

Hugin, *twentieth-century facsimile of fearful Viking longboats, stands a bare mile from the Cross at Ebbsfleet commemorating the landing of gentle St Augustine.*

robe and with his children kneeling in medieval sorrow about him. He died at forty, driven out of his mind by ceaseless work, his quest for perfection, and an unwarranted sense of failure. Next door stands his house. From its battlemented tower he watched anxiously for wrecks so that he might be the first to clothe and house the survivors.

The High Street will lead you past red-tiled roofs and the Norman tower of St Lawrence's Church to Manston, the Battle of Britain's front-line fighter station. Today, it is Yugoslav holiday flights and even occasional Concorde 'flips' that roar down its long runway – not Spitfires. But flanked outside the pavilion by sleek Canberra bomber and twin-jet and delta-winged Javelin interceptor, Spitfire and Hurricane, stand within it to remind us of 'The Few'.

West lies marshside Minster, prosaic enough save for its majestic cruciform Norman-Early English church and for its ancient nunnery, revitalized by Bavarian nuns fleeing Nazi persecution.

And on the A253 is Sarre. Its Crown Inn bears a long list of its customers' stage-names, from lugubrious George Robey to 'Two-Ton' Tessie O'Shea. Doubtless Margate's proximity and the Crown's own cherry brandy, still made from a Huguenot recipe as a condition of its licence, had something to do with it. A fitting boundary for Thanet!

9

Canterbury to the Coast

Scant in miles but rich in history and interest. Ancient cathedral city; Cinque Ports; bustling Channel ferry terminal; sea-faring town well known to Nelson; modern seaside resort; quiet villages set in peaceful Downland; cliffs and bays, beaches and bingo . . . and rapacious Goodwin Sands! All in one chapter!

Canterbury Cathedral is at its most magnificent when seen through Christ Church Gateway. The latter – bright with Tudor arms and shield-bearing angels; secure in Bishop Juxon's massive, carved doors; and dignified by octagonal turrets (once demolished so that a High Street banker could see the tower clock!) – is the perfect frame for the cathedral's most delicate and lovely profile. It is a soaring vision of towers, flying buttresses, myriad pinnacles and crockets etched against the sky. Floodlit, it is ethereal, spun gossamer . . .

It is a constant contrast in itself. The simple Romano-British church has, over the centuries, grown into today's magnificent cathedral of lovingly carved stone. It is a contrast that runs like a thread through the grandeur of the interior. One hundred and twenty-six feet above you is the lacy fan-vaulting beneath Bell Harry's lantern; a few feet below you, the cold horror of the defenceless Becket's murder, in the Martyrdom, by Henry II's four armoured knights. In the gilded splendour of the Warrior's Chapel, beneath tattered banners, Lady Margaret Holland reclines in spacious 'polyandrous peace' between her two husbands – and forces Archbishop Stephen Langton, architect of Magna Carta, to lie with his legs and feet stretched through the cathedral walls into the cold!

With glittering shield, gauntlets, jupon and leopard-crested helm above him, 'all armed in steel for battle', is the Black Prince, a paragon of honour, youthful hero against overwhelming odds at Crécy – cold-blooded slaughterer of the men, women and children of Limoges. On top of the cathedral's most ornately decorated tomb is Archbishop Chichele (founder of Oxford's All Saints in expiation of the slaughter at

Ernulf's Crypt, air-raid shelter in both Wars, contains the subtly lit chapel of Our Lady Undercroft, beloved by the Black Prince.

Agincourt) in his richest vestments; below it, his shrunken, naked corpse, shorn of all glory, lies on a shroud.

And in less obvious contrast, there is Prior Chillenden's screen, of stone carved like ivory, where kings and angels still live on, though its mitred saints were thrown down nearly 350 years ago by iconoclast 'Blue Dick' Culmer. Stone steps have been hollowed by pilgrims' eager feet; but the Norman piers of Prior Ernulf's crypt still stand, rock solid, beneath the vast weight of the choir above. And in the glory of the great west window, among kings and saints, Adam delves and sweats, half-naked.

Contrast is in the imagination too as it doubles through the centuries. Regal but evil-tempered Henry II, barefoot and clad only in an undershirt, is scourged before Becket's tomb by monk and bishop alike. King Canute fastens his crown to the Great Rood in expiation of the murder of old Alphege who steadfastly refused church ransom to the drunken Danes. Pilgrims, crippled, blind, scrofulous, thrust imploring hands into Becket's jewel-encrusted tomb. Dean Colet and a blushing Erasmus turn up fastidious noses in disgust when proffered

The Black Prince lies in Canterbury Cathedral: with replicas of his achievements above him – and a smiling little dog at his feet.

unsavoury relics to kiss. The clank of armour and clash of sword as Becket's murderers strike him down before his horrified monks ring in the silence of an empty cathedral. 'Blue Dick' on his firm ladder rattles down 'proud Becket's glassy bones'; and master mason William of Sens is thrown cripplingly down by rickety scaffolding from beneath his own Agnus Dei above the choir crossing. The Great Cloisters' 825 heraldic bosses look down on monks, blue-nosed and icy-handed, as they work and play; Prior Wibert's delicate 'tented' Water Tower spares them the rough scourge of plague; and up the richly carved Norman staircase poor pilgrims trudge for frugal fare in the North wing Aula Nova. . . . The list is endless.

Canterbury itself, despite the ravages of Baedeker raids and modern architects, still has much that is beautiful. St Martin's, where Queen Bertha worshipped and Augustine preached, has a bright splash of thin Roman bricks in its walls, a late-Saxon tub font, an air of timelessness, and a hurricane-cleared view over HM Prison's walls to St Augustine's Abbey and the cathedral.

The former, once a rival to Monte Cassino's magnificence, was more important even than the cathedral itself. After all, it was the acknowledged burial-place of kings of Kent and Canterbury's archbishops. Today little remains but the Decorated Gothic Fyndon Gateway, plain Cemetery Gate, a mere stump of what was once Ethelbert's Tower, its massivity broken by enriched Romanesque arcading; a lofty nave wall of Abbot Scotland's ragstone, and later Tudor brickwork; the crypt of Wulfric's octagonal rotunda; the Roman bricks of St Pancras' west porticus – and a lasting impression of vanished grandeur.

Only a stone's throw away, across what was once Mulberry Tree Walk, are the city walls. Behind them lies the Memorial Garden with its central cross and tiny Chapel of Remembrance in a D-shaped bastion. And behind the garden looms the cathedral, still whole and magnificent.

Canterbury's parks more than make up for their smallness with unusual charm. Dane John Gardens, once execution site and plague field, lie below the medieval city walls and the unusual, conical Dane John itself. On one side of its dignified avenue of lime trees is a robust Boer War obelisk inscribed by Eric Gill. On the other is the contrastingly delicate Marlowe Memorial. Its young Muse's scanty attire brought horrified glances – and her banishment from the old Buttermarket next to the cathedral gateway.

In the Westgate Gardens the shallow Stour is willow-fringed and, with dazzling flower-beds, leads the eye to the massive backdrop of the Westgate's drum towers. The entrance arch between them is so narrow that, when it threatened the arrival of Wombwell's Menagerie in 1850,

Pilgrim VIPs lodged in Meister Omers; lesser lights climbed Prior Wibert's impressive Norman Staircase to sleep on the floor of the Aula Nova above.

only the mayor's casting vote saved it from demolition. Today East Kent double-deckers cautiously ease through it – with only inches to spare.

There is still much to enjoy in the High Street, which changes its name almost as often as ambitious Hollywood starlet. Queen Elizabeth's guest chamber, with a double overhang, has a *mélange* of pargeted grapes and bibulous putti astride barrels, false rustication, bow windows and rich brick-nogging. The Beaney Institute was the bequest of a Canterbury surgeon settled in Melbourne whose skills (or presumably lack of them) led to two charges of manslaughter and one of murder. It is a mixed and overwhelming bag of tricks: heavy gables, oriel and latticed windows, half-timbering, red brick, a mosaic of tiny red and white stones, and a tiled porch supported by exuberantly carved eagles. Such grandeur might well have intimidated rather than encouraged the honest working man to further whose education it was built. Just across hump-backed King's Bridge the Weavers' five gables and window-boxes of brilliant geraniums reflected in a silvern river stop photographers in their tracks.

Stour Street, narrow and drab, is an unlikely setting for two such gems as Greyfriars Monastery and Poor Priests' Hospital. Of the former, all that remains is a tiny, steeply roofed building of black flints and grey ragstone generously patched with brick. Shaded by a copper beech, it straddles the narrow Stour on pointed arches set on round piers in the river bed. The Poor Priests Hospital, contrastingly massive, has since 1180 been in turn the home of Lambin Frese the Minter, hospice, gaol, workhouse and organ works. Today its enduring flints and oaken timbers have been restored with sensitivity to house a strikingly displayed Heritage Museum.

The castle, once one of the largest Norman keeps in England, is now sadly reduced in height and with no trace of perimeter walls or outbuildings. To Richard Barham, cleric and lively rhymester of medieval legend, it looked not unlike 'a well scooped Stilton cheese – but taller'. Its fighting record is equally undistinguished. Tame surrender to the Dauphin, 1216; capture by a handful of Wat Tyler's Kentish rebels, 1381; a token resistance by the Royalists in the Civil War; and, final humiliation, a nineteenth-century take-over by the nearby gasworks as coal store!

On each corner of Mercery Lane are rooted medieval buildings of such reassuring bulk and wide overhangs that they almost touch above it. On the left, thronged today by Debenham's eager bargain-hunters, was the Chequers of the Hope, where a hundred and more pilgrims found nightly lodging. Between its stone arches, the souvenir-touts of their day sold phials of Becket's seemingly endless blood or leaden brooches depicting his scalped head. On the right (now Boots the Chemists) lived prosperous Solomon the Mercer, his status-symbol house set over vaulted twelfth-century cellars.

Still further north of the triple gabled House of Agnes where David Copperfield stayed, towards the modern hill-perched university, is a church dedicated to St Dunstan, artist, musician, theologian and administrator – who pulled the Devil's nose with his metal-worker's tongs. In a vault below the Roper chapel lies the severed head of Sir Thomas More, once Chancellor of England and Henry VIII's close confidant – a head lost because, 'King's man' though he was, as 'God's man first' he refused to take the Oath of Obedience. Chillingly displayed on London Bridge for days, the head was finally thrown down at dead of night to his devoted daughter Meg, waiting in a boat below.

Canterbury is rich too in neighbouring villages of charm and character. Fordwich is approached over a hump-backed bridge, across a stretch of the Stour beloved by Izaak Walton. On its tiny quay, where Caen stone for the cathedral and wine for the abbey's thirsty monks were landed, is a tiny, jettied sixteenth-century town hall-cum-courtroom-cum-prison of timber and brick nogging – and a ducking-stool for scolds.

To the east, a road winds along a placid Stour to Wickhambreux and its towering white weather-boarded mill and huge water-wheel. Beyond it, pleached limes lead to a church with an Art Nouveau east window by Arild Rosenkrantz – all swirling angels and lilies. 'A real stunner; it stopped Archbishop Ramsey in his tracks, speechless. . . .'

Across the green, bereft of its tall limes and chestnuts by the 1987 hurricane, are dignified manor and rectory; sprawling whitewashed Rose & Crown; the former post office, chequered in flint and stone and with crow-stepped gables; and Old Willow Farm, with three plump bay windows and a rustic bridge across the shallow Little Stour.

To the south lies straggling, workaday Bekesbourne. First comes imposingly porticoed eighteenth-century Howletts, where gaming-club-owner John Aspinall regularly romps with Siberian tigers and heavyweight gorillas and plays generous host to other endangered species. A mile away, past the railway station, St Peter's is uniquely sited on a knoll above fruit trees and a shallow ford. Across the latter is the Old Palace where Cranmer wrote the Book of Common Prayer – and Ian Fleming, of 007, 'Licensed to Kill'.

Back on the A257, although Sandwich calls seductively, Wingham demands a halt. It has a kinked High Street, lined with copper beeches and Spanish chestnuts, an air of gentle urbanity, and the cleanest 'loo' in the county. It has too a distant memory of the King of France's gift elephant plodding to the King of England's Tower of London menagerie, and a twentieth-century one of once having had *three* railway stations. What's more, it reared both Bolívar's dashing cavalry leader, William Miller, and Best's son, the tanner of Wingham, a Jack Cade rebel. Of him, Shakespeare's Bevis cried: 'He shall have the skins of our enemies to make dog's leather of.'

Its buildings are equally dashing. The church, with conspicuous green copper spire, has a grandiose black-and-white Oxinden Memorial, live with ox heads, playful putti and cascading flowers and fruits. It has too, surely uniquely, piers of cheap chestnut rather than expensive stone – simply because a sixteenth-century Canterbury brewer embezzled the restoration fund! Dog Inn and Red Lion pub (as well as Old Canonry and The Chantry), imposing thirteenth-century timber-framed houses, have a surprising religious past – as part of a thirteenth-century College of Six Canons. And, just for variety, there are a couple of Kentish rarities – thatched cottages.

Across Ash Level, Roman Richborough fort is under siege. Its 1,700-year-old walls, twenty-five feet high and eleven feet thick, of stone and still iron-hard mortar, stoutly resist encirclement by muddy Stour, silted Wantsum channel and modern railway line. And beyond them, menacingly poised, are the vast parking-lots of today's invaders – German Volkswagens, Pfizer's sprawling pharmaceutical empire and Richborough power-station's three giant cooling-towers, already redundant.

Here, first protected by double ditches, was the Roman army's huge supply base. And here, in AD 85, the might of Rome was celebrated by a towering triumphal arch, set on foundations thirty feet deep and sumptuously decorated with marble columns and bronze statues. Two hundred years later, as Jutish pirates became even bolder, the flaunting monument became practical look-out post, part of the strengthened defences of a Saxon Shore fort. Today the glory has faded, but in early morning mist you can still hear marching legions and glimpse upraised eagles.

Just down the road is a *modern* pyramid. A scrapyard of Mini piled on Peugeot, of Daimler on Porsche, of Zephyr on Cavalier. An omnivorous crane with a grab like a dinosaur's claws seizes these once-prized cars two at a time and flings them disdainfully aside to be crumpled like old hats – and baled for scrap.

It is hard to believe that Sandwich, now a sleepy market town, was once England's premier port and had a turbulent history. Canute, in 1015, put hostages ashore here with their hands, ears and noses cut off; Becket fled in fear and returned in triumph from exile; the French harried it repeatedly; Huguenot refugees, fleeing the barbarities of the St Bartholomew's Day massacre, brought it new-found prosperity; and

Queen Elizabeth supped here in 1573, on 160 dishes, and was (or should have been) 'very merry' – but not merry enough to finance the dredging of Sandwich's silt-choked harbour.

To the east lies not only world-famous Royal St George's Golf Course but also the almost equally feared Royal Cinque Ports and Prince's Golf Courses. (The latter was 'holed out' during World War II as a bombing range!) To the south, Sandwich Bay became a Millionaires' Row; to the north, for bird-lovers there is a nature reserve, and for the hardy a nudists' beach.

The whole of russet-roofed Sandwich is uniquely covered by a single conservation order. Its web of narrow lanes is almost indigestibly rich in buildings. Dutch-gabled Manwood Court; St Clement's imposing tower rich in Norman arcading; the King's Arms, where a wild satyr acts as corner bracket; Luytens' Queen Anne Salutation house, specially sited near the gasworks to benefit the health of three asthmatic bachelor brothers; Old Dutch House and Flint House, which speak for themselves; tall, quayside Fisher Gate and chequered Tudor Barbican on which a tablet records that 30,000 Jewish refugees found safety here from Hitler's insensate cruelty; tiny Customs House and imposing King's Lodging, which has a Dutch-gabled gateway – and the friendliest of West Highland watchdogs.

With unusual charity, Sandwich has twinned with Honfleur whose men brutally pillaged it in 1547, in token of which the mayor still wears black robes.

Sandwich offers a choice of routes to Dover as different as they are delightful. The A268 hurries to Deal by a seaside route past mist-hazed and richly fertile fields and Worth's peaceful backwater.

A glimpse of the inland silhouette of Betteshanger's pithead-gear is a salutary reminder that Kent was once 'coal' as well as 'cherries'. With workings stretching a mile out to sea and a mountainous spoil-heap beside it, it is the sole but precarious survivor of the original quartet that formed the East Kent Coalfields. Nearby Tilmanstone's redundant winding-stock was sent crashing down in 1987.

Deal, once labelled 'villainous' in his famous *Rural Rides*, by the outspoken radical, William Cobbett, is to-day bright, breezy and bracing. Good enough for Julius Caesar's landing in 55 BC, it is today unfashionable – and so, mercifully, uncrowded. On the sea and of the sea, it has resisted the tawdry gimmicks that bring in quick tourist 'bucks'. Its retirement and its pleasures are taken quietly. A steeply shelving shingle beach crowned with a mini-Armada of assorted boats is, not surprisingly, more popular with discerning anglers than with timid bathers. So too is its gaunt concrete pier – England's only post-war one.

Four miles offshore, and ten miles long by two miles wide, but constantly shifting, the Goodwin Sands, 'the Shyppe Swallower', have for centuries been a grave for the unwary, the unwise and the unfortunate. In the Great Storm of 1703, thought by some to be the Day of Judgement, 'Fower ships of the Royall Navy, and others, and 1800 men were drowned.' And yet their very presence helped create The Downs, sheltered waters where fleets of sailing-ships 500 strong waited for favourable winds or rode out storms – and made Deal rich.

At low tide some of the hidden Sands shake off the sea like surfacing whales. Innocuous enough – except for the occasional chilling glimpse of mast or funnel. Or even of virtually a whole ship. For, on occasions, the Goodwins play cat-and-mouse with their prey, sucking them down, briefly relaxing their grip – but always reclaiming their own. In them, as Shakespeare wrote, 'the carcases of many a tall ship lie buried' – even, in 1954, ironically that of the guardian South Goodwin lightship itself!

In 1854 top-hatted men played cricket there, a feat repeated periodically, including 1985, when Kent's 'greats' swopped St Lawrence turf for Goodwin sand. But it is no place to be at the turn of the tide. In minutes it creates swirling quicksands that have suction enough to swallow men almost at a gulp.

Behind the broad promenade lies Middle Street, cutting across a web of quaint seventeenth-century alleys. Black-and-white Time-Ball Tower, whose Greenwich-controlled ball has long dropped precisely at 1 p.m. GMT to ensure chronometer accuracy on passing ships, is now a museum. White-cupolaed barracks are as smart as the Royal Marines themselves. St Leonard's Church, red-brick tower capped by trim white turret, has a gallery 'Built by ye Pilots of Deal' in 1658. So perhaps, if storm delayed, they could still, sea-booted and chimneypot-hatted, attend services without disturbing others. Classic St George's Churchyard is where Nelson wept at the funeral of 'dear, good, little' Captain Parker who died in great pain after an abortive 'commando' raid on Boulogne.

And, of course, there are Henry VIII's three revolutionary, low-profiled, Tudor Rose 'Bulwarks' (castles) that mounted devastating fire-power. Sandown was long ago overwhelmed by the sea. Walmer, as the official residence of the Lord Warden of the Cinque Ports (currently the Queen Mother), has become less bellicose. It has picture windows inserted by Wellington for Queen Victoria's visit, and a Georgian annexe, and in the moat, once filled with sea-water at high tide, are gardens and clipped yews planted by Pitt's niece, the egocentric virago, self-styled 'Queen of Arabia', Lady Hester Stanhope.

Deal Castle, however, looks as impregnable as ever. Drawbridge and

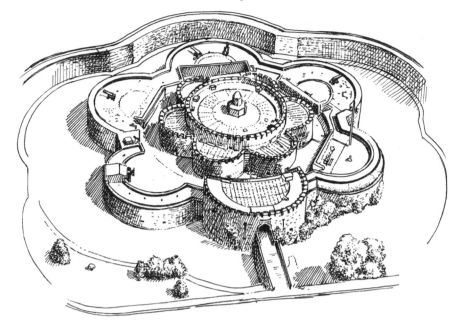

Deal Castle's curved bastions deflected cannon balls, its broad platforms gave unprecedented fire-power, and its very compactness, a small target.

portcullis are long gone but the deep moat, heavily studded doors and ominous murder holes above (for sudden pike thrust or boiling oil) still show blunt hostility. So do the broad gun-emplacements and black-snouted nineteenth-century cannon with their high-piled 'cascades' of thirty-two-pound shot. Inside, still more cannon were mounted to fire through deeply splayed embrasures in eleven-foot-thick walls.

Inside, passages follow the outer walls in a circular maze. They curve past cookhouse ovens, cool wine store and still cooler powder magazine with its copper-sheathed doors and copper-hooped barrels of gun-powder, then, bewilderingly, on again past half-moon chapel and deep central well.

Walmer, Deal's Siamese twin, is largely residential, but Kingsdown still has a nautical tang. This is the springboard from which Kent's too-often bungalow-bedevilled coastline rises to real grandeur: crisp turf, sheer drops, wide seascapes and towering chalk cliffs. Shortly before St Margarets-at-Cliffe, an imposing granite obelisk remembers the destroyers and crews of the Dover Patrol. In both wars, in all weathers and at no small cost, they kept open the Channel's vital sea lanes.

For me, St Margaret's *is* its wholeheartedly Norman church. There is power in the huge, almost windowless tower, the soaring chancel arch and the massive piers embellished with zigzag ornament and scalloped capitals. And there is added richness in the gable-protected west doorway. Inside, a wide modern window contrasts with deep-set Norman ones. In the former, Christ and the South Foreland cliffs flank a blue-green sea and red-hulled Townsend Thoresen ferry, the *Herald of Free Enterprise*, to honour three local men who died in the Zeebrugge disaster.

A narrow road zigzags down beneath the tiered houses of the wealthy to the little bay and its lone pub lying snug between steep headlands. From its rocky beach, groyned with heavy iron girders, a succession of Channel swimmers have headed hopefully for Cap Gris Nez, just twenty-one miles distant.

In the lee of the cliffs are the sweeping lawns and sunken pool, rockery and bog garden of the unusual 'Pines'. A pugnacious, nine-foot-tall Winston Churchill dominates its centre. Behind him lies the façade of 73 Cheapside, ornate and with its empty windows bright with flowers. As a lighter touch there is a barrel-shaped Romany *honeymoon* caravan, complete with frilly curtains, gilded fittings and a practical down-to-earth black stove. Making love can be hungry work!

On the cliffs above, the South Foreland is a lyric overture to a matchless clifftop walk to Dover. The old lighthouse, rigidly fenced off, teeters on the cliff edge. A white smock-mill, with delicate tracery sweeps, and the vividly green-tiled Dolphin's Leap keep it discreet company. Safely away from cliff fall – and remotely controlled – is a second lighthouse. Despite its twenty-six-mile, 1 million candle-power range, still higher tech has just rendered it redundant. Now it is 'Desirable Residence for Sale'.

So, on to Dover, sparing a dizzy glance down to Langdon Bay – accessible only by a steep stairway cut out of the cliff face itself. Further on, from a finely sited car-park, Dover Castle is silhouetted to the west. And the fascinating ceaseless bustle of Britain's major passenger port is at one's feet.

Those who like rolling, unspoilt countryside better than seaside will prefer the inland A256 route to Dover. Eastry's church, gloomy but richly ornamented, is full of interest and has a window uniquely dedicated to 'the wives and mothers of the parish'. And below Becket's there is a labyrinth of chalk caves where the archbishop, fleeing the King's wrath, may have hidden. Betteshanger's garden-set but fraudulent 'Norman' church is sheltered by a yew planted by Gladstone – just after he'd raised income tax to an 'iniquitous' 7d in the pound.

Rich and exuberant! The south door of Barfreston's tiny but incomparable Romanesque church – half hidden on a secluded Downland hillside.

Off-route Barfreston is a must. Little more than a hamlet, yet its church, perched between the lone yew of Yew Tree Inn and a hurricane-crumpled corrugated-iron barn, is unrivalled in England. It has a wealth of Norman decoration. Snarling animals, jousting men, a bear playing a harp, a monkey mounted on a goat, strange amphibians, the labours of the month . . . a frieze of heads grotesque enough to scare away the most demoniac of devils . . . Christ in Glory . . . a wheel window . . . and, inside, still more carving on the chancel arch. All this in a building not fifty feet long!

Although isolated and disused, Waldershare church is equally stunning. Outside there are yews and views, a vast Guilford family mausoleum and a quirk of brick bonding. But it is its dark and dusty interior, its north chapel, that holds its highlight, a monument worthy of St Paul's and the *Guinness Book of Records* . . . an exuberant, overweaning, four-tiered wedding cake of four differently hued marbles! At its corners, life-size women mourn wealthy Sir Henry Furnese who died in 1712. Above them, irrepressibly cheerful little boys stand naked and unimpressed amid ornate cartouches of arms. Above them more putti heads and impressively curling volutes. *And above them*, an urn – almost touching the ceiling! In the south chapel – and in much less ostentation – Susan Bertie in square-toed shoes, and her plump, peruked husband lie together – still fondly holding hands.

Sir Henry's second monument, a tall-windowed Queen Anne mansion, stands in the park below – a park in which the 1987 hurricane unceremoniously flattened a whole avenue of mature trees: the present Earl of Guilford has ceremoniously set them on their roots again with mobile cranes! It is not the hurricane but time, weather and, *of course*, local vandals who have taken their toll of Sir Henry's third monument, a lofty, balustraded belvedere.

Out of earshot, the A268 continues through dormitory Whitfield and the Knights Templars' Temple Ewell, crouched below the Downs on the infant Dour, to Dover.

Dover's main street, drab and narrowly confined by the Dour Valley, is at first glance frankly undistinguished. Yet it does contain the Roman Painted House with its 2,000-year-old walls still rich in colour; Hubert de Burgh's 1203 Maison Dieu, a hospice for 300 years but today aglow with Cinque Port banners, stained glass and portraits; St Mary's clasped-buttressed and arcaded five-stage Norman tower; and St Edmund's, England's smallest church in regular use and the only one to be dedicated by one saint, St Richard of Chichester, to another.

Dover is at its best on the curving spaciousness of Marine Parade. At one end, huge TIRs sweep down Jubilee Way, past precautionary 'escape routes', to the 'Gateway to Europe'. Six hundred acres of

Dover's Russell Gardens are a charming oasis of peace amid the bustle of England's busiest passenger port.

harbour are sheltered by two long breakwaters built of 60,000 huge concrete blocks. With a hundred arrivals and departures day, it is a veritable bus-station of a port through which in a single year pass a couple of million cars, half as many juggernauts and 14 million passengers. And yet in 1824 Dover, like Sandwich, had its silting problems. 'Not a nutshell,' it was said, 'could float in or out.'

Nearby, Charles Rolls, first man to make a return Channel flight, and Captain Webb, first man to swim it (on a nauseous diet of cod liver oil, beef tea, brandy, coffee and good old ale), gaze determinedly towards France.

At the other end, if you don't wish to risk a choppy crossing, the Prince of Wales Pier offers a sea-blow, a tangle of anglers, all-embracing Dover views and dramatic close-ups of giant Hovercraft. All whirling, whirring propellers and half-hidden in swirling spray, they heave themselves onto terra firma like primeval beasts.

Above all, of course, is Henry II's castle, 'Lock and Key to the

Kingdom', 'Cornerstone of England'. Within its encircling walls the massive keep towers 465 feet above sea-level. Saxon St Mary in Castro unfortunately suffers from Butterfield's Victorian and urinal-like mosaics once succinctly described as 'serviceable, durable – and damnable'. And the craggy Roman Pharos, only feet from it, whose beacon light guided Caesar's galleys safely into harbour, still stands over sixty feet tall.

The castle itself is honeycombed with passages and outerworks. Within its twenty-four-foot-thick walls are vast banqueting halls, in which French Napoleonic POWs froze and wretchedly carved their names and graffiti. *'Dieu tout puissant delivre moi'* ('Omnipotent God deliver me'). There are upper and lower chapels with sumptuous Norman decoration; a diorama of Waterloo; daunting arrays of improbably horrific weapons; and a 400-foot well, down which an obliging custodian will send a lighted rag swirling into Stygian blackness.

On the Western Heights, across a harbour big enough to give anchorage to the Grand Fleet (in the days when it *was* Grand), are the foundations of Pharos' twin, HM Borstal, Citadel and Drop Redoubt. The latter were vast enough for Cobbett to thunder that, used in 'profligacy most scandalous', their bricks would have made cottages for every labourer in Kent and Sussex. There is, too, the Grand Shaft with its triple interlocking staircases, reputedly for 'officers and their ladies; NCOs and their wives; soldiers and their women'.

Shakespeare Cliff, where men were once lowered on ropes to gather the delicacy samphire, now gazes down on frenzied Channel Tunnel borings. Behind it a mushroom town of drear hutments spreads up the valley.

Despite that, the North Downs Way offers a fine Folkestone finale. It is at its best along the cliff edge behind Capel-le-Ferne. At its best when an autumn sunset gilds the railway lines 300 feet below and, setting in a sky of beaten copper, turns the sea into a golden path to Copt Point.

Suddenly, almost at one's feet, there is a yawning gulf. Here in 1917 tens of thousands of tons of chalk slithered slowly down over underlying clay to block railway line and beach. Today this once white wilderness, the Warren, is now a green jungle, haunt of earnest geologists and adventurous small children, a sheltered haven for sun- and sea-worshippers.

Folkestone has three faces, each with different appeal. The Leas are elegance personified. Sleek hotels front onto its cliff-top lawns and gardens (part of Decimus Burton's townscape) and a curlicued bandstand, rated by Newman as a 'flimsy piece of confectionery'. Discoverer of the circulation of the blood, and inveterate coffee-drinker, William Harvey, one hand on his own heart, the other holding a deer's, gazes

Dover Pharos, within the Castle walls, was a guiding beacon for benighted Roman galleys;
a bell-tower for Saxon Christians.

out over the white faience of the Leas Hall clinging limpet-like to the cliff-face. Zigzag paths drop invitingly down to the beach past tamarisk, broom and pine. Inland are broad avenues, grass-verged and tree-lined, flanked by suitably handsome houses.

At the east end of the Leas is the Avenue of Remembrance. Down it, in World War I, a million men marched to embark for Flanders mud – and massacre. From the harbour, the Old High Street, steep and narrow, is a veritable staircase of souvenir shops and bingo arcades, pubs and cafés, and even Ye Olde Kent Original Humbug Shoppe.

It leads to St Eanswythe's Church. One of the latter's predecessors was built too near the cliff edge . . . another was sacked by the Danes. But the bones of the young saint and miracle-worker are still enshrined in a church richly decorated with wall-paintings, alabaster arcading and a Kempe window, honouring William Harvey – and paid for by the medical profession worldwide.

East Cliff too has acres of grass. Much of it, under the gaze of one of the 194 coastal Martello towers built to repel Napoleon, is dedicated to sport. From it, westwards, is a spectacular view of Old Folkestone, high-piled behind the harbour; of fishing-boats, at low tide sprawled on the mud; and of steamers berthed alongside the Mole waiting for boat-trains that crawl down Tram Road, a low-arched causeway not far from William Cubitt's towering nineteen-span viaduct. Northeastwards there is an unforgettable view of miles of curving white cliffs rising sheer from sea and beach.

Sandgate, awash with antique shops, is backed by a last kick of the Downs and the sprawling wasteland of Shorncliffe Army Camp. Its fifteenth-century castle has long been relegated to mere Martello-tower status. Mountainous seas helped to bring about its downfall, and today, when whipped to fury by south-east gales, they hurl spray high above the roadside cottages – in one of which a desperately sick H. G. Wells found new life.

Sleepy Hythe is another marooned Cinque Port. To the west, the crackle of rifle practice occasionally disturbs Romney Marsh peace; to the east, sunk below the broad sea-wall, is a billiard-table-flat golf course of seemingly little malice. The Royal Military Canal's banks offer shady strolling, somnolent fishing, dilettante oarsmanship and a grandstand view of Hythe's spectacular biennial, the Venetian Fête. And, at their terminus, the perfect one-third scale locos of the Romney, Hythe & Dymchurch Railway, amid billowing steam, wait impatiently for their Marsh odyssey to begin.

In the narrow High Street, a splendidly pilastered Nat West bank and a pedimented town hall on plump Tuscan pillars stand side by side. From beneath the latter a lane climbs steeply up the hillside between

A perfect one-third-scale locomotive of the Romney, Hythe & Dymchurch Railway,
part-brainchild of a Polish Count.

pleasant houses to St Leonard's. Even its lofty chancel and Bethersden
marble shafts are not as striking as the crypt – containing a seemingly
illogical and spine-chilling 2,000 high-stacked skulls and 8,000 thigh
bones of resurrected plague victims. Outside in the graveyard there are
not unwelcome sea-breezes and the tomb of Northumbrian Lionel
Lukin who still keeps an eye on the sea which he taunted with the first
lifeboat. On its trials it carried ballast – of opportunist contraband!

Sadly, Saltwood Castle, where in shamed darkness the four knights
plotted Becket's death, no longer opens its grounds to the public. But
Sandling Place, a Whitsun glory of azalea and rhododendron, certainly
does.

Inland from Sandgate lies hitherto unknown Cheriton. There the
Channel Tunnel terminal is already devastating hundreds of acres of
Kentish countryside. And, underground, twin rail tunnels are burrowing through the first of their thirty miles. Along them 'shuttles',
interspersed with British Rail expresses, will hurtle torpedo-like . . . at
100 mph . . . every ten or twelve minutes! A daunting prospect for the
1990s that may or may not steady Britain's erratic balance of trade. In

its wake? A wider web of roads? More fuel-belching juggernauts? More gaunt warehouses? More land-hungry suburbia? An ear-battering 180 mph railway that will certainly keep up with the French – but will give no help to overcrowded and frustrated commuters?

The Canterbury–Folkestone road too has its switchback moments. Barham Downs give a view of tumbled hills and a glimpse of the idyllic Elham Valley. Broome Park is field marshal's home turned time-share country club. A platoon of neatly ranged golf buggies does little to detract from the exuberance of its rose-red brick, scrolled and pedimented gables, soaring pilasters and deep eaves. From such peaceful Jacobean bravura Lord Kitchener left for his ill-fated voyage to Russia aboard HMS *Hampshire*.

Denton has a miniscule green, pretty cottages and The Jackdaw: a name that keeps alive the memory of Richard Barham's thieving 'Jackdaw of Rheims' so witheringly cursed by 'bell, book and candle'. Nearby Tappington Farm, a rambling delight of brick and timber, catslide roof and tiny dormers, set in a hollow between rich chocolate ploughland and wooded hillside, was Barham's own spectre-haunted home.

Much-bombed Hawkinge Aerodrome now peacefully displays, in the Dowding Memorial Hangar, grim evidence of the half-forgotten heroism – and horror – of Battle of Britain warfare.

East, in their own tight little valley, lie Alkham and what little castle-building Henry VIII left of the abbey dedicated to St Radigund. The latter was a German princess (and vegetarian) who delighted in caring for those 'with nauseous distempers' and who, even when married, wore a hair shirt.

West are the sweeping viewpoints of Sugar Loaf Hill and Caesar's Camp – the latter of Iron Age rather than Roman occupation. At their feet are Folkestone, sea and harbour . . .

10

Romney Marsh

Romney Marsh was Richard Barham's 'Fifth Continent', remote from civilization, to which, in 1821, he bade a joyful farewell with only a lingering backward glance at 'gooseberry wine, pear and codling'. Queen Elizabeth I dreaded the Marsh, where witches wheeled above Dymchurch Wall on broomsticks; ruthless smugglers infested its shores, and the very weather was apostrophized as 'evil in winter, grievous in summer and never good'.

For all that, it is a land of small miracles; a land won from the sea, below which much of it lies, with rivers that dramatically changed course; ports that became inland towns; a maze of lanes; a cobweb of dikes; fat pastures and fatter sheep; and churches that rejoiced even John Betjeman's critical heart. Yet, in this motorized age, it is still a place where silence and solitude can be found, where time stands still but the light constantly changes before burning itself out in majestic sunsets.

An obvious approach is along the A259 coastal road from Hythe, but here the Marsh is not at its best. Far preferable is the gentler backdoor route from Ashford. From it you are sped on your way in a swirl of roundabouts, dictatorial blue arrows and eager traffic. Then peace as the B2070 heads for Ham Street, the Marsh and Littlestone-on-Sea. It is a peace to be shattered only by the Kingsnorth Museum with a row of red-muzzled cannons set between Victorian lamp-posts! Orlestone Forest, its sombre winter branches spring-jewelled with catkins, hugs the road on one side, Ham Street Woods more distantly on the other.

Secluded Orlestone is a gem that straggling Ham Street finds hard to follow, but it does its best with the only railway station for miles (with oddly staggered platforms), a pondlet across which a drunken willow throws huge branches, black-and-white dormered Middle Platt and Keeper's Cottage and a lichened pill-box.

The B2067 sweeps you by Leacon Hall, a splendid Queen Anne mansion. But the heart of Warehorne lies down an Appledore-bound lane – a scatter of pleasant houses round a homely green. The wide-eyed Woolpack gazes, slightly startled, across to St Matthew's red-brick tower, whose predecessor was shattered by lightning in 1773. Sheep graze contentedly in its graveyard as if of indisputable right.

Here, just above the Marsh and its fevers, lived Richard Barham, lawyer turned clergyman, scholarly antiquarian and a future canon of St Paul's. And here, when confined to bed after an overturned gig had smashed his leg, he gave free rein to the lively verse and rumbustious characters, folk tales and legends which were later to make the *Ingoldsby Legends* a rollicking success.

Appledore surprises and charms by its very brevity. But along its wide, grass-verged street are buildings of brick and tile, plaster and timber that repay a leisured stroll. 'High Class Junk' faces 'Jone's [*sic*] – Greengrocer'. So too do stoutly timbered Swan House and Swan Inn. Outside the Red Lion, travellers lunch al fresco despite the menace of a grimly black Franco-Prussian War gun trained on them and the church from 'Wheelwrights' just across the road.

In front of the Early English church, a forsythia-surrounded notice board tells Appledore's history. A peaceful backwater? Backwater: maybe, for it was once on the now ten-mile-distant sea, known to traders and Viking invaders who made it their base. Peaceful: definitely not! The French in 1380 burned village and church; Horne's Place – but not its lofty little chapel and tunnel-vaulted undercroft – was sacked by angry Wat Tyler; and Jack Cade's men made their mark too in 1450.

Where then to find peace? The banks of the Royal Military Canal belie its name; walk in tranquillity on its grassy, raised embankments and see only the endless green peace of the Marsh. Or for a splash more spring colour visit 'Appledore's Answer'. Martin Clifton and his father, a Lincolnshire man, once carried coals to Newcastle by exporting bulbs to the Netherlands from their 150 acres! Today those acres are decimated, but beside a cathedral-like barn their formal, pooled garden is a patchwork of spring colour, of hyacinths rubbing shoulders with tulips, daffodils with narcissi. A miniature Spalding!

Enough dallying. The Marsh lies ahead. Snargate and Snave have all the sound of Dickensian lawyers or pantomime bailiff's men.

Snave, marsh-encircled, marsh-isolated, is small (fifty-nine souls in 1801) but possessed two manors – and the right to erect its own gallows. Nearby Hangman's Toll Bridge, beyond Walnut Tree Farm, probably refers to the charge levied to enter the burial field. The church's finely battlemented tower and porch are approached by a grassy, elm-flanked track. It is dedicated to St Augustine but was recently rechristened 'the Daffodil Church' because of a lavish gift of bulbs sent 'to that lonely church'.

Brenzett and Brookland follow. The former, a mere hamlet, has,

Legend, in an immoral age, said that Brookland's belfry toppled down to earth in amazement when a virgin *was married there.*

unless Brenzett folk have disproportionately large thirsts, a disproportionately large inn. And beneath St Eanswythe's shingled spirelet, on
a brightly decorated tomb-chest, lie, side by side, the effigies of two
Roundheads still in their riding-boots. Strangely, peaceful Brenzet was
the rallying-point for Wat Tyler's Marsh men – armed only with pitch-
forks.

Battle of Britain dog-fights in the jet-streamed sky above the empty
Marsh were a daily occurrence that scarcely halted ploughmen in their
work. The Brenzett Aeronautical Museum on the Ivychurch road is a
reminder and memorial of gallantry and terrifying death, German and
British alike.

Brookland church too often suffers the indignity of cursory visits
merely to inspect its belfry, all wood and shingle, three 'candle-snuffers'
piled one on top of the other and surmounted by winged dragon with

forked tail. No matter of climbing perilous ladders to view it. Because of the soft nature of its site, it is next to the timber porch – on the ground!

A return to the A259 takes us slightly above the Marsh along the old Rhee Wall which helped contain the sea, past tiny Old Romney, once an island and then a flourishing eleventh-century port. Today St Clement's is field-surrounded. It was damaged in World War II, and rain dripped through its shattered roof for years. Mortally ill, it might well have been demolished but for Canterbury architect Anthony Swayne and Rank Films. The former planned the stitching-up of the tower's gaping wounds; rotting beams were strengthened and refaced. Money ran out. And then a modern 'miracle'. Rank wished to film *Dr Syn*, Marsh priest and smuggler of Russell Thorndike's novels, in the church. Even commercialism's flint heart was touched by the still-uncured ills. Rank paid handsomely.

With Old Romney eventually landlocked, New Romney throve at its expense. Then, in its turn, it suffered the vagaries of Nature. In 1287 a freak storm blocked its harbour, and the Rother, for a second time, treacherously changed its course, to Rye. In a single night, maritime trade, New Romney's life-blood, was cut off. But along its neat grid-plan streets still stand buildings of charm and character: the town hall and assembly room, Southlands Almshouses and St John's Priory.

But it is St Nicholas's, last survivor of Romney's once five churches,

Once overlooking the town wharf, Old Romney church now dreams amid the pastures of which Cobbett said, 'I never saw such corn before'.

that is its joy and the Marsh's landmark. The Normans, repulsed in 1066 by Romney fishermen, came back in force after Hastings to exact revenge. And their descendants settled there and built its magnificent pinnacled and clasp-buttressed tower of pale gold stone over a hundred feet high above its lavish triple-shafted doorway. Steps lead *down* to it, and marks, still visible on its sturdy round and octagonal piers, show how high sea and debris rose 700 years ago.

The B2075 drives on to Lydd. On one side, small lakes have formed in old gravel workings, and piles of it make the only 'peaks' between here and the Lympne 'cliffs'.

On the other side is Walland Marsh, south of the Rhee Wall to the Kent Ditch (or county boundary), home of the black-spotted *Rano ridibunda* or Great Marsh frog. Great enough to eat field-mice and voles, as well, regrettably, as smaller members of its own species. Clamorous enough, *en masse*, in the mating season to warrant local protests to the Ministry of Health. More than amorous enough, too. In twenty years, a round dozen of them, a number which included only two females, imported from Hungary into a garden pond, multiplied and took over a hundred square miles of Marsh!

Lydd's narrow sandbank ancestry can be traced from its elongated plan and axial streets – lined with homely weather-boarded and tile-hung cottages. Its wealth, like New Romney's, can be seen in a church founded on wool. Fifteenth-century All Saints, 'the Cathedral of the Marsh', at 200 feet, it is the longest parish church in Kent. Its tower, whose final stages, with slender pinnacles, were commissioned by the rector, a certain Cardinal Wolsey to-be, overtops New Romney's by some thirty feet! In World War II, its chancel was virtually demolished, first by an HE bomb and then by flying bombs. The suggestion that, to save expense, a new chancel be formed from the nave was indignantly repudiated by its parishioners, and today its stands splendidly and harmoniously restored.

Lydd has more modern claims to fame: the invention of the explosive Lyddite, and an Army camp where today soldiers are trained for the IRA's shoot-in-the-back 'war' in Northern Ireland. To the north lies Ferryfield Airport; to the south, the modern ziggurats of Dungeness nuclear power-stations A and B.

If Romney Marsh is a fifth continent, as Richard Barham opined, Dungeness is surely a sixth. It is like no other area in Kent, probably in England. It is a mass of moving shingle with the sea scouring it from the west of the point and swirling it round to the ever-growing beaches of the east. Believe it or not, lorries shuttle from east to west carrying back to the power-stations shingle once swept from beneath them.

Winds are bitter; fog rolls in silently, secretively. But there is a living

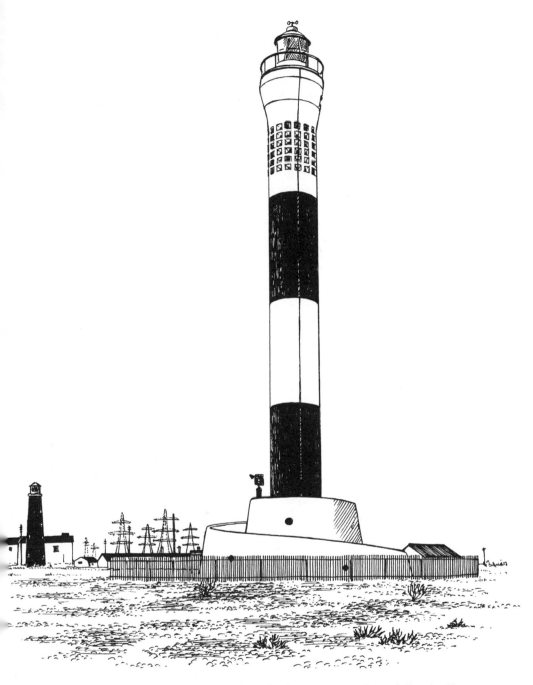

Third of its line, majestic Dungeness Lighthouse lends soaring verticality to billiard-table flat marsh.

to be made with rod and line, and nets. The only hoardings you see proclaim it: 'Fresh Lug' and 'Bait', 'Squid', 'Plaice, Shrimps and Dover Sole'. The shingle has spawned a shanty town of tarred sheds, down-at-heel bungalows, old railway carriages . . . some with flaking paint, some spruced up each spring.

There is even a single-storey concrete church. It started life as part of war-time PLUTO (Pipe Line Under The Ocean), which fuelled the Allies' invasion tanks, planes and trucks, and ended it, because of apathy and vandalism, as a meeting-place for the Royal Ancient Order of Buffaloes. Even the church bell was stolen! Today's Pilot Inn crouches squat and square against the wind. Its predecessor's saloon bar had the doubtful distinction, it is said, of having been a Spanish frigate lured ashore by locals who plundered its wine and gold and murdered the crew. On the beach itself, oil-caked winches, rusty oil-drums, duck-boards, nets, cable and chain, frayed ropes . . .

If the shingle desert is of little use to man or plant, it is a haven for birds. The RSPB reserve covers 1,200 acres and has logged 270 different species. Gravel pits have provided fresh water and island havens for reed buntings, sedge and reed warblers, and shelduck. Little terns, fire-crests, stone curlews and the far-from-common common gull too.

If birds abound, so seemingly do lighthouses. The first light here was in 1615, because 'a thousand perished there for want of light every year'. The base of Trinity House and James Wyatt's 1792 lighthouse is today part of keepers' cottages. The 1904 lighthouse, of black brick, looks immovable enough but was pensioned off because of the constantly changing foreshore.

The latest of the long line, built in 1961, is black-and-white collared. Frighteningly slim, it nevertheless beams its light seventeen miles. Its strident voice, three two-second blasts in every minute, is actuated by the very mist it thwarts. It bludgeons and nags the unsuspecting ear and would seemingly drive any resident to jibbering lunacy. The last possibility was, however, given a firm thumbs down by a svelte, black-trousered red-head who seemed to have strayed from another world. 'Totally immune,' she laughed. And should the foghorn be insufficient to warn off blinded ships, *Alice Upjohn* is half a mile up-coast, poised to uphold RNLI tradition.

Give me the clean desolation of Dungeness; spare me the ribbon development of Greatstone-on-Sea. Mile after mile of 'undistinguished and indistinguishable' bungalows reel past what to the uninitiated seems a social vacuum.

Littlestone is better. It was planned, whereas Greatstone just grew. Oddly, it owes something to the Hong Kong–Shanghai Railway. On the latter's completion in 1886, by a Littlestone-infatuated Sir Robert Perks, he found time and money enough to plan 'a maritime town', a second Eastbourne with Grand Hotel and sound Victorian houses, four and five storeys high, looking down on grass and sand. Chapel and golf course followed; so too did a handsome and lofty red-brick water-tower. Then, as suddenly as it started, development stopped. And today, still incomplete, Littlestone slumbers gently.

St Mary-in-the-Marsh – 'very much in the Marsh,' says Newman – has charm, a Norman church tower, two fine brasses and the grave of Edith Nesbitt (author of *The Railway Children*), marked with the single word 'Resting'.

Holiday camps, bungalows and shacks follow the coastal road to Dymchurch. That too has caught the contagion, but the eighteenth-century New Hall makes some amends with its court-room of the Lords of the Levels. The early twentieth century, by my book, turned up trumps only with its reinforcement of the old sea-walls along which coaches once ran. Today, inland, they tower grassily twenty feet above the road, and seawards throw out twenty yards of concrete defiance to the sea, culminating in a final concave coping. Even centuries of winter storms will find the going tough!

A Marsh 'round' can be completed, suddenly uphill, past the graceful modern Shepway Cross. Here Lords Warden for centuries dispensed salutary king's justice to those high-handed Cinque Ports-men, founders of the Navy, who had carried their royal privilege into licence. And so to Lympne – pronounced 'Lim'.

Here, 300 feet above the Marsh, on what once were sea-lapped cliffs, is a wealth of interest and beauty. Lympne Castle, on cliff edge, though 'lyke a castelet embatelyd', is really a medieval manor house that belonged to the archdeacons of Canterbury. For all that, the ghost of a Roman soldier is said to walk the east tower where once stood a Roman look-out. One for the fort below guarding Portus Lemanis, head-quarters of the 'Admiral of the British Fleet', facing ever-fiercer Saxon raids. The fort, undermined by springs, slithered down the hillside some 1,700 years ago. But, in the huge blocks of masonry of what is now called Stutfall Castle, you can see that Roman brick and stone are still as indissolubly wedded as ever by enduring Roman mortar. St Stephen's Church, with its severe central tower but no transepts, virtually rubs shoulders with the castle to complete the picture.

That should be more than enough for one small Kentish village. Nothing of the sort! Walks along the tree-lined ridge give breathtaking views across the Marsh and its villages, spread like a map below, to those distant enclaves of modern power, Dungeness A and B. It was from Lympne Aerodrome that Amy Johnson, in 1932, took off on her record-breaking flight to Cape Town.

And then, of course, there is Port Lympne, built with Sir Philip Sassoon's wealth and sustained by that of gambling-club-owner John Aspinall. There, in a 270-acre safari park, as kind to animals as any captivity can be, he seeks to save endangered species, as he does at Howletts, near Canterbury.

But Port Lympne is no mere 'zoo'. It is also a dream house of the twenties enjoyed by Douglas Fairbanks and Charlie Chaplin, by Churchill and Clemenceau and by French heavyweight champion Carpentier. It is rich in modern animal art treasures as well as a superb Rex Whistler period-piece *trompe-l'œil* mural. At the time of writing, Arthur Roberts is completing an even more ambitious one, with some 350 south-east Asian creatures brilliantly alive on the walls, even the ceiling, of the drawing-room. Rich too in splendid gardens, its chequerboard flower beds blaze with colour. (With 200 tons of elephant manure dug in, why shouldn't they?)

And so to Aldington, perched on a last fling of the Quarry Hills. Here Archbishop Warham once had 'a chase for beasts of the forest'. Here too he installed as rectors the Dutch humanist and theologian Erasmus – whose knowledge of English was as scant as his parishioners' of Greek and Latin – and Thomas Linacre, founder of the Royal College of Physicians, although he had taken no Holy Orders! None of which detracts from the church, which has a richly embellished and battlemented Perpendicular tower that houses six bells, the tenor inscribed:

> I mean to make it understood
> That tho' I'm little yet I'm good';

an east window bright with a sea of haloed heads; mass dials; floral misericords; modern stained glass; much imported panelling and, in particular, a fine made-up pulpit, its front rescued from harsh domesticity as a chopping-block but still dramatically showing 'the Pelican in her Piety' with three eager young drawing drops of blood from her breast. No, Aldington church has little cause to be retiring.

Even more memorable, for us, is its setting: a churchyard big enough for browsing sheep; the church itself half-hidden behind copper beeches and pines; and a low, tiled farm outbuilding kneeling almost at the west door, and another standing, more protectively, to the north.

Aldington, for all its peacefulness, has known high drama. At nearby Court-at-Street, the callously manipulated 'Holy Maid of Kent' wrought 'miracles' that ranged from 'lighting candles without fire' to 'moistening women's breasts that wanted milke'. Visions, and voices too, could be tolerated but prophesying Henry VIII's damnation should he marry Anne Boleyn brought poor, epileptic Elizabeth Barton to the Tower – and Tyburn Tree in 1534.

At the other end of the scale were the 'Aldington Blues'. Led by George Ransley, they became, of all ruthless Kentish smugglers, the most notorious. For the first three decades of the eighteenth century they came and went much as they pleased across the Marsh and high-handedly ruled the coast from Camber to Deal. And that despite 'Flogging Joey's' and the Coast Blockade's desperate efforts to apprehend them.

But in July 1826 several smugglers – 'armed with long duck-guns' – killed a Blockade quartermaster on Dover beach beneath their very barracks in the Casemates. £500 was far too big a reward for frail human nature. One of the gang turned informer. At 3 a.m. on 17 October, shadowy Blockade men and Bow Street Runners silently infiltrated Aldington; Ransley's barking dogs were cut down, his door was forced and he himself seized and handcuffed to the stoutest man in the party. Strangely, the death sentence was not demanded. Instead, Ransley and seven of his gang – all men 'of fierce aspect' were sentenced to transportation for life.

Nearby are a splendidly diverse trio. Goldenhurst, where Noël Coward lived, its view Marshwards inspiring his unforgettable 'Room with a View'; a detention centre where youthful delinquents receive the 'short, sharp shock' which too often merely galvanizes them into further and better-planned vandalism and villainy against long-suffering citizens; and Homelands, 'Canterbury Oast Trust for the Mentally Handicapped'. Here its patron, the Archbishop of Canterbury, takes board and lodging – for his pigs! Twenty-one-year-old Tracey, gardener, woodswoman, stock-keeper, art teacher and extrovert, grinned at our ill-concealed disbelief. And yet – if Wodehouse's massive Empress of Blandings could be the apple of the Earl of Emsworth's eye, why shouldn't an archbishop . . . ?

We paused to have a word with Jasmine, the Jersey calf; to stroke Gregory's Girl, a downy bantam sadly widowed only the day before, when an inquisitive dog made off and away with Gregory Peck. 'More in curiosity than in anger', it was stated in his defence.

Gertrude, as befits an archbishop's pig, a Kent Show Champion Berkshire and a Reserve Champion of all her vast kind, was the cleanest pig we'd ever met. At Tracey's whistle she came at a splendid semblance of a trot (whether out of affection or greed I hesitate to guess) and amiably accepted our tentative and inexpert scratching. Mermaid, her mother, was definitely not built for even such speed but was a superbly buxom specimen of her kind. And Clarence, although up to his hocks in mud, was, regrettably for an archiepiscopal pig, 'definitely not to be trusted'.

Bilsington is a crossroads village. Its church lies down a side lane past a once-moated farm and is surrounded luxuriantly – and luxuriously – by strawberry fields.

But it is in the churchyard that the main interest lies. A verdigrised fifteenth-century bell, Whitechapel-cast, too heavy at nine hundred-weight for a squat and ageing tower, is supported there under a tiled canopy. A touch of the knuckles makes music to substantiate its inscription: '*In Multis Annis Resonet Campana Johannis*' ('For many a year shall John's bell sound'), which doubtless was the wish of its donor – a London fishmonger. Tombstones record the death of five young Law children – and a member of Queen Victoria's private band.

Across the road – and the village cricket ground – is a lofty fifty-foot obelisk. Its top twenty feet are as ragged as a Gaudi pinnacle on Barcelona's famous church. It was struck in 1967 by lightning which plunged startled locals into darkness. It honours James Cosway, secretary to Vice-Admiral Collingwood, philanthropist and prospective MP, who helped ill-paid labourers change their luck in America. He died when the horses bolted on London Bridge and overturned the Brighton Mail.

Ham Street ahead heralds a return to Ashford. Keep the splendid round of Woodchurch and Tenterden, Wittersham and Stone-in-Ebony for another day. It is far too good to be rushed.

Woodchurch, whose derivation is perhaps unobviously obvious, is a village of some standing: Kent's Best Kept Village, 1983 *and* 1986. It is well worth peeling off a layer of creeping Ashford overspill to reach its vast triangular green near which there is much to be seen.

Among white weather-boarded houses spaced round it is Hendon Place: three-quarters of a Wealden house, with silver-grey timbers, bay windows, steep hipped roof, a top-knot chimney-stack, roses up the path, and a graceful ash tree giving it dappled shade.

Across the road soar the 105-foot church tower and shingled spire. Despite the sturdy efforts of massive and stepped angle-buttresses, it leans twenty-one inches out of true. Inside, there is a thirteenth-century stained-glass medallion of the Entombment, Roualtesque in dark blue and brown; an unusual brass of Nichol de Gore; and fraudulent shafts of Bethersden marble – that on closer examination are only freestone waxed to a grey-blue finish! Even so, Newman, not one to give easy praise, was moved to say: 'The nave is prose; the chancel, poetry.'

The church keeps good company: across the road are two inns in surprising amity side by side: the wistaria-veiled Six Bells and the

Tenterden, creation of rich weavers and wealthy ironmasters, is an intriguing palimpsest of styles with 'harmony in its very diversity'.

Bonny Cravat. Behind them towers Jack, a smock windmill, redundant since 1926, now happily restored to his former black-and-white majesty. Not yet up to working though, so no modern miller will suffer the fate of John Parton – beheaded by his own sweeps in 1831.

Tenterden calls. Sunlit and serene, it is something of a dream town. Warm and friendly in the knowledge of its time-gifted good looks and prosperity but never arrogant or overplaying its hand. As glad to welcome you as you are sad to leave it.

For Smallhythe, take the B2082. Pass, if you can, *two* cricket grounds; those of Tenterden and Smallhythe. Then, before you drop down to Marsh level, succumb to Spots Farm with herb garden, eighteen-acre vineyard and a Müller Thurgau well worth sampling.

At the far end of Smallhythe stands a splendid trio. Priest's House (actually, and rather less romantically, the shipwright's house), Wealden and fully jettied; a tiny red box of a church, Dutch brick (landed at the nearby quay nearly 400 years ago) from its foundations to the top of its stepped gables, which are its sole concession to ornament; and Smallhythe Place, the harbour master's old house. A small green pool in the latter's lawn is the last tiny trace of the arm of the sea that in the sixteenth century made it Tenterden's flourishing port. One worthy of a visit by Henry VIII himself to launch his ships of stout Wealden oak.

Smallhythe Place, set amid wide lawns and with daisy, marigold and lobelia adding bold slashes of colour against its silver-grey timbers and buff plaster, is a very special house. A museum filled with the mementos of the long career of Ellen Terry, greatest and most beautiful actress of the late nineteenth century, who lived here for thirty years, and also of David Garrick and Sarah Siddons.

On the ground floor, low, beamed rooms with huge fireplaces are still alive with Ellen Terry's presence. Tiny frayed ballet shoes which she wore in a childhood début as Titania; her serene death mask; the gleaming star of her Dame Grand Cross; the faded photo of a youthful Juliet with Mrs Stirling as the doting Nurse – and written under it, 'What joy to have seen them in this scene! John Gielgud'; and a dressing-table runner on which Sarah Bernhardt had gratefully scrawled in greasepaint '*Merci*, my darling!' after using Ellen Terry's dressing-room.

Precipitous stairs lead to four rooms, one opening into another and, like a ship at sea, with sloping floors and tilted beams. Here are the simple white cap for Viola; the purple cloak richly embroidered with gold dragons for Lady Macbeth; her travelling day-bed; her children's school desk which became her own favourite writing-table. Here too are Irving's bust, penetrating, intent; his death mask, gentle and at peace;

and below it the swords and 'jewelled' daggers he used on stage. Outside in the stables stands the coster cart on which Ellen Terry jaunted happily round the Marsh on picnics.

To the south, across the inelegantly named Reading Sewer (though for 'sewer' read 'drainage ditch'), lie the flat, flat, land of the Marsh and yet another Kentish island. The Isle of Oxney, some four miles long and two wide, has been stranded inland now for centuries. It rears up out of the treeless Rother Levels distantly water-encircled still by Kent Ditch, the Royal Military Canal, Reading Sewer and the Rother itself. And it is truly islanded again after heavy rain.

Clothed in gentle woods and parkland, Oxney rises like a Lilliputian mountain range. On the crest of its 214-foot ridge lies Wittersham, capital of Oxney. Even so remote, it too suffers commuter growing-pains. Nothing, however, spoils the grouping by the church. White weather-board and tiled cottages stand beyond it, Wittersham Court beside it, and across the road, behind a privet hedge, trim as an Army 'short back and sides', Wittersham Hall. The latter has indeed Newman's 'syncopated fenestration' but for the rest, with pantiled roof, wide pediment and loggia beneath, it has all Lutyen's smoothness. The Hon. Alfred Lyttleton, (1857–1913), for whom the house was built, was an aesthete who sought to bring soul into grubby politics, whose cover-drive was a thing of beauty and whose tennis had the same élan.

In the church his memorial tablet is surmounted by a striking bandeaued native head. Deeply gouged fourteenth-century octagonal piers contrast with plump modern hassocks, a recumbent gallery of oasts and flying swans, bells and crowing cockerels, bees and locusts . . . Communion kneelers are bright with wild flowers, field poppy and dog rose . . . Everything is alive with light from the clear-glass east window behind which tall trees sway.

Stone-in-Oxney, Stone-juxta-Ebony, Stone-cum-Ebony: take your choice of these ringing names. There is only one Stone-and Ebony, of which one expects so much, is only a signpost name, a name without substance.

The B2082 heads cheerfully east, as if intent on visiting Stone. But at The Stocks it does a right-angled jink to sweep over the Kent Ditch and head for Rye – a jewel to which Kent, alas, can lay no claim. But The Stocks, hamlet though it is, can offer you a white weather-boarded post-mill and a huddle of cottages, one of which is completely clothed in fish-scale tiles.

Straight on is Tighe Farm, where wide (but private) lawns afford an even better viewpoint round the rim of the Marsh as far as a hazy Folkestone. The lane ahead drops down the old cliff-face in a series of half-hairpins to a somnolent canal, haunt of anglers and algae, disturbed only by forays of lonely moorhens.

At last, to the left a deep lane, golden with daffodils in spring, descends to Stone until, suddenly, Tilmonden stands high-banked above you. Richly tiled on one side, it has a silver-and-buff façade, creeper-covered, with full overhang, and above – a tiny oriel window on a sturdy bracket in the coving beneath deep eaves.

As next-door-neighbour, high-perched too, is St Mary's, risen phoenix-like and Perpendicular from the fire of 1464. Inside, below its tower, Time leaps back 100 million years – to an iguanadon's tail found in a nearby quarry! And, in a hop of a mere 2,000 years, to outpost Roman legionaries worshipping before the stone on whose face is outlined a rugged bull; and on the top of which is a stained, saucer-shaped depression that may have known sacrificial blood. Known too the ignominy of being an inn mounting-block.

Oh, Ebony? Today merely a hint of dark mystery in the open Kentish countryside. Its only trace is a scattering of drunken tombstones on a hundred-foot hillside to the west, once an island in the Rother estuary in its own right. Its church has had a chequered career. Struck by lightning in Elizabethan times; rebuilt; taken down stone by stone and re-erected in 1858, with celebratory bell-cote, a couple of miles away at Reading Street. At a total cost of three months' work and £270! Across the old ferry over Reading Sewer, lanes wind back to Ham Street.

11

The North Downs

The chalk backbone of Kent. Thrusting in from Surrey shortly before unhappily named Hogtrough Hill, above Brasted, run the North Downs, with the ancient Pilgrims Way at their feet, the full length of the county, to end with a flourish in Dover's white cliffs.

Their steep scarp faces that of the South Downs across the Weald, which, together, they encompass. But none of Kent's authors or poets has sung their virtues as lyrically as Kipling and Belloc did those of their Sussex counterparts. Corn and cherries are grown on their flanks and at their feet; yew, whitebeam and especially beech surge along their crests. Yet in their long, dry valleys and steep-sided coombes, with few farms and yet fewer villages, there is, even today, a feeling of secrecy, of remoteness and isolation.

No one road runs their full length; only two cut boldly across them. You travel exhilaratingly by a disorientating maze of lanes: some sunken, shaded and alive with writhing beech roots, smothered with head-high meadowsweet; some plunging joyously down into deep coombes; some gleefully dipping and rising, twisting and turning, like switchbacks on holiday across the gently undulating northern slopes.

It is the latter which preclude dramatic 'two-way' views like those of the South Downs. Yet, even though 857 feet is their greatest height, the North Downs offer sweeping views over Swale, Medway and English Channel, as well as across Weald and Marsh.

Three rivers, Darent, Medway and Stour, breach the chalk rampart. And so, like near-neighbour Gaul, the Downs may for simplicity and ease of exploration be divided into three parts.

The Eastern Downs
Their gentler slopes and flat plateaux stretch pleasantly enough but without drama or ostentation from Canterbury to Folkestone, and from Deal to Wye. When Canterbury's streets and their ceaseless crocodiles of Continental schoolchildren and students bemuse you, there is no

better antidote than the rural charm of the Elham Valley, Dover's bustling port or Folkestone's sea breezes, the tranquillity of the Stour or the solitudes of the Downs themselves.

Bridge, three miles south of Canterbury, is the stepping-stone to the former. Two battles are numbered in its history. At 'England's Old Hole' the Roman 7th Legion was momentarily thrown back by desperate and bloody counter-attack by the Britons. And 2,000 years later, a thousand-strong 'sit-down' routed a foot-dragging Ministry of Transport. Too long had TIR lorries, no respecters of person or property, thundered down Bridge's two steep hills. A bypass was won!

Neighbouring Bridge Place, of hand-made Dutch bricks, is tall and impressive. So too is its massive mastiff watchdog, Dunstan. He weighs in some three stone lighter than Big Bear, his seventeen-stone grandfather.

Bridge Place looks out on the parkland of parvenu Bourne Park, a Queen Anne mansion which, with no fewer than thirteen bays of tall windows, under pediment and hipped roof, retains both proportion and dignity. It is equally beautifully sited too: on a tree-backed, grassy knoll that looks across a reedy lakelet complete with a Willow Pattern bridge. Beyond are the Barham Downs where Dinky Toy cars shuttle to and fro, ceaselessly and, mercifully, silently.

To the south, to Bishopsbourne, runs a magnificent lime avenue whose late-evening shadows slowly march across a pocket-handkerchief cricket ground – 200 years old. Here half Kent, on foot, on horseback or in waggonette, would flock to see twelve Gentlemen of Kent under Squire Sir Horace Mann, 'King of Cricket', face up to the Earl of Tankerville's Twelve Gentlemen of Surrey. For a 1,000 guineas a side (Sir Horace's undoing!) and with, as the posters proclaimed, 'Good Ordinary on the ground by Aylwood'.

Above, at the top of Bridge Hill, is Highland Court which, amid orchards, also has a secluded cricket ground. Staidly dignified in appearance, it was nevertheless the home of dashing Count Vorow Zborowski who, as a sixteen-year-old, inherited a cool £11 million from his father. The latter was a racing-car fanatic who, reputedly, died in 1902, when his gold cuff-links caught in the throttle lever – and sent his Daimler plunging over the Grande Corniche at Nice. Vorow shared his father's racing enthusiasms – and his fate, when he too died in a crash, on his beloved Italian Monza circuit.

As his memorials there are the ever-popular 'Chitty-chitty-bang-bang' racing-car which he designed and Ian Fleming immortalized; and the Romney, Hythe & Dymchurch narrow-gauge line with its perfect one-third scale Pacifics, *Green Goddess* and *Northern Chief*. He planned it with J. E. P. Hewey (an Australian whose grandfather's chance purchase of 128 acres of scrubland became the centre of boom-town Melbourne) but he did not live to see its creation.

From Bourne Park a lane strikes boldly past fields dotted in spring with crinkle-coated lambs in brown leggings frolicking to the querulous bleating of matronly sheep and the whistle of swirling flocks of starlings. In 1988 it was also to the harsh buzz of chain-saws cutting up once-majestic cedars now sprawled on their backs by the hurricane.

At Bishopsbourne there is the perfect village group. Nineteenth-century, no-nonsense Oswalds, once gleaming white, now an unassuming pale grey beneath greyer slates, lies back behind its low flint wall. Under Scots pine and yew lies the garden, crocus- and snowdrop-dappled in early spring. There for five at last contented years lived Joseph Conrad, Polish-born novelist, master of English prose. And there, in 1924, he died, refusing to see friends, in order to spare them anguish.

A chain-splinted chestnut tree, home of grey squirrels, and a war-memorial cross on a tiny green separate the house from the church with its sturdy west tower and delicate Burne-Jones window. Inside is a wall monument to Richard Hooker, black-capped and clad in his Oxford doctor's robes, which he forsook to marry, in mistaken gratitude, a slut and a virago. For all that, cogently reasoned and fluently written, his *Ecclesiastical Polity* routed Calvinist and Catholic alike in their charge that the Church of England had neither philosophical nor theological foundation. Even the Pope was moved to write: '. . . they shall last until the fire shall consume all learning.'

In the cottage-lined Street, you will find Conrad Hall, the Old Forge and, opposite, a plaque reminding book- and flower-lovers that Jocelyn Brook, novelist, poet and author of a definitive book on orchids, lived here also. It leads into Charlton Park with its plain Georgian-fronted mansion. Here in 1798, George IV, having reviewed his troops on Barham Down, returned for pleasanter 'skirmishes' with Lady Conyngham. Far sterner ones took place 150 years later, when villagers routed the mere suggestion of a pop festival. And far wetter ones when the temperamental Nailbourne, turning fields into lakes, roads into rivers, and itself from trickling stream into a creditable imitation of the Stour, sets neighbouring villagers hastily filling sandbags.

Legend blames it on a blameless St Augustine who, acting only for the best, created the stream in a time of drought, a usurpation of pagan privilege that so angered Woden and Thor that they forced it under-ground again with storm and landslip. And, in subsequent demarcation talks, held rock-solid, only grudgingly allowing the Nailbourne to flow one year in seven.

Barham Downs, bald and breezy, are steeped in history. Armies,

from Caesar's 7th Legion to the 'Old Contemptibles', have dug in there to throw back attack, both real and threatened. More happily, in 1635, Charles I picnicked there (although it was a fast-day) as he escorted his bride-to-be, Henrietta Maria, from Dover to London; and Canterbury citizens trooped out for the free ale of the hustings and the excitement of the race-course.

Elham has much to offer. A square of Georgian houses, one with fish-scale tiles, is quiet and unhurried except on Boxing Day, when it is filled with the clatter and whimper of the East Kent Hunt meet. Behind it rises the buttressed tower of the finely proportioned church. Its square-piered interior is full of light and interest: font and cushioned prayer-stool, painting and panelling, Dutch glass and French lectern. A delicate fifteenth-century alabaster triptych shows a raging Henry II . . . and Becket falling under the assassins' swords. Between them St Catherine is tortured on the wheel. In a quirky Victorian stained-glass window, David and Saul are facially changed into opera-singer Adelina Patti and historian Thomas Carlyle! Their attendants? Disraeli and Gladstone!

On the main road, the black-and-white Abbot's Fireside is breath-taking. It has everything. Steepling roof; carved bressummer; deep eaves; caryatids, grotesquely big of bosom and belly; lattice windows; and swallows' nests. Its oak door complainingly allows entrance to a ten-foot-long mantelpiece where the Five Senses are set above a barbarity of fork-tongued hounds and man-eating whales. Beside such ferocity Wellington once wrote his dispatches.

On the lonely Downs above is Acrise Place, part Tudor, part Jacobean. Its fine range of pedimented stables looks out of unseeing eyes from beneath sagging roofs. Yet, it was once the pride of Huguenot David Papillon and six generations of his descendants. The rough flint church with brick porch and toy-like shingled spirelet stands close by in a tree-shrouded clearing. It seems a little overawed, for all its minstrels' gallery, heavily moulded chancel arch and commodious squire's pew with a set of 200-year-old children's chairs. And yet, in 1502, the rector pleaded, 'Our stepull is at reparacon yf it be not holpe ryzt sone . . . it wyll fall down for it raynet in and rots the timber.'

Beyond Etchinghill, the B2065 sweeps down from nearly 600 feet past isolated Summerhouse Hill and a miniscule, half-hidden wildfowl reserve to Hythe and the sea. On the western side of this last Downland flurry is Postling, close enfolded by the hills.

Nearby, the Eastern Stour is born not half-a-dozen miles from the sea at Hythe. But perversely it swings west to join the Great Stour on their long journey to Pegwell Bay near Ramsgate.

North again, on the Pilgrims Way, is Pent Farm. Polish master-mariner Joseph Conrad rented it from his friend, and sometimes condescending collaborator, Ford Madox Hueffer. Despite the sweep of quiet countryside about it and the idyllic roses round the windows, his stay was not happy. He wrestled with ill health, recurrent debt and the moulding of the English language into the perfection for which he ceaselessly strove. For all that, *Lord Jim* was finished here in 1900 after a twenty-one-hour stint and celebrated at dawn by a triumphant chicken sandwich – shared with his dog Escamillo.

As at nearby Stowting, there is a Downs-enveloped tranquillity. Narrow lanes wind at their feet or slant across their broad flanks, giving glimpses of a tree-quiffed ridge, the dark sprawl of Lyminge Forest and a richer, redder soil. Then Stone Street, the Roman highway, runs arrow-straight (save for a gradient-reducing jink above Monks Horton) from Roman Portus Lemanis (Lympne) to Durovernum (Canterbury).

To the north-east, lanes criss-cross through five miles of forest. In the Forestry Commission's West Wood, evening sunshine dapples the trunks of seventy-foot spruce yellow-green and burnishes young larch with gold along the way-marked paths and broad rides.

The Minnises, Rhodes, and Stelling (to say nothing of Wheelbarrow Town) lie athwart the forest on hawthorn-dotted common splashed with the gold and bronze of gorse and bracken. Upper Hardres Court once lay behind Boulogne's town gates – granted by Henry VIII for wartime services rendered. Nearby, at peaceful Lower Hardres, dragoons, in 1830, clashed with unemployed labourers ousted by new-fangled threshing machines. And Captain Swing's nightfall notes threatened blazing ricks and smashed machinery.

So, through tranquil orchards, back to Canterbury.

Canterbury again is an excellent starting-point for the Downs west of Stone Street. The B2068 climbs gently past hospital, St Lawrence cricket ground and orchards; sends the splendid scenic Chartham Downs road switchbacking away westwards above Garlinge Green and Kenfield Hall.

Waltham's lonely church, drably rendered and brick-patched, is retiring; Hastingleigh's church is positively a recluse – a full mile and a half down a steep-sided valley, with only Court Lodge Oast Farm as neighbour. A huge and hollow yew acts as gate-keeper. The little church has a single slender pier and an altar cloth reminiscent of Van Gogh's sunflowers.

From the Bowl Inn back in the village, the road, high-hedged, lollops placidly along the Downland crest until suddenly, almost theatrically, there is Broad Down, sheep-dotted, lark-thrilled and with a stupendous view. It unrolls across a chequer-board of pale yellow and green fields, and darker green of woods to the hills beyond the Stour Valley, to Ashford and Bachelor's Soups and to the distant blue haze that is Romney Marsh and the sea. Immediately and dramatically below, the Devil's Kneading Trough is the narrowest of re-entrant valleys, tight squeezed by the precipitous slopes of Millstone Point.

At the foot of the latter, Brook, aptly named, lounges unhurriedly down to the massivity of its church tower. Inside are fourteenth-century tiling, low-set squint and an altar slab buried in fear of the Reformation – and ceremoniously reinstated in 1986. More memorable still, black on white, white on black, are tiered roundels, the faded thirteenth-century picture-book of Christ's life for the unlettered.

By the side of the church crouches a long, black-timbered barn with two entrance ports inset below its steep tiled roof: the Wye College Museum of the nineteenth century's simple farm instruments replaced by today's £50,000 hi-tech juggernauts. The crown carved in the downland above was the students' tribute to Edward VII on his coronation.

Further east, Mersham straddles the busy A20, hurrying to seaside delights. To the south lies the village: its church, from chapel to chancel, overflows with Knatchbull monuments, including Sir Norton – with 'a smile of conscious rectitude'. A magnificent fourteenth-century west window with thirteen lower lights for Christ and his disciples adds rich colour.

Further north, Brabourne, beautifully compact, may be found through a tangle of lanes under the Pilgrims Way. Its church is a palimpsest of styles, merging one into another, rich in the unusual: a wide tower that collapsed in the fifteenth century and is now massively buttressed; an Easter sepulchre; a heart-shrine of Balliol College's founder; a thirty-foot belfry ladder rough-hewn from two oaks; brasses, long secreted under the vicarage roof; Norman chancel and the oldest known *complete* Norman window; a Bethersden marble tomb-chest serving as altar; and a chapel dedicated to the Scotts!

Twelve generations of the latter lived near Smeeth at Scott Hall, now only hummocks in a field. Of that distinguished family, Sir Thomas was perhaps the most famous. He mustered 4,000 men in twenty-four hours to repel possible Spanish invasion; bred horses; improved both Romney Marsh and Dover Harbour – and still found time for seventeen children by the first of his three wives! Of him it was written:

> He kept tall men, he rydd great hors;
> He did write most finely.
> He used few words but could discuss
> Both wysely and dyvinely.

Westwards again to Wye. Though it is perhaps better met from the north where the road crosses the five-arched bridge over Great Stour, with weir and old mill on one side and Tickled Trout on the other.

The village has a quiet, unhurried, Georgian dignity. Local boy John Kempe – to become Archbishop of Canterbury – founded a College of Priests here and rebuilt the imposing church in 1447. (Its steeple collapsed in 1686 in mid-service but the vicar, noticing ominously twitching bell-ropes, shepherded his flock to safety just in time.) Today the former silver-grey stone, rich red-brick and tile, courtyards and greens, stone-mullioned windows, is an agricultural college well worthy of London University. Wye's other claim to fame is the local barber's daughter, Aphra Behn, (1640–89) who, way before her time, was abolitionist, authoress – and spy!

From Wye a scenic lane follows the east bank of the Stour, past Olantigh Towers to meet the A28 opposite Godmersham Park, where Jane Austen often visited her brother. Better, however, to explore narrow lanes to the right. They climb steeply up the opposing Downs, wind through the combe in which tiny Crundale village shelters, then up again to the church, high perched above valleys daubed lemon-yellow with rape. 'Not bad for its age': a youthful comment in its visitors' book sums it up pretty well. But the ridge walk beside it *is* undeniably splendid.

Sole Street has little to offer except a peaceful stretch of Lyminge Forest – and, nearby, the once aptly named Penny Pot Alehouse. Beyond the red-brick bulk of St Augustine's Mental Hospital are wide views across the Stour of Canterbury's encircling and regimented orchards.

The Central Downs

Set between Stour and Medway, these are remoter, more rural yet and still more a baffling maze of lanes, forever twisting and turning, dipping and falling, forcing the explorer to play an unwilling version of motorized snakes and ladders. Their peaceful countryside and sleepy hamlets and villages are best explored from Canterbury or Faversham.

Medieval and modern conflict in Chartham, five miles south-west of the former. By its two greens tower the knapped flint walls of thirteenth-century St Mary's. Its roof is a thickset forest of beams; its chancel windows are of Kentish tracery, and its brass of Sir Robert de Septvans is the fourth oldest in England. Bareheaded, indomitable even in death, he grasps his heavy battle-sword, and beneath the loose surcoat he wears chain-mail. Modern takes the not-so-pleasing shape of Wiggins Teape's mill, which, like its 1738 forerunner, straddles the Stour's three channels and, with its help, still makes fine paper.

Norma Fryer unerringly depicts Chilham's varied beauty, but discreetly omits tight-packed cars in its central square.

Industry is certainly not for Chilham, a couple of miles further on. Openly and unashamedly but never brazenly, it lives on the beauty that has made it Kent's most perfect, almost too perfect, village. Four lanes, each with its own charm, wind up to the knoll-top square. At one end are the gates and replanted avenue of the castle, or rather a Jacobean mansion rich in gables and chimneys, for little remains of the Norman keep and its Saxon foundations. Its terraced lawns, box- and yew-hedged, give memorable views of Stour and Downs.

In the summer, lance and sword clash against armour as modern knights do combat. And peregrine falcons, their high-pitched 'kek – kek – kek' stilled, their scythelike wings folded back, 'stoop' at 180 mph able to kill with a single blow of their talons. Falconry as well as jousting has been revived at Chilham.

At the other end of the square, at respectful feudal distance, are long-standing friends – the fifteenth-century White Horse Inn and St Mary's Church. In the latter, its flint tower chequered in Caen stone, the body of St Augustine rested after the Dissolution until – incredibly – it simply disappeared! Half-timbered and brick-and-tiled houses, each without an architectural hair out of place, encircle the other sides of the square.

From Challock's spacious, grassy Lees, a lane leads to the church. Past the new school, through a tunnel of beeches, a sharpish left turn, and suddenly, without let or hindrance of gate or fence, there stands the church of St Cosmos and St Damian. No man-made sound; only the rustling of poplars and the occasional harsh 'kok – kok' of a pheasant. Cornfields sweep down to it in a golden flood. Inside, in Stanley Spencer idiom, but by Kent's John Ward ARA: John baptizes Christ in Kentish Stour and countryside in front of an astonished parish council in modern dress!

Back at the crossroads, the Faversham road (the A251) and the B2077 head you through rolling cornfields towards the perfect archetypal hamlet of Throwley Forstal, and Throwley itself, or at least its church. A short lime-tree avenue and half-timbered Church Cottages point the way to it: four high-piled gables and tower, a nondescript porch with flaking blue paint, and gently nibbling sheep (blue-faced Leicesters?) give little hint of the beauty within.

Inside, sword in one hand, scroll in the other, stands the Brasted curate's son who became the first Baron Harris of Seringapaman and Mysore. Wounded by the American rebels at Bunker's Hill in 1775, he insisted on watching the operation through mirrors. Later he overthrew the traitorous and revengeful Tippo Sahib. The fourth Baron, cricket's examplar who outfaced 'The Demon' fast bowler Spofforth, is briefly dismissed in 'Captain Eton, Oxford, Kent and England'. In the south chapel it is the Sondes' turn: two fine tomb chests, and on each, devoutly kneeling, husband and wife.

Past Town Place (where the church key is kept) the road swings past New York and Belmont. No Manhattan skyscrapers here, only an isolated pair of cottages, American Colonial style with wide and shady verandas. Belmont, with curving bays and pavilions, walled gardens and unusual grotto (to say nothing of cricket ground and golf course), is the Harris mansion.

Cornfields and woods, hawthorn hedges, tangles of wild rose and towering meadowsweet line the way to Eastling. The manor there is a dream: through wrought-iron gates, looking down flagged and rose-lined path, one can enjoy the close-studded timbers, two-storeyed porch and half-hipped roof with slanting ridge and the first gentle hollowing of age. The sole approach to the church is between seemingly 'private' grass verges and Kentish cherry trees. Here are a massive yew (eighteen paces needed to circumnavigate it), roses, pessimistic triple buttresses, lozenge tombs and surrounding cornfields. Only the erratic threat of a distant bird-scarer momentarily shatters the silence. Outside the village is a novel notice: 'Caution! Free range children!'

Newnham boasts a trio of curiosities. A vineyard and nature trail;

Throwley church boasts two richly coloured Sondes tombs – and a tablet to Sir George, one of whose sons was hanged for his brother's murder.

Calico House, with its pargeted front of flowing leaves and tendrils painted in rusty red; and, on the hill above, Sharsted Court, with rich topiary, twenty staircases and two immaculate tennis courts, once used by the owner's daughter – Wimbledon champion Virginia Wade.

Wichling St Margaret's catches you off guard. A gap in a field-hedge . . . a mown path . . . and, at the far end, the tree-screened church. Quite alone save for distant views of a silvern Swale and Sheppey's green fields.

Unsophisticated Milstead is a little-known show-piece. Compact and leafy, it clusters round its church set on a bank beneath a vast yew. Hoggeshaws, a magnificent Wealden hall-house; Manor Farm House, pale terracotta plaster and timber with a forest of lupins and delphiniums above a pooled rock garden – and, best of all, the Elizabethan manor. The latter must surely arouse sinful covetousness in all who see its close-studded timbers, gables and gabled porch, oriels, clock-tower (just slightly tipsy?) and thatched barn. Unseen, unheard, the thunderous M2 races by just below.

'Cold and dreary country' Hasted called it. But Frinsted's church-yard is bright with buttercups and daisies – and its own rose garden. Wormshill has an imposing timbered porch; Bicknor, oil lamps, and chalk walls that shattered before 1861's bitter frost. And Bredgar greets you with a traffic sign 'Wild Fowl' near a sizeable pond. From it, imperturbable mallard and Aylesbury ducks hold up the traffic by waddling across the main street and immediately, without hint of apology, waddling back again! The B2162 will sweep you over the M2 to Sittingbourne . . . Faversham . . . and Canterbury.

Equally good things, but demanding less exacting navigational skills, lie below the Downs steep southern scarp. The A20 and M20 fence them in, though never too obtrusively – except for poor, bisected Harrietsham.

Canterbury again makes a good launch-pad. And what gentler prelude than the Stour Valley with its clear and shallow river which over the millennia have somehow worn their way through the Downs' massive chalk wall?

Beyond Chilham, the hills roll away to the south. On their lower slopes Julius Laberius, one of Caesar's tribunes, shared a long-barrow grave with neolithic man until recently, when, report says, it fell to the plough. And Godmersham church, tree-framed, sits quite alone, poised and assured, on a knoll just above the Stour.

Behind it, and behind long brick walls, is Godmersham Hall, once owned by Jane Austen's brother and more recently by a 'Black Cat' cigarette heiress. Handsomely symmetrical in red brick with stone dressings; pastoral with woodland glades and classical temples against a Downland backdrop, it still holds something of the spirit of Hampshire's Jane – who also had a soft spot for Kent.

Boughton Aluph, one of Kent's four Boughtons, is the musical one of the family, for here in its Downland sequestered church of rose-pink brick and subtle grey flints is held the annual Stour Music Festival.

Eastwell Park offers strange contrasts. To the east, a flamboyant neo-Jacobean gateway of rough flints and smooth stone, turreted and flanked by rampant lions. To the west, beside a forty-acre lake, home of

Eastwell Park has not only a 40-acre lake and thirteenth-century Lake House but also a four-star hotel and a derelict church.

moorhen and coot, is St Mary's Perpendicular tower, bomb-damaged and fallen into decay; its former magnificent tombs are now sheltered in Kensington's Victoria & Albert Museum.

At the mansion, a young bricklayer, covertly reading Latin, was held to be Richard III's natural son – fleeing from the Battle of Bosworth Field. Far less lonely surely was Heneage Finch who sired twenty-seven children by his four wives and whose descendants held Eastwell for 257 years! John de Fonblanqua Pennefather demolished it in 1928 – only to rebuild it with its original stones. Blindness robbed him of its completed beauty.

Westwell has known no such grandeur. Yet it nestles contentedly enough under the Downs. It has two small greens, one peacock-frequented, and a drably rendered church with a fine Early English interior. Its miniature forest of columns, some slightly drunken, smacks fractionally of Cordoba's far greater wealth of zebra arches.

There is also a mill, whose ancestry dates back to AD 858; a gently murmuring water-wheel; a mill-house whose frame of ships' timbers is rough with the depredations of mud-borers; and a first-floor sitting-room with the mill-pond lapping at its feet. Rose-hedged too!

A quiet lane, parallel with the busy A20, heads west for Charing. The latter's main street winds up steeply between half-timbered and eighteenth-century houses, to join the A252 – at the top of which, hard by the restaurant once backed by Canterbury's 'Red Dean', is a breathtaking view of the Weald.

But it is a cul-de-sac to the right that steals the show. First, a pleasing modern library. Then a farm, which once knew archiepiscopal grandeur. One into which Henry VIII and his vast – and doubtless hungry – retinue trooped on their way to the Field of the Cloth of Gold. And finally, to complete the picture, a church with a splendid Kentish Perpendicular tower. Its roof was burned down when a Mr Dios discharged his fowling-piece at marauding pigeons, missed – and set alight the tinder-dry shingles!

Lenham, in Holmesdale, also neatly sidesteps the traffic's hurly-burly. Even if it is not strictly 'Downs', its memorial cross is cut deep into them. Round its central square are a huge Wealden house turned drugstore, under which three Saxon warriors slept undisturbed for centuries; the cream-washed Dog & Bear boldly sporting the royal arms; a lock-up, with ashlar front and rusticated arch, charming enough to invite crime; and pollarded limes. On the south side, a magnificently timbered cathedral of a tithe barn, sole survivor of three, yields pride of place only to the church.

Is Lenham a second Chilham? 'Like Chilham? No, we're a *working* village,' Lenhamites will tell you, 'not a tourist trap!' And they're not unhappy that once they had a reputation for cantankerous women as well as fine watercress.

Harrietsham at first glance is all pubs, 'kaffs' and filling-stations. It is to the south of the A20, which slices it clean in two, that its highlights lie: a charming row of almshouses whose blue doors open onto a rose-lined lawn and whose rain-heads bear the crest of the Worshipful Company of Fishmongers; the close-studded and deep-eaved Old Bell House; and a vast, creeper-shrouded, almost Dickensian stone house behind whose dusty, net-curtained windows might well lurk a second Miss Havisham.

Hollingbourne too is cut in half by a leisurely rural railway – one that may become a multi-mph Channel Tunnel track which will cut an ear-piercing swathe through Downland peace. South of the bridge is Eythorne Street, a curtain-raiser, a blur of brick, a 'whiter than white' Sugar Loaves inn and a dab or two of half-timber.

To the north, Hollingbourne, rich in good things, takes it easy before its road climbs steeply through beechwoods to the Downs' crest. Its church is a Culpeper treasure-house. In their chapel Lady Elizabeth, 'Best of women; best of wives; best of mothers', lies alone – with her feet on a 'theow', an unlovely beast with heraldic spots cloven hoof, cow's tail and toothy leer. 1988 saw the church's 350th anniversary – and, hopefully, restoration. Even the *Star Exponent* of Culpeper, Virginia, USA, carried the appeal for funds – next to an article headed 'Argument Ends in Throat Slashing with Billhook'. Why Virginia, USA? The second Lord Culpeper, with six others, received a not ungenerous 5 *million acres* there, between the Potomac and Rappahannock rivers!

Rich in characters, Hollingbourne also sired Nicholas Wood – who suffered from *Caninus Appetitus*. He and John Taylor, the so-called 'Water Poet' (of whom it was said that 'he had but a pennyworth of poetry to an unconscionably large quantity of water') once engaged on a wager 'to eat at one time as much black pudding as would reach across the Thames between London and Richmond'.

Hollingbourne has much more beside. The overshot wheel of the Mill House, all warm brick and tile, is fed by water from a tree-surrounded pool above it. And behind that and its own cotoneaster-clad wall the manor is almost overwhelming with lofty gables, chimney-stacks and elaborate brickwork. Beyond is the Malt House, close-studded timber one side, red tiled cat-slides the other. And the Pilgrims' Rest offers a last hospitality.

The road, turning left here and closely following the Pilgrims Way, is as lovely as any in Kent. Rippling, golden seas of wheat and barley lead the eye to Downland grass and the long, beech-crested skyline. Past tiny Broad Street, park land and grazing sheep on the left, lies

Thurnham, a cricketer's mecca. Down a walled alley sheltering a king-size kitchen garden lies the church. In its gently terraced and Wimbledon close-cut lawns there lies, next to Eliza Susanna, his eighteen-year-old daughter, Alfred Mynn (1807–1861), the 'Lion of Kent'. A seventeen-stone round-arm bowler of bruising pace; a batsman of finger-splitting power. With the Downs and the scant remains of Thurnham Castle high above, no bad resting-place between innings!

The former Cock Horse, where extra horses could be hired for the stiff incline above, stands at the next crossroads. To the south is Detling church, with its unusual four-faced lectern. Here a one-time rector's inamorata sought sanctuary after their adulterous association had led to murder. To the north is the Kent County Agricultural Showground, once a World War II aerodrome from which squadrons 'scrambled' urgently to drive the Luftwaffe back from London. Today it knows no greater thrill than the Grand Parade, led by rectangularly chiselled bulls, show-jumping's race against the clock, monster cabbages and Granny Perkins' peerless crab-apple jelly.

The road switchbacks west beneath 'The Larches' to a mellow finale at Boxley. The cream-washed King's Arms gazes down a narrow green towards the church. On one side spacious houses sprawl in even more spacious gardens; on the other, fields sweep up to the wooded ridge of the Downs.

Inside the church are unusual, rotund chalk block pillars and a tablet that verifies that Sir Henry Wyatt 'of Allington Castle, Knight Barrenet [was] imprisoned and tortured in the Tower dungeons, where preserved and fed by a cat which killed and brought to him pigeons'. Richard III, alas, showed him no such pity!

The abbey lies almost cheek by jowl with the full fury of the M20. Originally a manor, it was obtained by Cistercians in return for absolution of the owner's many sins – and dissolved on the equally flimsy pretext that they grew too many gilliflowers. What remains of it is now a delightful private house with sunken rose garden and 600-year-old tithe barn.

The Western Downs
Cobham, easily accessible by the A2 from Rochester, must rank high in any 'Top Ten'. What better start than Cobham Hall (now a girls' school), a stately, H-shaped, turreted mansion of Elizabethan brick and Caen stone? It stands in a park of majestic trees where Dickens loved to walk and in which there is an ornate seventeenth-century mausoleum – shortly to become the centre-piece of a £500,000 twentieth-century mansion!

Inside: a landing big enough to hold a scarlet-and-gold coach; a Long

Gallery with towering mantelpieces; a breathtaking Gilt Hall – in which
I have watched leotarded girls in graceful ballet practice and trampo-
linists making close inspection of the gilded plaster on the lofty ceiling
above twin minstrels' galleries.

Here the Hon. Ivo Bligh, having, in 1882, avenged England's first
defeat by Australia, brought back the famous 'Ashes' and, with them,
as his wife, the girl who had teasingly burned the bail of which they
consist. Here too, in a torrential storm, as bride-to-be, came La
Belle Stuart, who had diplomatically side-stepped Charles II's
persistent invitations to his bed but yielded to his whim that she pose as
Britannia – for our coinage.

A hard act to follow? Not for Cobham. Down its single street lie the
maroon-and-white Darnley Arms, happily haunted by Sir Thomas
Kemp who received a last-minute execution reprieve; Mr Pickwick's
Leather Bottle, half-timbered in buff and brown and packed with
Dickens memorabilia; a towering black pump that celebrated an Earl of
Darnley's coming of age; a single wistaria-covered house with two front
doors; proud oasts, intriguingly named Fuggles, Bramble and Bullion
after hop varieties; the seventeenth-century National Trust Owletts,
home of Sir Herbert Baker, co-creator with Lutyens of Delhi's splendour; a College of Priests, designed by Henry Yevele, now turned into
almshouses for 'the poor and needy . . . no common swearer, adulterer,
thief, hedge-breaker or drunkard'.

Oh, and there is, of course, the little matter of the church of St Mary
Magdalene. Not content with the impressive arrogance of a superb
alabaster tomb-chest of the ninth Lord Cobham and his lady, encircled
by their fourteen kneeling children almost within the sanctuary, there
are the brasses. Stretched across the width of the chancel, like wall-to-
wall carpeting, they are the finest collection in the world – matchless in
detail of fourteenth- and fifteenth-century armour and dress.

Sole Street's claim to fame is the 'singularly perfect' Yeoman's House
restored and given to the National Trust by Sir Herbert Baker.

And so, reluctantly perhaps, to Meopham ('Meppum' locally). Now
not quite sure whether it is town or village, it vies for 'longest' tag as it
straggles along the A227 for more than a couple of miles. The church, a
little overweight, with a tower that sports bold lucarnes and blue-faced
clock invites exploration – but its notice-board gives no hint as to the
key's whereabouts, only a chilling query 'Will Pollution Seal your
Fate?'

A mile further on is the inviting village green, triangular and
white-railed. From as far back as 1776, cricket has been played on it.
The balconied pavilion, sheltered by tall limes, looks across to the
white-fronted Cricketers Inn, whose beams are reputedly ships' tim-

Meopham windmill, on land leased for 999 years, is said to be built of ships' timbers from Chatham Dockyard.

bers. Its sign depicts top-hatted and bow-tied players in front of surprisingly modern stumps. Behind it rears up an unusual hexagonal smock-mill, jet black but with gleaming white sweeps and fantail.

Between green and church a narrow lane plunges downhill above a half-glimpsed valley to Luddesdown Court, oldest continuously inhabited house in England, where Saxon, Norman and Tudor work mingle. Its yard-thick flint walls still look stout enough to withstand a second millennium. 'Restored to the limit of endurance' is Newman's opinion of its knoll-perched church!

Neolithic farmers lived here in sheltered Downland folds; so too do orchids, pheasant's eye and ground pine, to say nothing of *Cernuela neglecta*, the fast-disappearing Luddesdown Snail. Today on the encircling Downs' steep slopes toy tractors score long lines on vast hedgeless fields, tilted prairies of dark ploughland or golden stubble. And in the woods above, lanes and paths offer ways as secluded as any in Kent.

One leads to Dowde – or is it Dode (no two signposts agree)? – a valley where birdsong and windsong are the only sounds. A tiny two-cell Norman church, ancient thatch replaced by tiles, is the sole remaining building of a hamlet wiped out by the Black Death in 1348. Stinging-nettles and rank ivy grow at the foot of its splotched walls of flint and drab rendering; birds, sated on the lush elderberries festooned on the wire-mesh fence that safeguards it from vandals, fly in and out of its slit windows. Only once a year does it again know prayer and devotion – by Catholics for whom it is 'Our Lady of the Meadows'.

Nearby is Holly Hill, one of Kent's finest viewpoints – to rolling hills across the Medway, even as far as Kingsnorth power-station on Sheppey. Below, Vigo Village, like New Ash Green, is a not-unsuccessful modern creation in an age-old rural setting.

With the A227 regained, Stansted lies to the west, Trottiscliffe to the east. The former is a scattered hamlet in peaceful seclusion north of Wrotham Hill. On a knoll stands St Mary's, notable only for William Webb, sixty-seven years a chorister, and a zebra-striped chancel roof. Delicious Church Cottage, all white weather-board and rendering, tiny latticed windows and big brick chimney-breast, clings to its steep bank. Across the road a miniscule green, with a seat-encircled ash tree, looks down on a cricket ground of such vast expanse that even the Oval might envy it. And above, the Black Horse, contradictorily yellow-stuccoed, is of size enough to warrant unworthy doubts about the village's sobriety.

Yet more striking, at the foot of the hill on Malt House Lane, is the war memorial: a splendid bronze affair of a naked man (unless a discreetly draped belt counts as clothing) holding aloft the branch of a palm. Proudly mounted on a podium and set in a tiny garden, it is worthy of a city centre. And yet it went AWOL. Stolen at dead of night, it was recovered a year later from a South London scrapyard – unmelted and unharmed.

North again is Ash-cum-Ridley, a name as pleasing as its church tower outlined against the red brick of the Jacobean manor; New Ash Green, another attempt at a town in rural setting; and Fawkham's St Mary's, demurely white but with a flirtatious bell-turret, set, unfenced, by the roadside.

Trottiscliffe has even more going for it. A name mercifully slimmed or slurred to 'Trosley'; a 160-acre country park of down and wood with wide Wealden views; a house lived in by artist Graham Sutherland; a Norman church; a former bishop's palace and a neolithic long barrow.

The church of St Peter and St Paul stands aloof from the village, below the Downs and Pilgrims Way. On one side are eighteenth-century cottages of rich rust-coloured local sandstone. On the other is Court Lodge Farm, on the site of the old manor whose splendidly rusticated brick gateway and front wall alone remain. Here Bishop Hamo de Hethe sought refuge from the Plague, only to see it kill thirty-two of his household.

The ground stage of the church's tower serves also as a flower-filled porch. Within, red-brick aisle, box pews and wide reading-desk (probably cannibalized from the old pulpit) lead the eye gently up to the vivid red, green and blue of a Victorian east window and much splendidly crafted timber. But it is the pulpit that seizes and holds the eye. Sneered at by ecclesiologists, rejected by the Dean and Chapter of Westminster Abbey and smuggled out in 1824 without their knowledge, it is nevertheless overwhelming. A spreading stem raises it high above the congregation, and a veritable palm tree supports the inlaid canopy and its finial – only inches from the roof. A giant of a pulpit! A hundred years later a faded scrap of paper and a farthing were found tucked in its finials. It told of the pulpit's near destruction by plumbers 'careless with their fire' and of the subsequent 'discarding' of both master plumber and clerk of works!

A jolting apology of a lane leads to the National Trust's Coldrum Stones or long barrow. They are best viewed from the front – where a memorial plaque fittingly dedicates them to Ightham grocer Benjamin Harrison (born 1837) who became England's leading archaeologist. Destruction of the eastern half of the 4,000-year-old barrow has left stones precariously perched at the entrance to the burial chamber. Monster sarsens (some twelve feet by ten), rich red-brown in colour, loom dramatically above you. On the close-cut grass behind them a score of such stones, prone now, once formed an upright ritual circle.

With a temptingly well-surfaced farm road 'Strictly Private', it's back to Trottiscliffe and thence on by-roads to Ryarsh and Birling. They are only a mile apart but, according to water-colourist Rowland Hilder, who has made Kent's oasts and barns, furrowed fields and towering elms loved worldwide, each regarded its neighbours as 'foreigners'. Hilder's father was butler at Birling Manor – long since destroyed by fire which raged unchecked for lack of mains water. The straggling village is dominated by the church, perched high above the road on a steep knoll. Its tall tower, buttressed and battlemented, has red tile-caps on tower and turret. Inside, the broadest of chancels, without screen or arch holds something of the drama of a modern stage set.

To return to Rochester involves a very different scene – below lonely, wooded Downland slopes, populous, greyed 'cement country' lies alongside the Medway. Snodland has the drab practicality of Victorian industrialization, relieved only by the cement-powdered ragstone bulk of All Saints set on the river's edge above its evil-smelling low-tide mud. Along the main road: Blue Circle Cement . . . pale blue-green lake in old quarry workings . . . Rugby Cement . . . skyscraping chimney . . . scarred chalk cliffs above Halling . . . Cuxton . . . views to the slender M2 bridge . . . and beyond to cathedral tower and castle keep . . . To the east, sloping down to a leaden Medway, an artist's palette of burnt-umber plough and ochre stubble, of *terre verte* pasture and veridian woods.

The other half of the Western Downs lies to the west. Wrotham Hill, even in the 1940s, had a slightly sinister connotation for motorists.

Today they swish up its 761 feet in top gear. It is crowned with a BBC transmitter mast and offers one of the finest views in the county.

Now, with the M25 taking the traffic strain, the road sweeps comfortably enough through harum-scarum West Kingsdown. Once all cafés and filling-stations, an anarchic sub-topia, it was given a Peacehaven shanty-town image. Today it has outgrown its adolescent thirties rash. It can even offer, at a distance, a smock-mill that has journeyed from Farningham; and St Edmund's, a little Saxon church lurking in a wood and with a lean and unfashionable south-east tower as well as medieval glass and twelfth-century wall paintings. And, oddly enough, some of Kent's loveliest and loneliest scenery is close by.

A mile or so further on – Brands Hatch! As noisily crowded as Knatts Valley is peacefully solitary. A mecca for motor-racing fans. A place to be braved by others at least once in a lifetime. Cars park in their thousands. Ford, Peugeot, Toyota, Shell, Ferrado, Dunlop . . . all fly the advertising flag over a small 'town' of kiosks, offices, sheds and stands. Spectators crowd every vantage-point. All of this and 2¼ miles of track lie in a grassy, wooded hollow.

It is a rural idyll – until shovel-nosed cars, low-slung, high-tail-winged, huge-tyred, move out from amid their overalled acolytes at the pits. Engines are blipped, revved to thunder – and they're off! Down the straight, round, up behind a tiny wood, to reappear, disappear, snake upward again, disappear yet again and finally sweep tight round the bend, snarl downhill and then hurtle into the straight. Cars of rainbow colours flash past like angry hornets. Drivers are mere blobs of red or blue helmet.

Who's leading? I've no idea – and it really doesn't matter. All that does is noise, more noise; speed and still greater speed. Noise wins. Engines scream and whine; exhausts boom; tyres screech. A car spins desperately like a beetle on its back; a steward frantically waves a warning flag to the next car swooping down . . .

In addition to Formula 3 cars, Brands Hatch plays host to skate-boards and giant trucks, power-bike and pedal-bike, mud-spattered Land Rovers and spotless vintage cars. Even L-plated hovercraft have been known!

Give your ear-drums and your curiosity a chance. Explore intriguing Knatts Valley. From off the A20, and despite warning signs, 'Unsuit-able for Motors', take the tree-shaded, single-track lane that corkscrews down into the valley. Here, in absolute seclusion, are huge weather-boarded stables and small bungalows and chalets with bright but flint-infested gardens. South, in a grassy basin, tree-dotted and tree-rimmed, is Woodland's Golf Course. And south again, below the Pilgrims Way, lies Kemsing.

There, three ancient brick-and-tile houses huddle companionably above the war memorial, set in a Lilliputian garden, and key-hole-shaped St Edith's Well, whose waters encircle another tiny garden. You will see her, with a sheaf in her arms, beneath the curving tiled roofs and green cupola of Kent's finest village hall. With its specially marked hop-scotch court, it caters for all ages.

Nearby, creeper-covered Wheatsheaf and white stucco Bell gaze amiably enough at each other. The butcher's shop, sporting in its empty window two straw hats and an upstanding young china pig in blue-and-white apron, is bright with hanging baskets. Little Wybournes is big enough, for all its name, to have a handsome bracketed clock and a pedimented white door-case. And St Mary's, aloof up a short lane, has a wavy crinkle-crankle wall below it and a rambling graveyard above it, where begonia and marigold, geranium and salvia, aster and ageratum bring life and colour to the graves of parishioners long dead.

Four miles of cornfields rolling down the broad flank of the Downs to a hidden M26 and a Quarry Hills skyline bring you to Wrotham. A tight (no pun intended) little village with four pubs, all black-and-white painted, within a 200-yard miscellany of white weather-board, colour-washed plaster and brick-and-tile houses. Enmeshed in a web of traffic-loud roads: the M20 to the north, M26 to the south, A227 and A20 – maybe the locals need them?

Its narrow High Street, once thunderous with Gravesend-Tonbridge traffic, is quieter now. And the visitor is more able safely to take stock of worthwhile buildings as close-packed as the pubs. St George's, perched on a knoll above a tiny paved square, is a sturdy bulldog of a church. Porch and tower are both impressively battlemented. In a niche on the former, a grave St George by Willi Soukop RA replaces, thanks to the Royal Academy of Arts, one stolen in 1971. In the latter, a seventeenth-century clock not only played hymns but could also on occasion lapse into 'The Captain and His Whiskers took a Sly Glance at Me'. An arched passageway through it ensures that the processional holy cross does not have to traverse unconsecrated ground. There is, too, a most unusual and seemingly impractical passageway *above* the chancel arch connecting north and south aisles.

Companionably near, the Three Post Boys, top-hatted, black-booted, red-, green- and blue-jacketed, blow a resounding gallop. Across the road, behind low stone walls and wrought-iron gates and amid manicured lawns, stands Elizabethan Wrotham Place, starting a new life as discreet offices.

Opposite the Place, overgrown bushes almost obscure a plaque: 'Near this place fell Lt Col Shadwell who was shot to the Heart by a

Deferter on the morning of the First day of June 1799. The Afafsin with another Deferter, his companion, were immediately secured and brought to justice.'

Nor is Wrotham's tale yet finished. A further hundred yards on, scrawled display boards offer 'Semi-Dwarf; Mixed Colours; Baby Rabbits – £2.50'. A remarkably down-to-earth approach to the former archiepiscopal palace! Little enough remains of it – except in Maidstone, where in 1349 Archbishop Islip built a fine new riverside palace from its old stones.

The Weald

For many the Weald is Kent at its richest. Yet once it was an unpeopled and impenetrable forest set in a great bowl between North and South Downs; a region of '-dens' (clearings) and '-hursts' (wooded knolls); a cradle of English industry where wool was woven in cottage and grandiose cloth hall alike, and iron ore smelted and worked in the woodlands. It was a Black Country that knew the flames and fumes of furnace and forge. Today it is the Garden of England; from the Quarry Hills, a 'blue dimness' of fields and orchards, hop gardens and woods. Its only railway line runs arrow-straight from Ashford to Tonbridge. But Beult and Teise, lanes and minor roads, twist and turn across it past a wealth of small towns and charming villages, of fine manors and lush farms.

Its very clay has given rise to the taunt that Wealdmen have speckled bellies and webbed feet, and to a tradition of evil roads. 'I saw a lady of very good quality drawn to church in her coach *by six oxen*,' wrote Defoe in the early eighteenth century. Centuries later Victoria Sackville West added: 'But only a bold man ploughs the Weald for corn.' It is indeed 'hard as iron in summer, thick as soup in winter'. Yet it was that same much-maligned clay that gave rise to the dark oak and to the rich red brick and tile which are the hallmarks of its houses.

The Weald is far too big and lovely to be downed in a single gulp. For convenience, east and centre are explored first. It is a journey of delight that should be divided and subdivided, sipped and savoured as your mood and its beauty take you.

Where better to start than with the unfailing delight of Smarden, south-west of Charing and Quarry Hill country, on the B2077?

A writer's nightmare: so much to enthuse over; so difficult to turn into evocative words. Virtually a single street with almost *too* many houses of charm or distinction in it. A rambling black-and-white house smothered in roses; a white weather-board cottage whose jumble of tiled roofs seems to sink ever lower in diminuendo; Zion Chapel, discreet in pediment and white and pale green paint; Dragon House,

Close-studded Headcorn Manor stands behind a church even richer in timber with a
magnificent rood-screen and a splendid roof.

half-timbered with a striking frieze of galumphing young dragons; a
clapboard cottage swathed in wistaria; Whim House, plain weather-
board gleaming white; and even, Smarden's only false if fervent
gesture, a Union Jack front door.

At the right-angled turn of the street, the church path disappears
between Pent House and Parsonage House, making an unusual lich-
gate. Beyond it is St Michael's, 'The Barn of Kent', plain but not
unexciting with its thirty-six-foot-wide, pillarless nave, and only scissor
beams and walls to take the strain of the roof.

And, past it, Smarden's valedictory gesture, two more splendid
houses. Hartnup House has gable over oriel, is half brick, half
close-studding and has miniature windows, irrational but charming.
The Cloth Hall, towering brick flues at one end running up the tiled
wall, and hoist and loft doors at the other, rings the changes with a
mellow façade of ochre plaster and close-studded beams. Beyond,
dappled orchards and grazing sheep. Not bad for one small village?

Headcorn is well worth a short country lane detour. Once modern
'semis' are dispatched, its main street grows in stature: wide pavements
and a squat war memorial lie beneath chestnuts heavy with autumn

conkers. An agricultural merchant's towering silo underlines Head-corn's present and proud name; two splendid weavers' houses, its past. The Chequers is silvered timber and buff plaster on a ragstone foundation; Shakespeare House, as tall and steeply gabled as a fairy-tale castle.

At High Street's dog-leg turn, a tree-lined path leads to the church and ends at the hollow father of all oaks, with a sixty-foot root spread and forty-two-foot Cyril Smith girth. King John held bear-baiting beneath it; a prisoner escaped from his cell over the battlemented porch along its branches; and, more recently, twenty-seven school-children clambered carefully into it. This year vandals set fire to it!

Modestly, behind the church, in Gooseneck Lane, is Headcorn Manor, once Cloth Hall and Parsonage, as firmly rooted, if not as anciently, as the oak. With close studding, jettied ends and oriel windows pouring light into its double-bay hall and with a steep, tiled roof, it is a joy to the eye. The charming cottages of Church Walk lead back to a still bigger timber-framed building with all-embracing eaves.

That Headcorn is not wholly rooted in the past is evidenced along the A274 to Biddenden. On the left, small planes – and daring parachutists – take off from Lashenden Aerodrome; on the right, huge tankers sweep into Unigate's modern creamery.

Biddenden, in the nicest way, makes no secret of its charms, Hendon Hall, with garden gazebo, and Biddenden Place, with fine hipped roof, graciously sandwich the village green and its Maids of Biddenden sign. For thirty-four years at the beginning of the sixteenth century, Eliza and Mary Chalkhurst lived together – and died together – as Siamese twins. Their memory is still honoured each Easter Monday with portrait-embossed cakes.

On one side of the curving main street is a magnificent row of half-timbered houses, with oriel windows peeping from beneath what is surely the longest and largest unbroken sweep of undulating red tiles in Kent. On the other side, from Chequers to Red Lion, white timber and red tile hold sway. And at the end, as a splendid finale, All Saints rears up, a geometrical delight of gables about a no-nonsense battlemented tower. No, not quite final, for behind The Street stands the Old Cloth Hall, where Biddenden's wealth was woven. It mounts a superb double surprise act: one side, seven-gabled, oriel-windowed, all glowing red tiles; the other side – gleaming white plaster and black timbers!

Only The Bull catches the eye in Sissinghurst's Milkhouse Street, and Newman pithily damns even the church: '. . . a poor thing . . . with a lean West tower . . . and stunted chancel'. For all that, Sissinghurst Castle is a Kentish, an English, show-piece. One both famous and infamous.

Sixteenth-century Siamese twins welcome travellers to a village of compact beauty and a High Street 'very short and very perfect'.

Infamous for Sir John Baker (Bloody Mary's Chancellor), 'that human vulture who under the cloak of religious zeal won by torture and pillage sufficient wealth to build this place' – and gain the Queen's cold favour. A Tudor manor turned by his son Richard into an Elizabethan palace. One well worthy to receive Queen Elizabeth herself – on three-quarters of a mile of Biddenden broadcloth laid to keep the royal feet from being mired.

And yet it became sufficiently derelict to be a prison for Napoleon's captured sailors, who made it yet more derelict. Despite the pleas of a disgusted Edward Gibbon (author-to-be of *Decline and Fall of the Roman Empire*, which was criticized for its lack of sensitivity!), they were so ill-treated that one killed a guard by dropping a pail of water on his head – from the top of Sissinghurst's four-storey turreted brick tower. This and the gatehouse range, at the end of the long drive lined with Lombardy poplars, are all that are left of its former glories to welcome visitors to those more recently added.

Glories created by the back-breaking toil of 'effete' Bloomsburyites of remarkable sexual mores: diplomat Sir Harold Nicholson and his wife, Vita Sackville-West, granddaughter of Pepita, a poor girl from Málaga; daughter of a vividly attractive and totally unpredictable mother; a scion of Knole. Together they cleared 'old iron bedsteads, old plough-shares, old cabbage stalks, old broken down earth-closets, old matted wire . . . with only omnipresent bindweed, ground elder and nettles in common'.

On such an unpromising site they created a home – and gardens within a garden, each a formality of design but within each an informality of planting. Herb garden and azalea-lined moat; cottage garden and thyme lawn; yew-ringed roundel and rose garden: all were their creation. Lace-cap hydrangeas rubbing shoulders with the gentle blue of ceanothuses; tree paeonies and columbines; evening primroses and fritillaries; even fig and vine (because, for Vita, Sissinghurst held a faint echo of something southern): all were of their planting. Gardens of softened squares and rectangles, each planned for perfume, season or colour.

And 'the most beautiful of all, the most beautiful in England', the white garden, the garden of cream and white and grey flowers: froth of gypsophila, spears of delphiniums, cascades of rose *longiciopis*. . . .

Resist the lure of Goudhurst and first swing south-west on the A229 to Cranbrook, 'Capital of the Weald'. H. E. Bates described it as 'a town trying to remember what once made it important'. The answer is simple enough: Romney Marsh wool, Cranbrook water, fuller's earth – and Flemish weaving and dyeing skills.

St Dunstan's huge and splendid church of golden sandstone

Vita Sackville-West '. . . fell flat in love' with Sissinghurst Castle. Its stately tower, of rich Tudor brick, houses her book-lined study.

enthroned above the turn of the L-shaped main street personifies the zenith of the wool trade. Vaulted porch; massive tower on which is poised a purposeful Father Time with curving scythe (reputed to have helped out on occasion with the mowing of the graveyard); long, battlemented aisles and a huge clerestoried nave beneath a splendid roof speak volumes.

Inside are richly carved 'Green Men'; a glittering candelabra – bought secondhand in 1716; a towering obelisk which lovingly commemorates the unloveable Bakers of Sissinghurst; and a ten-foot-long tablet showing a recumbent Thomas Webster RA, still besmocked and brushes in hand, with angels at his head and feet.

Beyond the graveyard, Cranbrook School, an Elizabethan foundation in varying shades of red brick, drops down to the main street. School House has a wide loggia on Tuscan columns; Big School, a steep roof, cupola-crowned. And beyond that, on the Benenden road, almost opposite the quaintly named 'House at Home', is Cranbrook's masterpiece: its Union Mill by Henry Dobell, 1814. Tallest in Kent; largest working mill in England; most photographed in the world. It's all there: the black brick base, the white weather-boarding, Dutch-made sails of grace and power, galley-shaped cap and fantail. All seventy-two glorious feet of it. Still working, yet with time to watch over the red-roofed town below.

Stone Street and High Street bear Cranbrook's hallmark – white weather-boarding – but with brick and tile too for warmth. Lloyds Bank is a charming, half-timbered twentieth-century impostor; the tile-hung George Hotel, genuine fifteenth-century.

The B2085 or, better by far, quiet paths will take you to Glassenbury. Angley Woods, once part of the impenetrable Forest of Anderida, now offers a delightful way through pine and beech and past outcrops of Wealden sandstone to its half-hidden beauty.

The Lodge supplies the initial fireworks. Its fence is aflame with scarlet and gold nasturtiums, and its beds are as brilliant as a Guards' parade with meticulously aligned *Begonia semperflorens*. From it, a drive meanders gently down the hillside between newly planted limes, as if to give the eye time to enjoy the unfolding scene of sleek horses in railed-in paddocks, rolling parkland and moated mansion snug at the end of its secluded green valley. Walter Roberts, a Scot, built the original house in 1473 – as well as enclosing 600 acres of open land and a trifling thousand of woodland!

It is not so much the house, brick with sandstone quoins and a wide, broken pediment, that catches the imagination. It is its moat with neat bridge and neater lawns encircling it. On one side, water-lilies, skiff and black swans; on the other, the reflections of Scots pines and even darker

Cranbrook's Union Mill: nearly 200 years old but still working.

conifers. Llamas once roamed the park, and it was the resting-place of Jaffa, Napoleon's thirty-eight-year-old charger.

A lane opposite will take you alongside Old Park Wood to Colliers Green, whose name serves as a reminder of the agricultural Weald's industrial past. There too lived and died much-travelled Charles Doughty, who wrote so richly of austere 'Arabia Deserta'. Nearby Curtisden Green has, some hold, a very different connotation: once perhaps Courtesan Green, when it discreetly housed nearby Glassenbury's mistresses! And more recently Richard Church, one of Kent's staunchest literary upholders, lived contentedly there in a converted oast.

Goudhurst, south-west and on the A262, is a village with a view. Hill-top St Mary's with battlemented tower and a blue-faced clock of mellow chime, stands reassuringly solid in golden sandstone. And yet its tower has suffered fire which melted the bells, and bombs which shattered its glass. Below it, once connected to it by tunnels, is the impressive, balconied, black-and-white Star & Eagle. And below that, picturesque tiled and weather-boarded houses on banks above the road tumble down towards the duck pond. Here, near the tiny brick-nogged Nat West bank, the road pauses to look at the view before dashing downhill again. And what a view! Hop gardens, orchard and pasture. Rolling woods, pink-roofed barns and white-cowled oasts. Grey churches and steeples. Tiny hamlets. All harmonize without a discordant note as far as the eye can see up the opposite slope.

The church tower has the widest view of all – sixty-eight towers and spires on a clear day, it is said, though surely with exaggerated pride. In it are fittingly splendid tombs of the Culpepers. Take your choice: marble or alabaster, brass or wood, profiled or in the round?

At the foot of Goudhurst's long hill, with oast and hop fields as near neighbours, is Finchcocks, a rarish building, for it is Kentish baroque – but lacking real flamboyance. Imposing, with its broad, red-brick, three-storey façade and with two-storeyed wings, yes. But its flourishes are modest: warmer red dressings, darker red chimneys overtopping the tiled roof; modest pediment and pilasters with enlivening touches of white; and a rubbed brick niche housing a slightly time-worn Queen Anne from the Royal Exchange. Within it, pianist and collector Richard Burnett has brought together a wide variety of historical keyboard instruments to be seen – and to be heard – playing the music specially written for them.

Kilndown – don't miss it – is best reached along a nearby lane. It owes its reputation 'as a whole of colour, unique in England' to Alexander Beresford Hope. To improve the church which his stepfather, Viscount Beresford, had built with sandstone from what is now

the village pond, he embellished the broached spire with bold lucarnes and masked the deficiencies of a low-pitched roof with a pierced parapet. That, in 1841, was only a start.

Internally, he beautified the church still further with marquetry panels of the saints made by local craftsmen from local wood; brass candle-holders; high on the wall, an ornate pulpit (modelled on one at Beaulieu Abbey), to reach which the priest has to disappear into the vestry to reappear in it moments later like some clerical jack-in-the-box; two crown candelabra; a finely carved rood-screen; an altar, a copy of William of Wykeham's Winchester tomb; an east window of dramatic stained glass from the Munich factory founded by King Ludwig of Bavaria; and, above the font, a German wood-carving of a splendidly moustached St George. Everywhere there are touches of rich and vivid but never obtrusive red, blue and gold.

A sporting switchback lane frolics past the unusually named Globe & Rainbow, shady woods, red-tiled farms, cottages, orchards and oasts to Bedgebury. To England's National Pinetum.

In the 1920s a survey at Kew's Royal Botanic Gardens showed that, while most of its trees could shrug off the effects of the Great Wen's ever-increasing air-pollution, its conifers couldn't. They were definitely ailing, beyond hope of real recovery. Forestry Commission and Royal Botanic Gardens started an urgent search for a healthier site. It ended in Kent, on the western edge of ancient Bedgebury Forest. On a hundred acres of undulating ground rising to 300 feet are a former hammer pond, now the haunt of wild fowl and fed by two streams, grassy avenues, tantalizing vistas and a glory of trees – Pine Hill, Sequoia Grove, Cypress Avenue, Cedar Bank . . . All yours for a few pence!

The Pinetum offers subtle colours of leaf and bark at all seasons. Richer ones in autumn: the russet of swamp cypress; deeper reds of Chinese Lawn redwood, rich orange of golden larch; and the crimson and gold fireworks of Liquidambar and maple. In winter, with snow layered on the branches of the great firs and Marshal's Lake leaden with ice and snow-flecked, Bedgebury gives you a glimpse of Scandinavia.

Above the Pinetum are Forest Plots. Here, on 126 quarter-acre sites, ninety-six species from the temperate zones of Europe are scientifically and commercially evaluated. Kentish soil and air work wonders. The Leyland cypress grows two feet each year; Silver firs tower a hundred feet high, only to be outstripped by Grand firs, one of which, at 150 feet, is the tallest tree in Kent.

Encircling Bedgebury Forest played its part in World War II. In 1940 47° of frost wrought icy havoc. And, contrastingly, in 1942, it lost

360 of its 2,500 acres not by the axe or incendiaries but by the equally lethal stub of a carelessly dropped cigarette. It was a holocaust fought through a long and dangerous night by Home Guard and troops as well as fire brigade. Today the scars are healed. But its eighty-foot watch-tower still stands as a silent reproach: 'Don't Smoke!'

Nearby is Bedgebury Hall, now a leading girls' public school. The old Hall lies under the lake-water in the grounds that once needed the care of forty gardeners. Its successor had its original brick encased in sandstone from nearby Prior's Heath.

It has known great owners. First, Kent's omnipresent Culpepers, seven generations of them, one of which cast guns that fired on the Spanish Armada. Then Sir James Hayes, once secretary to Prince Rupert, whom Pepys characterized as 'a mighty brisk blade'. The recovery of a sunken Spanish treasure ship and a marriage with the wealthy Viscountess Falkland enabled him to rebuild the house.

Still more remarkable was the illegitimate Viscount Beresford, who captured Buenos Aires, became Commander-in-Chief of the Portu-guese Army and received high tribute from Wellington for his part in the Peninsula War. His stepson, Alexander Beresford Hope (already met at Kilndown), was an idealistic philanthropist, scholar and poet. He planned a chapel, a hospice for clergy, almshouses and a reforma-tory in the best sense of the word. Sadly, it all came to nothing. But he did rescue Canterbury's St Augustine's Abbey, degraded as brewery and 'scandalous pleasure gardens', to transform part of it into a missionary college. And it was he who gave Bedgebury Hall a French flavour by adding the mansard roof with its two rows of dormers, to accommodate under it a score more servants to look after a steadily growing family.

East, where the A268 and A229 meet in a 'breathless nexus of traffic', Hawkhurst sprawls on a ridge amid tumbled Wealden hills. Divided into rural Moor and more urban Highgate, it boasts two churches: bomb-blasted, Perpendicular St Laurence and Gilbert Scott's Victorian Gothic All Saints.

Although eighteenth-century Dunks School, plum-red brick with a pyramid roof and clock-turret, and its flanking almshouses catch the eye, Hawkhurst's history is richer than its architecture. Here, in 1747, ex-Corporal Sturt and his militia outgeneralled and outgunned the villainous Hawkhurst gang of smugglers; Sir William Herschel scanned the heavens; William Rootes, later of Hillman and Humber fame, opened a cycle shop; and Dr Barnardo established his largest country home, Babies' Castle.

North and east, quiet lanes take you to Benenden, past High

Wealden farms at their best: Four Wents, Great Nineveh and Scullsgate. Almost in the shadow of the Forestry Commission's conifers in Hemsted Forest, at the highest point in the Weald, stands Benenden School for Girls.

In 1921 three teachers, with all the optimism of youth, took over this huge red-brick-and-sandstone house. Had they visions then that it would become one of Britain's most famous public schools for girls? That one of its aims, 'service to others', would be so well exemplified by a former pupil, the Princess Royal?

Originally it was an impressive Elizabethan mansion owned for 400 years by the Guldefords – and, for a shorter spell, by Admiral of the Fleet Sir John 'Foulweather' Norris. Virtually rebuilt in 1862 by the future Viscount Cranbrook, finishing touches were added by Lord Rothermere in 1912.

The village has a generously proportioned green with an appropriately long cricketing history. Edward Wenman, wheelwright and Kent cricketer, was born here. In the 1840s he and another Benenden man once challenged an entire Isle of Oxney XI to do battle. And trounced them by sixty-six runs!

Below the green are white weather-board and tile-hung cottages. On one side, the old brick-and-sandstone primary school, with cheeky half-timbered turret and tiled spire and, cheekier still, a tiny bellcote balanced on top of a buttress, is an interested spectator. At the top of the ground sprawls St George's Church, palely aloof in its sandstone.

En route to Rolvenden, a trim post-mill contentedly suns itself on Beacon Hill to your right, whilst to the left are the gardens of Hole Park: topiary and water-dell, daffodils and roses. Nearby Great Maytham Hall, an impressive neo-Georgian house by Lutyens, saw the creation by Frances Hodgson Burnett of *The Secret Garden* and that famous, or infamous, tear-jerker *Little Lord Fauntleroy*.

Rolvenden itself, though virtually gutted after the Great Plague, is pleasantly high, wide and handsome. Its sandstone church, with a contrastingly darker brown ironstone tower with white quoins, and a red-faced clock, rises out of a swirling sea of white weather-boarded cottages (one with a splendid bow window) to dominate one end of its broad street. Maybe the clock blushes for the sheer and unashamed arrogance of the church's vast manorial pew. Not merely does it contain eight comfortable chairs and a table big enough for a sit-down meal or a game of blackjack but it is accessible only by a curving staircase. And to crown all, it flaunts brass rails along which blue curtains can be drawn when ennui is brought about by the over-zealous minister below.

Rolvenden can boast modern marvels too. Korker's factory – brainchild of the village butcher – turns out mile-long links of sausages each week. And C. M. Booth's Motor Museum boasts no fewer than ten vintage models of the pre-war car that every red-blooded young man, and not a few red-blooded young women, coveted – dashing three-wheeler Morgans.

Tenterden may or may not have relinquished its title 'Capital of the Weald' to Cranbrook but it clings firmly – and justly – to that of 'Jewel of the Weald'. Its broad main street, widening still further between plane-shaded grass verges, offers a rich display of buildings from down the centuries. There is the fifteenth-century Woolpack Inn; the town hall (Tenterden has had a mayor since 1449 and, despite undignified incorporation with 'upstart' Ashford, still has); the black-and-white Spinning Wheel with, sign of the times, Laura Ashley next door; the Tudor Rose, a typical Wealden hall-house; and the Eight Bells, with mathematical tiles primly concealing some of the beauties of its original timber framing.

Modestly standing back is St Mildred's, strongly buttressed, of sandstone and ironstone and blessed with – it makes no bones about it – 'Kent's finest tower'. Where its tall angle-buttresses stop, octagonal turrets rise and are splendidly capped with crocketed pinnacles. And yet such splendour, fifty years in the completion, led to the old jingle 'Tenterden Steeple Made Goodwin Sands': a fallacious belief that funds for sea-wall defence were diverted to its glory and that, as a result, the fertile Isle of Lomea, 'very fruitful and had much pasture', became that infamous 'Shype-swallower' the Goodwin Sands.

Tenterden's obvious attractions do not end there. From Tenterden Town Station the Kent & East Sussex Railway will gladly take you on the *Wealden Pullman* or *Santa Special* for a leisurely four-mile rural journey to Wittersham Road, once islanded. And in due time its volunteer enthusiasts will clear the line as far as Bodiam and its magnificently moated castle. At eighteen-acre Spots Farm you can inspect vineyards and herb garden after a glass of excellent English Müller Thurgau, Reichensteiner or Huxelrebe, before journeying on, hardly a hiccup away, to Smallhythe, where there is so much in so small a hamlet (see p. 118).

High Halden sits too much in Tenterden's shadow. But The Chequers, with unruly creeper brazenly peering in at its dormers, was reputedly built from ships' timbers. And there is timber again – fifty tons of Wealden oak – beneath the unusual octagonal church tower, topped by a splay-footed spire, in its thirty-foot-long vestibule, in-geniously constructed by fourteenth-century carpenters in a web of scissor beams.

Bethersden is a village of leisurely houses, each with plenty of elbow-room, that tucks its centre unobtrusively away down a side turning. Its Perpendicular church's graveyard contains unusual oven tombs, an eighteenth-century 'economy barrow' with three graves in one!

Its 'marble', not Michelangelo's finest Carrara marble, is a limestone, to create which millions of freshwater snails, *Viviparus Paludina*, laid down their lives. Worked in mottled greenish-grey slabs from eighty feet below the dark Wealden clay, it makes fine paving-stones, as sturdily demonstrated in Biddenden. But smoothly polished it finds far higher status as gleaming floor slabs, pillars and tombs not only in Bethersden, Stone and other Kentish villages but also in Rochester and Canterbury Cathedrals.

Much more recently, Bethersden has achieved press and television fame as a rocking-horse centre. The go-ahead young Stevenson brothers, Marc and Tony, inherited Uncle James Bosworthwick's Suffolk carving skills and grafted them onto modern techniques. Now dapple-grey as well as superbly grained and gleaming walnut and mahogany Dobbins gallop wild-eyed, with nostrils flaring, not only into Britain's stately homes but also into those of King Hussein of Jordan and Sheikh Mohammed in Dubai. In the rocking-horse hospital, Longleat's 'Sir Jumpitty Gee-Gee Boy' and a hundred other weary nursery favourites have been given new life.

Just south of Ashford, Singleton Manor, moated and close-studded, is threatened by the advancing tide of urban development. But neighbouring seventeenth-century Singleton Barn, second biggest in Kent, tactfully restored as a pub, is a fitting place in which to toast the Eastern Weald.

Royal Tunbridge Wells, although not really of the Weald, is an excellent springboard for its western end. The dissolute and dying Lord North's chance discovery of the healing red ochreous spring in 1606 is too well known to bear repetition. So too is that of Queen Henrietta Maria's camping on its breezy Common and bringing in her wake a train of quacks and charlatans, pimps and sharpers, reckless young blades and familiar romps. Only with the coming of *soigné* Beau Nash in 1735 and formidable Sarah Porter, 'the Queen of the Touters', did raffishness give way to respectability. And later still to Queen Victoria's 'dear Tunbridge Wells', and to the apoplectic outbursts in *The Times* of 'Disgusted of Tunbridge Wells'.

Uniquely dedicated, the church of King Charles the Martyr has a riot of interior baroque plasterwork which is not matched by its plain, brick exterior. And Decimus Burton's simplistic terraces, crescents and colonnades cannot rival the stateliness of Bath's Queen Square or Royal Crescent. But the Pantiles, on two levels, paved and colonnaded,

Fops and beaux, familiar romps, pimps and toadies, sharpers and touts all frequented the colonnaded Pantiles in their seventeenth-century heyday.

with bandstand and music gallery and shaded by towering lime trees, is still the elegant and unchallenged Queen of Shopping Precincts.

Few towns in Kent have a more splendid exit than Tunbridge Wells. Pembury Road is regal, with its wide grass verges, magnificent trees, lavish Victorian mansions and spacious gardens that once earned it the title 'Millionaires' Row'. Today one of those gardens has become Dunorlan Park. Soaring Scots pines and cedars point the way down grassy slopes, past the ubiquitous rhododendrons, to a lake rippled by rowing-boats – and flotillas of deftly navigating mallards.

Regain the B2015, for north-east and east lies rich Kentish hop and orchard country. At Five Oak Green, Stepney's Father Richard Wilson (who had heard 'them *bloody* hops' so frequently that he thought they were actually red) founded the bright-tiled 'Little Hoppers Hospital' after he had met a distraught woman cradling her dead baby in her arms.

Whetstead Farm, with a mere eight oasts, is the herald of Whitbread's thousand-acre Beltring hop farm. Here, beside the dark green curtain of hop gardens, rear the biggest massed regiment of white cowled oasts in Europe – over twenty strong. From a distance they are armoured knights with lances uplifted; from the rear, tonsured friars Canterbury-bound.

A fascinating museum vividly recounts the story of the hop: the 'wicked weed', a distant cousin of cannabis; suggested fomenter of Jack Cade's rebellion; anathema to traditionalist Henry VIII; eccentric climber that alone spirals clockwise; fastest of growers, in that it can add a foot to its height in a single day; rival, in youth, of asparagus, for the delicacy of its first shoots; and inspirer of the Wood Conservation Act passed when the ever-increasing forests of hop-poles (there was no 'wirework' or 'stringing' then) threatened Wealden woods as had the ironmasters' charcoal-burners centuries before.

The Kindeley Hop, *Humulus lupulus*, went from strength to strength in Kent, 'the Mother of Hop Grounds in England'. Eighty thousand acres were under them in England. In the 1870s 36,000 slum-dwellers from London's East End poured down to Paddock Wood, the hop-pickers' Crewe Junction, there to be triumphantly transported in ribbon-decked wagons to the hoppers' often slatternly huts in Kent's rich countryside. It seemed an idyllic holiday with pay, but London's 'Thunderer' was moved to denounce its toll: Maidstone's back-alleys 'blocked with prostrate, human bodies; mothers immoral; 14 and 15 year old daughters debauched and ready for the streets; little children glib-tongued in obscenity and blasphemy'.

Today it is almost a closed chapter in Kentish history. Whitbread's own acreage is down from 300 to 100, England's from 80,000 to 10,000. The enemies? Trained biologists who have created a hop three times stronger than its forbears; the Common Market that demands duty-free entrance for Bavarian hops – and Chinese too; mechanization that at Beltring sends tall machines rumbling along the dark green alleys, to cut down the bines and transport them to the stripping-house where even bigger machines peel away, with metal loops, the light yellow-green hops, just as dextrously as once did finger and thumb.

But if mechanization rules the hop garden, London streets still echo and thrill to the clatter of Whitbread hooves. Their magnificent greys draw behind them not only barrels of beer but, on occasions, the Speaker of the House of Commons and the Lord Mayor of London. And it is to Beltring that these great horses come for a holiday, for Kentish grass beneath their feet, and final retirement. What a heart-warming sight to see a ton of grey Shire galloping joyously round a Beltring paddock, mane flowing, 'feathered' hooves raised high, strong neck arched! 'Ajax', 'Prejudice', 'Footman' and 'Saturn' frisk like colts.

'Gracie' proved that they are head and heart as well as bone and muscle. When her driver, mid-round, suffered a partial stroke, six-year-old 'Gracie' knew it. She urged her sluggish senior, 'Quota', into action and headed back for the stables in Garrett Street. Three times she waited for the green light, then three times crossed without hesitation – or mishap. Back at echoing stables, she whinnied and stamped until help came.

Matfield, Brenchley, Horsmonden, Lamberhurst and Bayham all call – and should not be denied. Head south now on the B2160. Paddock Wood has grown apace with a huge grain drying store, the equally huge English Hops headquarters and now a freight terminal which has a warehouse a quarter of a mile long, Transfesa and Pasqual. No wonder modern St Andrew's is red-faced without . . . and discreetly colourful within. For the rest, it is a growing sprawl.

A couple of miles south, Matfield restores the rural seemliness of Kent. Georgian brick, red stretchers and blue headers, and white weather-boarded cottages are randomly dotted round the back of the big village green. Between them is Georgian Matfield House, dignified with close-set windows, bold Tuscan pilasters, welcoming doorcase on elegant fluted Doric pilasters, and ornate lead down-pipes. Its stable block also cuts a bit of a dash with sleek white turret and a patterned black-faced clock which admonishes 'Mind the Time'. Surely, in Matfield, Time is in no hurry?

The manor's three pedimented dormers can just see the pond at the west end of the green. It has all the qualities a good village pond should have: a sandy beach, an island just big enough for a weeping willow, and a notice that announces 'No fishing – except for the children of Matfield and Brenchley.' At the other end, the white weather-boarded Wheelwrights' Arms has its own tiny green, bright with hydrangeas and two pensioned-off carts, one red, one green.

Retrace your steps to the Standing Cross Inn, and a sharp right turn heads for Brenchley. If Matfield delicately veiled its charms, Brenchley flaunts them almost brazenly – if you can use so metallic a word of a village so rich in timber.

For a start, Brenchley surely warrants a Guinness Award for the Smallest Village Green, a single oak, of no aldermanic girth, comfortably shades the miniscule triangle. Across the road, ten great cylinders of yew (once hand-clipped by men who surely earned their quart of beer) form a narrow avenue to the church. In 1703 its tower, 'whose altitude exceeded most in Kent', was 'by the rage of winds levelled with the ground and made the sport and pastime of boys and girls'. It has a strikingly wide chancel arch, text-encircled, a blue panelled celure and a fine crown-post roof.

And on the 'Square' stands Kent's most splendid butcher's shop, a close-studded, aggressively black-and-white building that was Queen Anne's hunting lodge – or so a local informed me. Church House makes pretence that its painted wood blocks are really ashlar. The Old Palace, curving itself round the corner, is, with gables, brick and upper storey half-timbering, too good to be true – and has indeed been recently restored with an almost indecent cleanliness of line. For all that, it once housed Nell Gwynn's bastard, the Duke of St Albans.

Restored too, though much less blatantly, is the seventeenth-century Old Workhouse, close-studded half-timber with projecting porch and oriel windows above and three gabled dormers. A veritable galleon of a house! And today, although divided into three, it is surely the council house to end all snide concepts of council house drabness! Only the red-and-yellow brick Bull sounds a false note – one atoned for by the nearby white weather-boarded Rose & Crown with its bow windows looking out across a red-brick path.

Brenchley lies in the centre of a skein of lanes. Eventually luck, bump of locality or Ordnance Survey map will bring you to Horsmonden. One to the south passes two fine houses, sixteenth-century half-timbered Brattles Grange and Marle Place.

To the north, a lane passes under Castle Hill, from which in the hop's heyday could be seen no fewer than ninety oasts, and past Furnace Pond, a quarter of a mile of rushy man-made lake. To see it, you must penetrate the screen of trees and cross the spillway down which its waters once raced to drive the huge wheel that worked the hammers, and the bellows which fanned the furnaces to red heat. Today the stream is a trickle, and the wheel a thing of the past. But here, amongst gentle greenery, was once part of Kent's improbable Black Country. And here, quite by chance, from among the crumbs in a hop-picker's lunch basket, was first planted Fuggles, most famous of all Kent hops.

Beside Horsmonden's unusually square green stands the equally unusual Gun & Spit Roast – a martial reminder of the days when John Browne, ironmaster to Charles I, employed 200 men making iron and casting guns. With splendid impartiality and doubtless a good sense of profit, he made them also for Cromwell.

In October you will find The Gun, most other pubs within a six-mile radius, and locals suddenly deciding it's time for a short break. These are the days of the Horse Fair, days when gypsies and *didicois* head for The Heath. Its green grass disappears not under picturesque Romany caravans but under huge chromium, mobile palaces complete with lace curtains and Crown Derby china, set amidst the detritus of scrap-dealers' lorries. True, horses are dickered over, hands slapped and bargains made but now it is more a clan reunion. And as with all reunions, beer often speaks all too loudly.

At the first crossroads on the B2162, south of the village, you are faced with a delightful choice. Ahead, the oddly named 'Sprivers'; to the left, Horsmonden's lonely church. The former's spacious gardens were walled and hedged, I'm told, to commemorate a Grand National victory. Oak from the estate was used in the building of the House of Commons – and, a century later, in replacing the same, now bomb-damaged timbers.

Horsmonden churlishly left the church behind when the village spurned the peaceful meadows of the Teise for nearby iron and quick profits. But St Margaret's still stands as imposingly and strikingly as ever, a mile and a half away as the crow flies – and in Kent that bird often seems to pursue a distinctly erratic course. 'Strikingly' because it is first seen framed between corrugated-iron barns and four worthy oasts. Nothing else. East and west windows were shattered simultaneously by a single flying bomb in 1944. Today, in the evening sun, its fine west tower arch is dappled in the 'hot colour and hectic shapes' of modern stained glass.

Much history is enshrined in it. A bust honours the rector's servant, John Read, who invented the stomach pump – and proved its worth on a dog. And a tablet records Simon Willard who emigrated to New England – to become a major-general as well as founder of Concord and of Harvard University. Recently forty Willards, from the length and breadth of America, sought their roots here. Old and ill, Horsmonden's last Willard was reluctantly persuaded to say 'a word or two' of welcome. Forty minutes later, her 'congregation' were still spellbound by her reminiscences.

Back on the main road (the A262) our way lies west. Then, after East Wood, a left turn onto the B2162 sweeps us down towards Lamberhurst. Here, high above the village, stands the church – virtually the golf course's nineteenth hole! In its unkempt graveyard lie man and wife, ninety-six and 101, doubtless tongue in cheek, beneath the inscription 'Surely, I come quickly.'

Halfway down, a lane turns sharp right for the Owl House. From its steep earth banks, grey-trunked beeches stretch a green canopy over the road which, in springtime, emerges, blinking, to a waving sea of apple blossom. 'Take Care,' pleads a roadside notice. 'Heavenly Pekinese With Suicidal Tendencies.' And there is the Owl House, oldest cottage and crookedest chimney in Kent! Its tenants once paid a yearly rental to the good monks of Bayham Abbey – of one white cockerel. Its owl is not that unblinking stone-carved bird in the Rhododendron Circle at the end of Owl Walk which leads to the Wistaria Temple. It was the warning cry of the smugglers ('owlers') who used the lonely cottage as a hide for wool to be smuggled to the Continent.

In 1952 Maureen, Duchess of Dufferin and Ava, a Guinness and a bright and beautiful young thing of the carefree twenties, bought Owl House and its garden – then, a single plum tree and a cabbage patch. Today it is one of the most serene gardens in Kent. Massed daffodils and camellias precede Purple Heart and Purple Splendour rhododendrons. With a laburnum backdrop, azaleas are reflected in broken colour in Moomina's Water Garden – just one of three delightful pools. (Entrance fees provide holidays for arthritics at Maureen's Oast.)

Down in the lush valley of the Teise lies Lamberhurst itself. Here Wealden ironmasters made a rich living. Proof enough is that in Lamberhurst 200 tons of railings were forged to surround St Paul's in London. And some have recently returned there. On local maps you find Furnace Wood, Forge Farm, Cinder and Steam-hammer Hills nearby.

Here, in the heart of the Weald, was England's sixteenth-century Black Country. Iron ore was present in Wadhurst clay; Andreaswald provided seemingly endless timber to be slow-burnt into charcoal, as well as used for ship's timbers. Yet not so limitless but that Henry VIII passed a statute ordering that in every acre be left 'twelve standels of oak' for his Navy's use.

Elizabeth I went a step further, forbidding the felling of invaluable oak for charcoal. England must have a navy. But the furnaces flared day and night; huge hammers sounded a noisy rhythm, and the oak was still felled. Cannon were a major product but, as logical Queen Elizabeth pointed out, cannon without ships to bear them were but half-cannon. When coal was mined in the north in the eighteenth century, the iron industry migrated to it – before the Weald was irretrievably destroyed.

Such medieval industry happily left few scars on Kent's face. Indeed, it improved rather than blemished it with hammer-ponds, needed to work bellows and hammers. The masonry of old furnaces below sluices and chute make picturesque minor ruins. And, if not beautiful, the iron tomb slabs of proud ironmasters at least lend an unusual touch to graveyards filled with stone ones.

Today Lamberhurst is widely known too for the biggest vineyard in Kent. It is owned by civil engineering genius Robert MacAlpine and was managed by cheery Karl Heinz Johner who commuted to his own Swiss border vineyard by car and plane – in a bare five hours!

Calculatedly picturesque, Scotney Castle in its lily-covered moat, made a perfect setting for a TV production of A Midsummer Night's Dream.

Grander but no lovelier than the Owl House is the National Trust's Scotney Castle. Or rather two castles. For Edward Hussey, an authority on fusing fine architecture into fine landscape, added his own controlled destruction to Nature's to turn the original Plantagenet castle and Elizabethan mansion into a romantic Gothic ruin. Its single machicolated Ashburnham Tower, with red-tiled and trimly lanterned roof, merges with the jagged walls, blind windows and gables of the mansion. A perfect combination of weathered brick, stone and tile reflected in the moat formed by the diverted Beult . . . As much photographed as a nubile Hollywood starlet, the old ruins have also a past of hidden priest-holes and dramatic Jesuit escape, and of ghostly cries still heard long after a murder in the moat.

Above them, Hussey carved out the hillside to provide stone for a new castle. Austere save for a battlemented tower but one much less dark and dank than its predecessor had been and with far wider views from its grassy belvedere. The resultant eyesore quarry was turned into a giant alpine rock-garden.

Only a mile further on lies Bewl Reservoir, the largest stretch of water in south-eastern England, with 6,900 million gallons of water, a hundred feet deep, covering 770 acres within a fifteen-mile shoreline. No mean visual acquisition because, with fields and rich woods surrounding the shoreline, it seems Nature's work as much as Man's. Only inlet and outlet towers and the thousand-yard-long dam, despite its landscaped embankment, give the game away.

Dunster's Mill House and fifteenth-century Ketley Cottage were both moved, beam by beam, to safer sites. Tindall's Cottage is now a fine museum-piece in the Open Air Museum near Chichester; and a Bewl oast flies the Kentish flag – in Montreal! Chingley Forge, where iron tools were made for nearly five centuries, was drowned. So too were farms, but nature trails and reserves help conserve, not destroy, plant and animal life, whether it is massed bluebells or spotted orchid, damsel fly or dragonfly, sweet chestnut or alder, green woodpecker or dunnocks.

If its banks shelter wildlife, its waters are dotted with 'wet bobs': wind-surfing and dinghy sailing; rowing and canoeing, even sub-aqua diving, on Bewl's deep waters. For the less energetic, ss *Frances May*, once the pride of Loch Lomond, steams sedately across to Goose Creek Jetty. But, pre-stocked with 12,000 brown and rainbow trout each year, it is as an angler's paradise that Bewl is most famous.

A right turn at the crossroads above it takes you pleasantly back via the B2169 to the remains of Bayham Abbey – and Tunbridge Wells. The former lie strictly in Sussex but it would be churlish not to mention them. Premonstratensian monks, white-habited in undyed wool and never knowing Benedictine wealth, lived there in 'pitiable poverty and abundant want'. But their verminous clothing was a penance rather than a necessity. Such dedication, it was held, doubled the efficacy of their prayers. They sought isolation and with it freedom from the world's, if not their own, cares. And they sought it on sites like Bayham, sheltered, well-wooded and watered. Poor though they were, they caught Henry II's building-mania when they added a choir and presbytery in the Westminster tradition: an innovative, individual masterpiece of handsome stonework. Today its chancel is grass-carpeted and in the friendly grip of a majestic beech tree; its broken walls, arches and windows are aubretia-speckled.

Above it, just in Kent, a new Bayham Abbey looks down on the medieval one. Set in spacious gardens and park, with its own tiny church, the sandstone Victorian mansion with shaped gables and tall chimney-stacks, for all the Marquess Camden's wealth, comes a poor second to the straitened monks' abbey below it.

The Vale of Eden

A Garden of Eden, even for Kent, sounds just a little too good to be true. Nor would the capricious River Eden itself make such sweeping claim. Its countryside is certainly still Wealden – and therefore lovely: well-wooded, with orchards and oasts to be found among its tree-shaded pastures.

Eden itself knows the magic of Hever and Penshurst; Bough Beech Reservoir, man-made though it is, is a fine stretch of open water; Cowden, Chiddingstone and Groombridge are three of Kent's loveliest villages; and what better backdrop than the Greensand Hills? For all that, Eden's countryside is rather too enclosed, too seldom given to the grand gesture, and its meandering lanes seem a little unsure of themselves.

South-west of Tunbridge Wells strange outcrops of tawny sandstone provide an unusual playground for the young – and not so young. On the common, between Higher Cricket Ground and Mount Ephraim, Wellington Rocks, flat-topped, with narrow 'passes' between them and sandy 'beach' in front, provide endless hours of chase and scramble for youngsters. It provides too a challenging long hit for Mad Hatters and Linden CC from their beautifully sited ground just below them. And on nearby Rusthall Common, solitary Toad Rock still squats malignantly . . .

Best of all are High Rocks, a perfect halt on the way to Groombridge. Here is a mini-Switzerland where outcrops, like blunt-nosed whales, rear up amongst trees which flourish almost as well *on* them as at their feet. Narrow paths and miniature canyons, spanned by rustic bridges, wind between them. Here, where simpering Victorian ladies had the vapours, children (with care!) can re-enact the Britons' stand against the Emperor Claudius's troops.

Opposite the entrance to High Rocks is the High Rocks Inn – and the Julie Tullis bar – with its unusual sign of climbers above a glacier. But then Julie Tullis was a very unusual woman. One who could hold her own with the finest male mountaineers of her day. One who, when her party was snowbound by howling blizzards, died near the summit of K2.

Along the edge of Broadwater Forest, the road winds down to Groombridge. A village divided – by Kent Water, the county boundary. And here Kent definitely gets the better of Sussex. Its rakishly sloping green is hedged about with interest. Above it, behind pleached limes, are The Walks: eighteenth-century cottages, tile-hung second storey above blue-and-red-brick first, and with the dashing Crown Inn conveniently on the corner. Equally charming houses and cottages, with silver-grey weather-board, line Ashurst Hill on the left.

Along it are two most unusual houses. Burrswood is Decimus Burton in Tudor garb, with, as Newman puts it, 'an unbelievable gallimaufry of sham gables, lancets and eyebrow pediments'. But it is its use rather than its appearance that counts.

As a teenager, Dorothy Kerrin was desperately ill – and was convinced that her miraculous overnight recovery was due to prayer. Today, run by the Kerrin Trust, the house is a Home of Healing, where prayer, psychology and medicine challenge illness. As if such work were not enough, Dorothy, at one swoop, adopted nine war orphans – and housed them a little further up the hill, at Lodge Court.

The latter is a superb house in its own right and with a story to out-rival Burrswood's. It consists of two long ranges, half-timbered with silvered beams and buff plaster, set at right angles to each other with lawns in front, and a low archway through each. By one, a blue-and-white ceramic Virgin Mary, copy of a della Robbia, the gift of a grateful patient to Dorothy Kerrin; through the other, a glimpse of the garden, once an orchard, sloping down past roses to a yew-hedged swimming-pool and fields rising up to Crowborough. A perfect whole? But the shorter range is modern; the longer, Tudor – and much travelled! It came from Udimore Court, near Rye, and was once visited by the Black Prince himself. But 1912 found it derelict and decaying, used as a hop-pickers' tenement. Steam traction engines hauled its beams, tiles and bricks through thirty miles of winding country roads to this perfect site.

The rescuer was no knight in shining armour – but a comic postcard artist! More astute than his fellows, he was perhaps the first to keep the copyright of his work . . . and so have the means to restore the battered house to its former beauty. Older readers will remember the striking signature of Lawson Wood. Remember also his too-human chimps and his comic, red-nosed policemen: 'The Nine Pints of the Law'.

On the other side of the green is Groombridge Place, and near its gate, its chapel of ease. A heartfelt cry of thanksgiving, it was erected in

1625 by 'That Worthy Patriot' and staunch Protestant John Packer, to celebrate Prince Charles' return from abroad – *without* becoming engaged to the Spanish and – worse still – *Catholic* Infanta. Repaired in 1754 from a 'very ruinous condition', it is today in splendid shape. Stained glass, nearly all by Kempe (spot his wheatsheaf 'logo'!) except for some fine original armorial glass, fills the church with a rich but sombre light. One window records the confinement at Groombridge Place of John, Count of Angoulême. With his older brother, the Duke of Orléans, also ransomed, after Agincourt, it took twenty-five long years before money was found to secure the younger one's release, though not all were passed at Groombridge.

Dark pews and Jacobean pulpit with sounding-board are so lovingly polished that they reflect the gleaming brass of candle-holders, swivel lectern and four chandeliers. Contrastingly, high up in one corner is the marble figure of a half-clothed young man, legs crossed, with an open book on his knee – and with his head lolling grotesquely on his shoulder! It is said to represent Philip Packer as he died in an arbour on Christmas Eve, 1686!

The Charles II Place is one of Kent's loveliest and most endearing moated houses. A drive leads past a lake over which leans a gravity-defying Scots pine. At its head is the best view of the house. Four Wellingtonias tower in front of the bridge that spans the wide moat and leads you to the mellow red-brick and russet tiles of the H-shaped Jacobean house. Peacocks strut on the steps of the classic sandstone porch supported on Ionic columns. Tall chimney-stacks, with plump projecting chimney-breasts, rise from the hipped roofs of the two projecting wings, boldly brick-quoined. And on the detached stables, a charming ogee-capped turret is silhouetted against the trees.

If there is any doubt as to whether or not Wren designed the house, there is little that Evelyn (of 'Diary' fame) helped to design the garden. Paths and steps flanked by clipped yew and hazel hedges; wrought-iron gates and fat urns; stone basin and sundial; roses, heathers, orange and yellow marigolds are set in terraces that leisurely climb the wooded hillside. Groombridge Place drowses secure and comfortable in peaceful isolation within its generous moat.

Up on the main road, Ashurst's little St Martin's, with its white weather-boarded bell-cote, gilt cockerel weather-vane and deep, tiled roof hides modestly among trees. Only a quarter of a mile away are the old furnace and mill-race in Pond Field.

Medway, Ouse and Mole rise within a few hundred yards of each other at Turner's Hill, across the Sussex border. Down Ashurst Hill and beyond the Bold Faced Stag, the infant Medway swirls between banks rich in rosebay willow-herb over a weir set between creeper-covered brick walls spanned by a frail bridge. Below is a broad pool, haunt of seemingly somnolent anglers.

Further on, the B2062 on the right invites you, irresistibly, to Cowden, a village which gives little indication of its seventeenth-century fame as an iron-centre. Thirty-acre Furnace Pond to the west once supplied power to make the falconet gun for Cromwell. Today even the clang of hammer on anvil at the Old Forge near the church gates has long been stilled. With the long, low Crown Inn, colour-splashed with hydrangeas, setting the pace at one end of the twisting street, and the equally strategically placed Fountain at the other, Cowden is as peaceful and white weather-boarded a village as you'll find in Kent.

St Mary Magdalene is rich in interest. In the churchyard, once oak-fenced by local farmers, each contributing in accordance with the value of his property, are two rusted iron tombstones. Bold, raised lettering still honours Mary and Richard Still. The latter, in 1726, left 20 shillings a year to the sexton for 'ringing the great bell at 5 o'clock in the morning and 8 o'clock in the evening from Michaelmas to Lady Day for ever'. The slender 127-foot spire has modern cedar shingles unusually covering walls and tower as well as the spire itself. Inside, six

Seventeenth-century Haxted Mill, hard at it again, is too good to miss – even if it is just in East Sussex.

massive beams, with arched braces in both directions, confidently carry its weight. The church once housed a statue of St Uncumber, whom unhappy wives besought to 'uncumber them of their hosbondys', for, in her youthful beauty, her desperate prayers for release from persistent suitors were speedily answered and chaste celibacy was found – in the overnight growth of a beard!

Edenbridge, straggling down the Roman Lewes-London road, might once have had something of Cowden's rural peace, but GLC overspill housing, industrial estates and *two* railway stations have put an end to all that. Nevertheless, it still has its moments. In August it goes back to its roots with a huge agricultural show, and in November it lets down its hair with mammoth Bonfire Night celebrations.

On one short stretch of traffic-ridden main street (which, at weekends, is only for the fleet of foot) it has buildings worthy of mention. Ye Old Crown is unique in Kent for a sign that completely spans the street. The inn was used by the notorious Ransley smuggling gang – and from dark passages upstairs concealed pipes ran duty-free spirits down to the tap-room – until inquisitive excisemen ended it all. Set back a little, and opposite a weather-boarded mill, the black sheds of the old tannery, the Leathermarket, are now garden-encircled. Taylor House, one of several Tudor buildings, still carries on its door the arms of Sir William Taylour, Lord Mayor of London in 1469.

And beyond black-and-white Priest House, gratefully just out of earshot of the ceaseless traffic, is the church of St Peter and St Paul. The rough-textured sandstone can glow like gold; marguerites and hydrangeas flourish round the porch; and the vastness of the diagonal buttresses, added later to its west tower, suggests either undue alarm or downright pessimism. As light and airy inside as it is reassuringly solid outside, the church has a stained-glass window from which the generously bearded local station-master looks out in the guise of a prophet.

From Edenbridge, Hever greets you with *two* signs on its inn, once known as Bull & Butcher, an oblique attack on Henry VIII. On one side of the building, a scowling, unwelcoming monarch; on the other a double-faced board shows back *and* front of a rather happier king. (Even backs can be expressive!) The ragstone church with its graceful shingled spire stands at the entrance to the castle park. Inside there is much to see: a Lifeguards' standard; a glowing Astor window, rich in colour, arms and saints; a brass of a woman in butterfly head-dress; and a simple wooden lectern which replaces that of 'convoluted ingenuity' made by the local blacksmith.

Finest of all is the tomb chest, with canopied niches, of grasping Sir Thomas Bullen; it was his ill-fated daughter Anne who fastidiously

Hever Castle: 'She brought me here every year a child', wrote an unenthusiastic Thomas Bullen. One of them changed England's history!

changed 'Bullen' (but not the armorial three bulls) to 'Boleyn'. The brass on top of it shows the 'Erle of Wilscher' armoured and splendid in his robes of Knight of the Garter, with his feet resting on a two-legged, winged dragon with barbed and knotted tail. Not the old man who after his daughter's downfall died broken and shunned.

How to describe his manor in a few words? The square, sandstone mansion within a wide moat was crenellated by good old Sir John Cobham in 1384 . . . sold to the Bullens in 1462 . . . and bought in 1903 by an American millionaire of taste and vision, William Waldorf Astor, descendant of a German butcher's boy. (Punning locals then nick-named it 'Walled-off Castle'.) Drawbridge and double portcullis now give, and doubtless once refused, access to a small inner half-timbered courtyard. Embattled and with arrow slits in its side turrets, Hever has all the look and charm of a toy fort.

Compact though it is, it holds countless treasures in fittingly beautiful rooms. Their ornate pillars, rich panelling, delicate plaster-work and sturdy beams make an ideal setting. The list is almost endless: portraits by Holbein, Mabuse, Cranach, Clouet; Flemish tapestries; German silver chairs; Delft china; K'ang Hsi vases; Italian armour; Venetian glass; Florentine sculpture; a Doge's biretta ... and instruments of medieval torture. The effect is stunning!

If the house is compact, the gardens are overwhelmingly spacious. And overwhelmingly beautiful. A thousand yew bushes made the maze – and hundreds more were clipped into unique life-size chessmen. Eight columns, seven in imperial porphyry (two from the Temple of Venus in Rome) and one of rare white, settabassi marble, echo the lines of Half Moon Pool. Rose Garden, Golden Stairs, Smugglers Way, Sixteen Acre Island, Chestnut Avenue, Spring Garden, Cascade, Sisters' Pool, Blue Garden and Anne Boleyn's Walk . . . but even these are outshone by the beauty and the Roman treasures of the Italian Garden. Clipped hedges and sandstone walls, broad lawns and flower-beds, pergolas and banked shrubs are the setting for an incredible wealth of statuary and sculpture: sarcophagus and cinerary chest; fluted column and marble pinnacle; Venus and Cupid; Pompeian storage-jars; a Graeco-Roman Pan; Venetian well-heads; four Byzantine lions . . . A modern loggia offers refreshment and a splendid viewpoint down the lake, which is statistically impressive even if only knee-deep in places.

The work needed to create the lake was on a mammoth scale. So too doubtless was the expense. Thirty acres of low-lying meadow were drowned by contractors' 'working night and day if so ordered' with the help of 800 men, six steam-diggers and seven miles of railway. To landscape it, hundreds of tons of rock were imported; trees were uprooted to flourish again on higher ground; and Scots pines were brought twelve miles from Ashdown Forest by sweating teams of four horses and ten men.

Even a castle may not be big enough to accommodate one's friends. So, from Tudor timbers, Astor built a Tudor village, each house different, even to the chimneys – copied from Hampton Court!

A mile north, off the B2027, lies Bough Beech Reservoir. The flooding of a tributary valley of the Eden below Ide Hill to store water for *Surrey* raised a howl of Kentish protest. But today sailing-buffs, bird-watchers, anglers and naturalists make full use of its 280 acres. Without pangs of conscience too, for Bayleaf, a splendidly timbered house, and Winkhurst Farm, a medieval house, were spared a watery grave and transported to the good company of other aged buildings at the Weald and Downland Open Air Museum near Goodwood.

A couple of miles east is Leigh ('Lye'). Set round its friendly, cricketing green, it is a charming fraud, full of Victorian bogus half-timbering and whimsy, of 'rustic musical comedy scenery'. All is in deliberate keeping with Nottingham philanthropist Samuel Morley's Hall Place, which Newman categorized as 'sonorous pomposity'. 'Fanciful Disneyland' would be kinder.

More immediately to the east, a mile by footpath, a mile and a half by road, is the National Trust's village of Chiddingstone. Its single street of tall sixteenth- and seventeenth-century houses, shops and an inn stands opposite the church. It runs the architectural gamut with a fine display of beams and barge-boards with pendants; tile hanging and brick-nogging, generous overhangs and symmetrically balanced gables.

Chiddingstone's beauty is such that the National Trust bought the village lock, stock and barrel – except for its drab castle.

Opposite, St Mary's makes a counter offer of impressive west tower with crocketed pinnacles; gargoyles with all Picasso's disrespect for the normally accepted number of eyes and mouths; iron grave slabs; a big sandstone mausoleum designed by a Streatfeild for succeeding Streatfeilds; and a Streatfeild chapel with a small tablet to Sophia, blue-stocking friend of Dr Johnson – and with the unusual but doubtless useful ability to weep at will.

In 1679 ironmaster Streatfeild built a red brick Carolean mansion. In 1805 dissatisfied Streatfeilds encased it in sombre sandstone and gave it tower, turrets and battlements to turn it into a Plain Jane of a castle that could never put on a really aggressive show. They also high-handedly diverted the village High Street and equally high-handedly demolished a few cottages to improve their view. All this as well as creating sandstone grottoes and a three-acre lake in which, incidentally, in 1945, was caught the largest-ever British bream. Today the castle houses Buddhistic images, Japanese armour, Egyptian artefacts and royal Stuart mementoes.

Roundabout lanes are in no hurry to reach Penshurst. But they do finally drop down past the vineyard, where, as the proprietor is of Australian stock, you will find wallabies as well as wines.

Comparisons are odious, but perhaps Penshurst Place's slower, slightly haphazard growth over seven centuries has given it a greater dignity than Hever's. And, with tower and unbroken crenellations, a 'fine stateliness'. Its red brick, tile and golden sandstone blend as smoothly as its different architectural styles.

Inside, its spacious rooms are rich in the diversity of rococo harpsichord and armorial china, of Brussels tapestries and crystal chandeliers, of towering canopied bed – and portraits of suitably inviting royal mistresses. Yet more impressive is the contrastingly austere hall, sixty feet high, with dramatically steep-pitched roof and life-size grotesques. Below, the medieval scene is set with trestle tables at which Henry VIII dined, central hearth, roof-vent high above, carved screens, minstrels' gallery silver-grey with time – and Sir Philip Sidney's porcupine-crested tilting helmet. In 1586, 'that perfection of man' showed well-known gallantry at Zutphen and less known diplomacy at Court. There he regained a furious Elizabeth's favour with 'a whip to show he had been scourged; a chain to chain himself to her majesty; and a heart of gold to shew he was now entirely hers'.

Penshurst's gardens offer equal diversity and delight. They range from a soberly impressive Tudor parterre, through Theatre Garden and Diana's Bath, to the unrestrainedly patriotic Flag Garden. To say nothing of a mile of clipped yew hedges and a Kentish orchard!

Neighbourly Penshurst church is approached through the tiny,

Penshurst owes its superb Great Hall to Sir John de Pulteney: merchant prince and four times Lord Mayor of London.

open-ended Leicester Square of timber-framed houses: surely the very antithesis of London's maelstrom? Through one of them is cut an entrance, a kind of super lich-gate, which leads past the handsome rectory of chestnut and blue bricks to the churchyard.

St John's, with buttressed tower topped by heavy turrets and pinnacles, is suitably impressive. Inside, a bas-relief Albigensian woman smiles enigmatically from behind a foliated cross. The Sidney chapel is a show-piece, with armorial shields and Sidney and Leicester tombs, including those of Sir William, the first of the Penshurst, Sidneys and Viscount Gort VC, C-in-C of the 1939 British Expeditionary Force, who married into the family. The Becket window is a tapestry of rich colours and ecclesiastical arms, of kings and queens, of commoners and saints.

And Eden, its course run, joins Medway near the bridge which swishes the B2176 up gently rolling hills to well-groomed Bidborough. From its narrow ridge, there are fine views northwards towards Ide Hill. Its Norman church tower has massive masonry but only a stunted, shingled spire – and a prodigiously long clock pendulum that, hypnotically, almost sweeps the floor.

And so back to Tunbridge Wells.

Green Hills – or Sevenoaks Ridge?

Take your choice of name. Both promise – and deliver – breezy, well-wooded uplands. But they modestly say nothing of Sevenoaks and Westerham themselves; of quiet hamlets such as Godden Green or Ivy Hatch; or of good neighbours, Vale of Eden, Weald, Medway and Downs. Or for that matter of Kent's finest cluster of great houses. Chartwell and Squerryes Court, Quebec House and Chevening, Knole and Ightham Mote, Mereworth Castle . . . Can any other county boast such an unbeatable septet?

Squerryes Court, almost on the Surrey border and just off the A25, looks across lawns (once the site of three kitchen-pavilions – set some ninety cold yards from the dining-room!) sloping down to its half-moon trout lake, source of the Darent itself. Beyond it are the remains of the 300-year-old lime avenue . . . and the Surrey hills. Its beautifully crafted bricks glow softly in the setting sun. Rectangular panelled chimney-stacks top the hipped slate roof where the line of six dormers is broken by a pediment rising from the projecting central bay and a Tuscan-columned portico. It is a picture of well-mannered William and Mary architecture. Its symmetry is as faithfully repeated at the back, where gentler lawns and flower-beds replace the once stiff formality of regimented trees and geometric gardens. An unusual and peaceful setting for Paul Daniel's TV *Murder by Magic*!

In the spacious hall, Sir Patience Warde, red-robed and bewigged, greets you from above the mantelpiece. His father, after siring six boys and a single girl, vowed that, even if the next of his brood was a boy, he should be named Patience. But a boy sent at fourteen to Cambridge to study for the ministry and who deserted it for London to make his fortune and become Lord Mayor in 1680 was not likely to be handicapped even by such a name.

Paintings by Stubbs, Wootton, Zaccharelli, Opie, Romney, Roos, de Ring, Rubens, van Dyck, and Joshua Morris floral tapestries, give added charm to the finely proportioned rooms. Our undoubted favourite – by a couple of lengths – was John Warde, Father of Foxhunting, MFH for fifty-seven years, with his twenty stone set deep in the saddle of 'Blue Ruin' – bought from a Newbury gin merchant!

Back on the A25 is Pitt's Cottage, home of Britain's youngest premier (twenty-four), whilst his Holwood mansion was being restored. Its thirteenth-century timbers, *jointed* not nailed, are still iron-hard despite generations of marauding beetles. Traces too can be seen of windows 'glazed' with transparent rabbit-skin, and of oak beams – painted green to evade the Oak Tax and confiscation.

In Westerham, Tudor George & Dragon, black-and-white painted, with ornate porch and balcony and with bottle-glass windows (where General Wolfe stayed in 1758 on his last night in his home town), stares across ceaseless traffic at the more genteel Georgian King's Arms, delicate pastel green with royal arms over white portico.

Beyond them lies the sloping green, focal-point of Westerham. There, it is not the wide variety of buildings that ring it which holds the attention. Nor is it St Mary's, lying just behind it, for all its three east gables; a fine octagonal wooden staircase spiralling up inside the west tower; and a rare Edward VI royal arms still showing, despite the passage of dimming time, the leopards of England, the lilies of France and a fiery Welsh dragon upstaging the lion as supporter. It is, of course, the statues of Westerham's two heroes. A cock-hatted Wolfe, who often went into action carrying only a cane but now brandishing his sword, urges his troops heroically into battle. Churchill, siren-suited, in rough-cast-greening bronze, slumps uncharacteristically in his armchair, looking pensively towards Chartwell. It was given as a mark of respect by Tito and his rugged Partisans – but Oscar Nemon's sculpture does Britain's great leader scant justice.

Quebec House catches you unawares on the first corner before the Chartwell turn – and offers no car-park. With three gables on each side, and tall chimney-stacks, it rears up gracefully from its small encircling garden. Here Wolfe (commissioned – at Squerryes – at fourteen; a lieutenant-colonel at twenty-three) spent his boyhood years. And here today in its light and spacious rooms are a collection of prints and other Wolfiana that includes his heavy field canteen and the dressing-gown in which his body was returned to England.

But it is in the stables at the rear that the bloody and see-saw culmination of the Seven Years War by the capture of Quebec is brought vividly to life. It is an excellently mounted and displayed account of the campaign that led to the death of both commanders, 'both men of sensitivity' with deep regard for their men.

Impatiently, the B2026 winds up the Greensand Ridge. Impatient to

Squerryes Court contains memorabilia of General Wolfe – including his mother's cure for consumption: sliced worms and ground snail-shells!

reach the deep combe, crested with tall woods above sloping sheep-dotted pastures and gleaming with the water of two small lakes, in which lies Chartwell. It was this view rather than the Victorianized fourteenth-century manor which brought Churchill here – and kept him here for forty-three years. It is the garden façade, with its added wings, crow-stepped gables, soaring vertical lines and triumphant lantern, that alone gives it real character. And Churchill himself saw to it that doors, windows and patios made Chartwell one with its garden.

It is a garden that charms you with its slowly unfolding delights: Golden Rose Walk (thirty-four yellow and gold rose species in two borders), given by the Churchills' children to celebrate their parents' Golden Wedding anniversary; the amazing eight-foot-high brick wall, capped and cleverly stepped down the hillside, that was built largely by Winston's own frustrated hands in the 1925–32 years when he was alone in a political desert; buddleias haunted by peacock and red admiral butterflies; three wagon-loads of Cumbrian rock down which splashes a cascade to the lake below; a cyclopean chestnut; lawns where Churchill walked with a malodorous pet sheep and where Montgomery ('long on strategy; rather shorter on accurate play') tried his hand at croquet with Lady Churchill. The empty garden chair that still stands beside the goldfish pond where Churchill used to watch, and perhaps commune with, his favourite golden orfe is strangely moving.

Lack of space, certainly not unwillingness, precludes adequate

description of Chartwell's interior. Even as one enters, it is obviously a
house lived in – loved; and a house worked in, with a book-lined library
and a study with its large mahogany writing-table dominated by
photographs of Winston's family.

Churchill is brought to life still more vividly in the Museum Rooms.
Gifts in recognition of his greatness: a crystal Cross of Lorraine from de
Gaulle; a silver shako (military dress hat) from his old regiment, the
Queen's Own Hussars; a green-glazed Persian bowl from Roosevelt; a
green-and-white malachite cigar-box from the Belgian Congo. His
uniforms: Colonel of Hussars, Elder Brother of Trinity House, Knight
of the Garter and Lord Warden of the Cinque Ports. To say nothing of
siren suit, ten-gallon hat and embroidered slippers. A dozen men in
one!

Most poignant of all perhaps is the half-drunk glass of whisky beside
the unfinished canvas in the garden studio. Beside it are broad brushes
and a hundred fat tubes of rich colour: 'Splash into the turpentine,
wallop into the blue and white, frantic flourish on the palette and then
several fierce strokes and slashes of blue on the absolutely cowering
canvas . . .': Lady Lavery's panache and advice were never forgotten!
'I seized my broadest brush and fell upon my victim with berserk fury.'
In art, as in life, Churchill faced his problems head-on.

After the crowding joys of Chartwell, the simple pleasure of Toy's
Hill above is the perfect foil. This, at 800 feet, is the highest part of the
Greensand Ridge. Increasingly overgrown though the crowning woodlands are becoming, its half-dozen viewpoints still yield splendid
panoramas: to the north, the Downs ridge and Chevening; to the
south-east, friendly Ide Hill, the gleam of Bough Beech and the Weald;
to the south, Ashdown Forest; to the west, the hills of Surrey.

It is a place of brown beech-mast underfoot, black and tangled roots,
grey-green trunks limned against the delicate green of spring leaves.
Silence. Mystery. Timelessness. Then, surprisingly, the faint traces of a
long-dead drive and lodge, of garden, terraces and house . . . Little
more: a wide swathe of close-cut grass amid encircling rhododendrons
and beeches, a circle of thirteen young Scots pine, seats dedicated to 'a
lifelong cyclist' and to 'a lover of views', and an unobtrusive plaque that
records that the land was given by W. A. Robertson in memory of two
brothers killed in World War I.

It is land where, in 1906, Lord Weardale, of the Stanhope family,
raised an improbable, sprawling black-and-white gabled mansion with
tall chimneys – which only thirty years later came under demolition
hammer and crowbar. It left the incomparable view as it should be, to
stillness, solitude and the occasional enchanted walker.

Back past the Fox & Hounds and, on the right, the woodlands

dedicated to Octavia Hill, co-founder of the National Trust, then down to the long, tree-lined descent of Brasted Chart. Here, Domesday Book records, was 'pannage for 20 hogs'. But today even its sandy heath, bracken- and heather-clad, is falling prey to the advance of sapling oak and birch.

Brasted struggles so far along the A25 that, were it not for the low range of tile-hung Manor Cottages behind it and the 'spreading chestnut tree' above it, its pocket-handkerchief green and solemn black pump might be overlooked. Not so the heavily timbered Victorian White Hart Inn. Fortunately so, for it has a peaceful garden and, much more important, a facsimile of the old bar's black-out board. On it are scrawled the signatures of World War II's new knights, the fighter pilots of nearby Biggin Hill who gathered here when they could, to forget both past and future, to live for the moment. Among the boldly scrawled names there stand out the unforgettable: 'Sailor Malan', Johnny Johnson, 'Shanghai' Brothers, Sandy Sandeman, Lord Tedder . . . as well as the thirty-three others who between them won fifteen DSOs and twenty-four DFCs – and put the 'many' deep in the debt of the 'few'. (The original is in the RAF Museum, Hendon.)

At Sundridge you have close-studded Old Hall – and interesting choices: to the north, Combe Bank and Chevening; to the south, a worthwhile sortie onto the ridge again, to the church, Emmetts and Ide Hill.

The church you approach quietly by leafy lane, lich-gate and war memorial and between fittingly lofty cedar and yew, only to be overwhelmed by a prodigally broad-shouldered west tower. The clerestoried nave boasts the tomb of Anne Damer, sculptress, whose hammers, chisels and apron are in her coffin, and also that of Beilby Porteous, bishop, scholar, benefactor and abolitionist, one of an American family of nineteen who came to Britain to educate his children. It was he who gave the fine brass chandelier.

Further up the road is Emmetts, the National Trust's lovely five-acre garden. It has long been famous for its spring and autumn colours and for its 'exotics' (including castor oil trees) set in a 'wild' countryside with conifers. One of them, a majestic hundred-foot Wellingtonia, fittingly crowns one of Kent's highest points, said to be visible from Crowborough, twelve miles away. Even though not open to the public, the nineteenth-century house warrants mention – its roof was raised by jacks to accommodate another storey beneath it!

Ide Hill village, with its spiky Victorian church, is set round a spacious, sloping green. St Mary's was built by Beilby Porteous to save his parishioners the long walk down to Sundridge – and back. Behind it and the rectory, a path leads to a viewpoint. Its once-sweeping panorama of Bough Beech Reservoir, Vale of Eden and Weald is now partly obscured by the luxuriant beechwoods that crown the two-mile-long escarpment to Bayley's Hill.

Immediately below lies Sevenoaks Weald. Architecturally there is little to tell, but it does hold memories of great men. Colonel Lindbergh, in 1926 the first man to fly the Atlantic solo, in the *Spirit of St Louis*, came here after the kidnapping and murder of his two-year-old son.

So did Edward Thomas, Lambeth born and bred, but with a fierce love of unchanging rural ways that brought him to Else's Farm by the railway line. He earned a bare living not by the poetry ('Yes, I remember Adlestrop') which was to gain him recognition only after his death in Flanders in 1917 but by interminable and badly paid hack-work. For all that, it was he who settled W. H. Davies in a down-at-heel cottage in Egg Pie Lane. And it was his children who were 'the ravens that fed him' as he (Davies) worked on the *Autobiography of a Super Tramp* based on his American hobo experiences.

Had you chosen 'north' at Sundridge, a by-road off the B2211 would lead you to secluded Combe Bank, a huge, white-rendered Palladian building of varied elevations, now an independent, girl's school. It was built by Colonel John Campbell to receive his bride, a maid of honour to Queen Anne. In its 350-acre park he planted a beech walk, and cedars which, until half-throttled by steel braces, were the finest in Kent; and cannily he had a small pond turned into large lake by using soldiers quartered on him while waiting to march north to crush the 1715 Rebellion. Rock garden and Grecian temple, however, were the brainchildren of Robert Mond, a penniless German immigrant – who created ICI and gave forty Old Masters and a cool £1 million to the National Gallery.

In 1815 Combe Bank was bought by a West Indies merchant. In resplendent coach-and-four and attended by liveried black servants, he took the countryside by storm. His son missed the carriage narrowly with cannon shot, fell into the lake and robbed the vinery – in company with two of Wordsworth's nephews, embryo bishops both . . . Excellent experience doubtless for Lytton Strachey's future 'Eminent Victorian' Cardinal Manning.

The Walter Crane room is an artistic *tour de force*: stamped and gilded wallpaper; a frieze of plump Florentine cupids pulling carts and Crane's own 'leaner androgynous *amorini*'. A ceiling of bronze-and-silver splendour depicts seasons, planets and signs of the Zodiac. The bow-ended Adam Room, with its eighteenth-century décor restored, and the tunnel-vaulted ballroom, now the chapel, offer a contrastingly peaceful pastel elegance.

Chevening is a mere handful of cheerful brick estate cottages set between a simple ragstone church and an imposing 'big house'. Some handful!

Inside, St Botolph's gives up all outward pretence of simplicity in the Stanhope Chapel: in hanging monuments, ornate alabaster tomb chests and Chantry's sculpture of twenty-three-year-old Lady Frederica Stanhope, who died in childbirth, with her baby peacefully at her breast.

Stanhopes have made their mark in British history. The first Earl captured Port Mahon in Minorca; the fifth founded the National Gallery; and the seventh gave Chevening in trust as residence for royalty or Cabinet minister.

The third played the eccentric with real panache. A 'Minority of One' in the Lords, he was dubbed 'Citizen' Stanhope for his fervent support of the French Revolution. But he displayed much less sympathy for a rebellious daughter and, unabashed, lectured the Lord Chancellor on law, and the bishops on religion! He was an inventive scientist but a poor architect: his greyish mathematical tiles on the house, all-pervading and limpet-like, have only recently been replaced.

With the Foreign Secretary 'in residence', armed police do not encourage visitors. Unless, of course, one of them can generously vouch from experience that your schoolmastering had shown no leaning towards either fanaticism or assassination.

Out of the Inigo Jones stable, the tall brick house is linked to flanking pavilions by curved quadrants. Elegant wrought-iron gates and railings enclose the resultant forecourt; and an informal park and tree-fringed lake encircle formal gardens. The Downs, steep and tree-crested, are a worthy backdrop – enhanced by the famous 'Keyhole' viewpoint cut in the trees exactly on the house's main axis.

Lucky as well as lovely, Chevening suffered a direct hit by a war-time bomb – that didn't explode!

Sevenoaks is a cricketing entrance, for it takes you past British Rail's 'Bat and Ball' station (to say nothing of the oddly named Railway & Bicycle pub). And then, along St Botolph's Road, on to one of Kent's oldest cricket grounds, The Vine, given to the town in perpetuity by its sporting neighbour, the third Duke of Dorset. An elegant white pavilion looks down the sloping ground towards a simple, lawn-encircled war memorial and, more distantly, the North Downs. Beside it is that cricketing rarity, a bandstand. Surely more grounds should emulate The Vine's fine example so that thunderous Wagner could accompany heroic last over onslaughts; Strauss waltzes lend wings to sluggish feet; or 'March of the Gladiators' stir stonewalling batsmen into masterly action.

Although rather swamped by the Victorian mansions of London

commuters who followed the railway when it came to Sevenoaks in 1868, the town still retains something of its former breezy, hilltop, country-town image. And retains too, down its long High Street, buildings of charm too numerous to detail: 'idiosyncratic' Chantry and gabled Temple House; self-assured Royal Oak Hotel and the shy tile-hung and timbered post office; Red House, bold of cornice and chimney-stack, and Bligh's Hotel, once isolated Bedlam Farm.

At its southern end stand Sevenoaks School and its flanking alms-houses – the gift of a foundling who fought at Agincourt when over forty and became Lord Mayor of London, succeeded by Dick Whittington. Rebuilt in 1724 in gaunt and galletted ragstone, they only just escape an undeserved institutional look.

Opposite, St Nicholas's Church makes generous amends. Its angled buttressed, three-stage tower soars above a fine two-storey porch which, not to be outdone, is also turreted and battlemented. In it are memorials to William Lambarde, Kent's own Elizabethan topo-grapher; Dr William Fuller, who researched eruptive fever – and flea-bites; Field Marshal Lord Amherst, who took Montreal; and John Donne, rector and later, in 1621, Dean of St Paul's. The latter fought at Cadiz, wed a sixteen-year-old girl without her father's consent and wrote not only sermons and satires, elegies and epistles of erudition and wit but also love poems of delicate – and sometimes not quite so delicate – passion.

Close by is Sevenoaks', and Kent's, trump card – Knole. No imposing wrought-iron gates greet you: the entrance is almost incon-gruously modest. The drive winds through the thousand undulating acres of parkland, graced with avenues of beech, oak and chestnut. Then, suddenly, in front of you is the grey bulk of Knole, which Vita Sackville-West describes as 'a town rather than a house'. And, of course, the famous red and fallow deer.

For all its shaped gables, tall chimney-stacks, gentle towers and battlements, cupola and oriels; for all its seven courtyards, fifty-two staircases and 365 rooms, covering three acres; for all its labyrinthine passages and creaking stairs, Knole is seemingly 'a town not built hither and thither at this man wished or that, but circumspectly by a single architect with one idea in his head'.

It owed its Tudor splendour, 'fit for the princes of the Church', to three archbishops of Canterbury: Bourchier, Morton and Warham. A fourth, Cranmer, grudgingly but fearfully had to deliver the house into the King's hands. Elizabeth I gratefully gave it (on thrifty lease) to her cousin Thomas Sackville, later Earl of Dorset. A poet in an age of poets, 'a master of sombre magnificence', he became a Lord Treasurer so diligent that he actually died at a Privy Council meeting. And one so

Knole's famous deer graze contentedly enough beneath its equally famous trees – but they aren't too aristocratic to share picnic sandwiches.

diplomatic that he was entrusted with the thankless task of carrying the news of the signing of her death warrant to Mary, Queen of Scots. On the altar of Knole's private chapel, there is still testimony of the gentleness and compassion with which he did it – a Germanic triptych of the 'Procession of Calvary', given him by the ill-fated Queen.

And here, Lady Anne Clifford, wife of the third Earl, heiress to vast Cumberland estates, who spent fourteen unhappy years successfully fighting her spendthrift husband's attempts to seize her fortune, was 'all blubbered with weeping' as she listened to John Donne preaching.

It is to Thomas Sackville that much of Knole's Jacobean magnificence is owed. In a year he spent the equivalent of £1 million, imported 300 Italian workmen, had his own orchestra . . .

Pass through Bourchier's turreted tower from Green Court to austere Stone Court. Beneath the latter's flagstones is a reservoir; on its walls, elegantly shaped rain-water heads bear the initials and date 'T.D.

1605'. And in the great hall, ruffed and grave, Sir Thomas gazes down from above 'My Lord's table', eyeing still perhaps his ninety or so retainers seated below him, hierarchically ranked from chaplain down to scullery maid. Behind them towers the gargantuan oak screen surmounted by his arms. Double caryatids, carved with 'barbaric vitality', span its width. Leopards prowl there and goats graze unsuspectingly. Even a snarling alligator warrants nothing more than to be carelessly wedged between screen and side wall.

Slightly overwhelmed, you are overwhelmed again by the Great Staircase and its aristocratic leopards, now an architectural feature, not a mere utilitarian necessity. One great enough to be copied at Hatfield, Blickling and a hundred other mansions. At its foot, in cold, marmoreal nudity, though certainly not chastity, sprawled – though with some modesty – across plump cushions lies ballerina Gianetta Baccelli ('Miss Shelley' to the tongue-tied servants). She was the third Duke's mistress – and just one of his numerous beautiful Italian souvenirs. On his marriage, her statue was diplomatically banished to obscurity, if not entire oblivion, in the attic.

Space allows no more than a glimpse of Knole's treasures. In the Brown Gallery, there are seemingly unending rows of Sackville portraits, similarly framed. Spangle Bedroom contrasts strikingly with the simplicity of Lady Betty Germaine's cosy little four-poster and bowls of pot-pourri. In the Leicester Gallery, Van Dyck has caught the pensiveness of old age and the fine bones of the Countess of Desmond – who lived to be 104 in an age not noted for longevity. And contrast again in the Reynolds Room, where there are portraits of exotically dressed Wan-y-Tong, page to the third Duke, and modish Lord George Sackville. Branded as 'unfit to serve His Majesty in any military capacity whatsoever', the latter surely epitomized Vita Sackville-West's castigation of male Sackvilles: 'a race too prodigal, too amorous, too weak, too indolent, and too melancholy'.

In the Cartoon Gallery, endless Raphael reproductions are far outshone by the juxtaposition of swaggering Henry Howard, Earl of Surrey, and Henry VIII, old and tense – who was to bring him to the block for high treason! The Venetian Ambassador's room is diplomatically magnificent, with a towering green velvet-hung four-poster. The silver-grey ballroom, in which ten generations of Sackvilles survey with not unwarranted pride gilded wall lamps, seventeenth-century French furniture, ornate fireplace, Persian carpet, Sèvres china and an oak frieze of gryphons, mermaids and grotesque monsters, is yet more sumptuous.

But it is the King's Bedroom that is Knole's *tour de force*. Dimly lit, it holds the mystery and magic of a dream castle. An ostrich-plumed

At the foot of Knole's Great Staircase there lies 'in cold marmoreal nudity' the third Duke's mistress, Gianetta Baccelli.

four-poster with a brood of brocade stools at its feet towers to the finely plastered ceiling. Its hangings contain *miles* of gold and silver thread – restored to their former splendour after thirteen years' work by 150 volunteer needlewomen. And everywhere, elaborately ornamented silver . . . tables, mirror, salvers, sconces, vases – in which even the flowers are silvern.

One can only thank Providence that in the first place Jack Cade and his Cheapside mob snatched Knole's owner, the repressive Lord Say and Sele, from the Tower where the King had placed him for his own safety, and put him to 'a messy end'. Thereby, perhaps, they encouraged his son to be rid of the ill-fated manor (for £266.13s.4d) to Bourchier, who magically transformed it from medieval muddle to Tudor symmetry. And that, in the second place, neither a Molotov breadbasket of 700 incendiaries nor a parachute land-mine, which shattered 500 windows and, snapping their iron bars like twigs, blasted open the massive oak doors of both Outer and Inner Wickets, inflicted irreparable scars on Knole.

At the southernmost corner of Knole's vast park is Riverhill House. It is a sprawling country mansion of unobtrusive charm set in a hillside garden that owes as much to Nature as to man. The Rogers proudly trace their descent back to John Rogers, the Martyr. Thunderous against Popish ways, he met Mary's furious displeasure head on – and unfalteringly preceded Latimer and Ridley to the stake. The Merchants Taylors Company, Lloyds Coffee House and the Army are the Rogers' more recent background. But times change, the days of gracious Edwardian house-parties are over. So too are the days of twelve servants, eight gardeners, seven farm labourers and a dairy-maid. Today the hundred-acre farm is run single-handed – by a Rogers, of course.

Just above Riverhill House a minor road ambles round Knole Park, thence to Bitchett Common and Bitchett Green, where beechwoods put on dazzling autumn displays. A slight detour takes you to inappropriately named One Tree Hill, which affords wide Wealden views and still better ones south-west to Penshurst and beyond.

And so, on to Ivy Hatch. It is a hamlet of charm and enthusiastic gardeners whose exuberant flowers spill out onto the road itself. North lies Ightham: south, Ightham Mote.

The former makes an ideal aperitif for the latter. Sixteenth-century half-timbered and brick cottages cluster snugly together where roads dip down into the village. A little aloof on its own knoll stands the Norman church. It is built of rust-coloured ironstone, with brick-patched and battlemented tower, orange-brown lichen on its tiles, and brick again (ten inches long, not the standard nine inches) in the rebuilt north aisle. Inside, the wagon roof is of local oak, and the south aisle has little grotesques as corbels.

It is, however, its monuments and memorials that make St Peter's memorable. Sir Thomas Cawne, a fourteenth-century armoured giant of a man, unbending even in death, lies beneath an unusual chancel window. Equally unusual, two Sir William Selbys share the same alcove, one above the other. The upper knight is the more peacefully relaxed, although, in the unruly Scottish Marches, he had 'put down 1500 desperate and wicked thieves'. In the same dark corner, hunched and peering out myopically from between curtains parted by lissome angels, is Dame Dorothy Selby. A fine needlewoman, she used her skill to depict but not, as legend exaggerates, to *discover* in 1605 the Gunpowder Plot. William Lambarde married his seventeen-year-old bride here – and here buried her, disfigured by smallpox, just three years later.

South again, past Ivy Hatch, is Ightham Vineyard, with as fine a view between heavily wooded hills down towards the Mote as eye could wish. And as good a blend of Müller Thurgau, Reichensteiner, Huxelrebe and Schönburger as palate could desire.

Then, suddenly, in a heavily wooded dell, it is there below you: 'perhaps the most perfect medieval moated manor in the country'. Ightham Mote, 'a poem in stone' and half-timber, rises sheer out of the water. Lawns, tiny cascades, gardens, old stables and a majestic, deeply fissured Scots pine complete a picture that halts you in mid-stride. It appears solitary, almost withdrawn, jealously hiding its inner courtyard beauty, but, as Andrew MacIntyre wrote, 'Where else in the world would this house be – but in Kent?' And, Kentish through and through, it held a young American, Charles Robinson, in thrall until, with fortune made, he returned to buy it, restore it and give it for posterity to the National Trust.

A double-span stone bridge carries you across the moat to the gatehouse and cobbled inner courtyard. There, all is a picturesque confusion of stone and timber, gable and barge-board, chimney-breast and oriel window, clock and cupola. And an enormous half-timbered kennel to match!

In the great hall, a picture of the Mote by Churchill, grotesque corbels, panelling, armour, tapestry and splendid carving of rose and pomegranate set amidst apes, chained watchdogs and snarling lions. On the landing of the seventeenth-century staircase there is Dame Dorothy again, black-gowned, lace-ruffed and with thin mouth pursed in disapproval. Beyond lie better things. Painted wagon roof, linenfold panelling and glowing stained glass give the Tudor chapel a warmth that Dame Dorothy lacks. The drawing-room, for all its obese fireplace

Ightham Mote: 'A poem in stone and half timber'.

and overmantel, with swaggering Selby arms above, and its Jacobean oak frieze of Saracens' heads and birds of prey, has gentler, more homely touches: a huge reflective mirror and rare and delicate Chinese wallpaper. On the latter, 200 years old, exotic birds live a paradisal life amid flowers and trees. Sadly, it is under expensive siege by gourmet silverfish.

Back to Ivy Hatch, then a fine ridge road takes you to sleepy Plaxtol with its crossroads church, doubly unusual in having no dedication and in being Cromwellian-built. Equally unusual are the Rorty Crankle pub, the huge leathern furnace bellows outside forge-turned-restaurant, and a modern but half-timbered Nut Tree Hall.

To the west is Fairlawns where the Cazalet stables once trained the Queen's horses. To the east, along a narrow lane, is Old Soar Manor (NT), the remains of a rare thirteenth-century knight's house: solar, chapel, *garderobe* and vaulted undercroft. Today a handsome farm-house of rich red brick replaces the rest of the building.

East lies Gover Hill (NT), a splendid Wealden viewpoint on the tip of Mereworth Woods. South again, the shock of Mereworth Castle! A castle that is no castle but a coolly symmetrical (and *very* private) Palladian villa. And half a mile away a church (replacing the ancient one casually demolished in 1720 by the earl of Westmorland to improve his view) that is an architectural pasticcio of famous London churches

Mereworth church was razed to the ground to improve the view from this elegant Palladian 'castle'

but one whose close-set Doric columns and barrel-vaulted roof are painted frauds.

The villa has steps and statuary; Ionic columns in pedimented porches on all four sides; elegant flanking pavilions with contrasting dark cedars; and a dominant central dome between whose 'skins' run twenty-four ingenious flues – into the necessarily blind lantern above. (A sop to the English climate!) Below it are sumptuous plaster coffering, an encircling gallery and, in the long gallery, a bewildering display of illusionistic paintings.

The church flaunts St Martin-in-the-Field vigorous spire; Covent Garden's St Paul's over-generous eaves; and Deptford's St Paul's semi-circular porch. But all its own is a lunette of rich armorial glass that floods the wide nave with golden light.

West Malling (to rhyme with 'falling') lies three miles north-east. But first Offham, known better for its ancient quintain (a device for tilting target-practice that demanded keen eye and steady hand as well as swift reactions to avoid a retaliatory blow) than for its handsome Queen Anne houses.

At St Leonard's, the lone, knoll-perched tower is probably part of Gundulf's fortified manor; and the nearby pub, the 'Startled Saint', doubtless got its name from the Spitfires which in World War II roared roof-high into urgent action from the Malling fighter station. Their pilots found brief relaxation at the Twitch Inn in the cellar of Douce House on the outskirts of the town – and wrote their names on its ceiling in soot from guttering candles.

West Malling itself has a wide High Street of largely Georgian façades and, were it not for the traffic, a leisured Georgian atmosphere. St Mary's Abbey, built by architect-prelate Gundulf in 1090, still shows a massive Norman tower with pyramidal pinnacles, blind arcading and richly arcaded thirteenth-century cloisters within much simpler twentieth-century ones. It lies behind a double-arched fifteenth-century gatehouse in spacious gardens. Across the latter a well-mannered stream snakes its way past the almost windowless but effectively lit modern chapel (simply and specially designed for the returning twentieth-century nuns) before cascading through an arch alongside the main road.

East Malling's best offerings, St Mary's, Court Lodge and a Wealden house, cluster together self-effacingly in the cul-de-sac of Church Street. Equally retiring, in spacious walled grounds, is Bradbourne, with its crescent, tree-lined lake. It is a masterpiece of Queen Anne brickwork, of subtle variations of colour and texture, that stands amid the almost too perfectly aligned plots of the world-famous East Malling Fruit Growing Research Centre.

The Darent Valley

Born in the aristocratic surroundings of Squerryes Court trout lake and pools, near Westerham, the Darent finally runs its course through industrial Dartford and across dark marshes before it joins the Thames. Most of its course is a joyous one; a favoured site of the Romans; beloved by author, artist and angler alike. 'The silver Darent on whose waters clean, ten Thousand fishes play and deck his pleasant stream,' wrote Edmund Spenser. But Darent can be workaday too, revolving mill-wheels and making paper.

Its infancy more easily ties in with Westerham and Holmesdale (p. 177). Its loveliest reaches as it glides, clear and tranquil, through the gap it has gently cut through rolling fields and downland are best visited from Sevenoaks. To start from Dartford would be like reading a book backwards.

Past Vine Cricket Ground and Bat and Ball Station, the A225 takes the M25 in its stride, and so to Otford, the real Otford. Its free car-park throws in a ringside seat for weekend cricket – and impeccable 'loos'. From it, turn left for a weeping-willow-shaded pond in the middle of which a thoughtful council has raised a very detached, timber bungalow for the local ducks. It is also used on occasion for emergency landings by long-legged heron!

Beyond it is a church whose foundations are awash; whose west wall is richly decorated with no fewer than eight Polhill funeral hatchments; whose sanctuary has one of Kent's finest Easter Sepulchres bearing Tudor roses in abundance – and a single Aragon pomegranate; and whose twilight is made on occasions more golden yet by gleaming candlelit chandeliers.

Nearby is – was? – Otford's trump card, the magnificent palace. It was, so the cynics said, built, in 1515, by Archbishop Warham's 'minding to leave to posteritie such glorious monument of his worldly wealth and misbegotten treasure'. He did just that. It was so splendid that Erasmus spoke of it with awe – and Henry VIII extorted it from an aggrieved and reluctant Cranmer. Only, with regal pettishness, to dispose of it as quickly as he had acquired it, for '. . . it standeth low and is Rheumatick and is like unto Croiden which I could never be without sickness.' Still, while he revelled in the 'sound, perfect and wholesome ground' of still more magnificent Knole, it was quite good enough for his luckless courtiers.

Becket features, equally pettishly, in Otford's earlier history. Nightingales, singing out their hearts, so disturbed his devotions that he decreed that, '. . . no byrde of that kinde should ever be so bolde as to sing thereabouts'. Amends, perhaps, were made when, to improve sanitation, he struck the ground with his staff, and water gushed forth abundantly. Not so miraculous really, for Darent's valley has an unusually high water-table.

Today, with bricks stolen, lead stripped and panelling spirited away, little remains of archiepiscopal splendour: a single tower, asters and flapping washing about it, and a low cottage wall of rich Tudor brickwork with tomatoes ripening in its sheltering warmth.

Much, though, still remains down the High Street: Forge Restaurant with latticed dormers; the largely twentieth-century Bull (just one of four pubs in a bare quarter-mile) set in a sunny beer-garden and boasting a sixteenth-century fireplace magnificent enough to have once graced the archbishop's palace; a Lutyens church hall; ibex on one side of The Horns sign, and musical instrument on the other; splendid but begrimed Pickmoss, half-timbered, jettied, with stained glass and handsomely carved door; Little Oast and Water Mill eyeing each other across a clear and sparkling Darent.

The road to Shoreham swings uphill, becomes a broken white line scrawled between high hedges and opens out into little Darent's surprisingly wide valley between green fields rolling up to the Downs. Off the A225, Shoreham itself is far removed from Otford's bustle . . .

At the King's Arms, a waxen 'ostler', with billy-cock hat, striped waistcoat, clay-pipe in mouth, and brushes at the ready, still waits, ever hopeful, for the clack of horse's hooves. Beyond is the famous willow-shaded flint-and-ragstone bridge. On it, schoolboys, well provisioned with crisps and coke, 'angle' for roach, chub and gudgeon – and perhaps an errant trout from the private pond downstream. Flint Cottage, all brick and warty flints, catches the eye, but it is white-stuccoed Water House with its blue door that is famous. Here Samuel Palmer lived and painted from 1827 to 1833. And here he welcomed his 'master', visionary William Blake, when he was sick and neglected. It was the latter's mystical fervour that inspired Palmer to paint the smallest creatures as living proof of divine power. Later his contrasting masses and boldness, as in 'In a Shoreham Garden', heralded the post-Impressionists.

To the west, carved out of the chalk, is a huge war-memorial cross. The church lies past a silvern weir where the Darent emerges from beneath a densely ivy-clad wall, past the half-timbered Olde George and up a long yew-lined brick and cobble path to a porch, its arch fashioned from a single huge up-ended oak. Inside are black leathern fire buckets used by Shoreham's eighteenth-century fire brigade; a 200-year-old Parliament clock deliberately set to face the pulpit (the latter, with crocketed gables, and the organ both came from Westminster Abbey); and a Burne Jones window with graceful Botticellian figures, the only one to survive in what was one of the most bombed parishes in the south-east. Across its width runs a finely carved rood screen, 'wide enough to park a small car on'. An oil painting, surely unique, vividly depicts a surpliced vicar outside the church in 1875 welcoming a sun-tanned naval officer standing up in a carriage hauled by wildly cheering villagers. His son, Verney Lovett Cameron, Commander of the second Livingstone Relief Expedition – and first man to cross Africa from coast to coast – has come home.

On then to the diverse attractions of Lullingstone: a dead Roman villa brought to life, and a mansion steeped in living history. They are best reached through Eynsford, which lies athwart Darent at the foot of a long hill.

Eynsford has its own attractions. Its narrow hump-backed bridge,

Eynsford's hump-backed bridge, shallow, grass-banked river, and close-studded Plough: ideal ingredients for a family picnic.

younger than it looks, and behind it the close-studded gable-end of The Plough have appeared, photographed at all seasons, in more Kentish calendars than Marilyn Monroe in pin-up books.

A mile further along, a fine railway viaduct, brick-built and balustraded, strides above the valley and its peacefully grazing Highland cattle, superbly shaggy and with enquiring, upturned horns. Beyond, modern wood and perspex, centrally heated, house the cold, grey skeleton of a fourth-century Romano-British house, which beat this cocky twentieth century to saunas and under-floor heating by 1,600 years. It showed more religious tolerance too, for above its pagan deep room, with its holy spring and painted water-nymphs, was later built a chapel in 385 on whose walls are painted six figures with arms outstretched in early Christian prayer.

But the main features that make Lullingstone outstanding in Britain are the mosaics. In the dining-room, Bellerophon, murderer, slighter of a queen's passion, bestrides the winged horse Pegasus, spawned from the Medusa's blood. Beneath its feet writhes the Chimaera, lion-headed, goat-bodied, dragon-tailed. In the adjacent sitting-room there is a seemingly happier story. In carefree innocence the Phoenician princess Europa rides a white bull. Little does she know that soon the idyll will end, when Jupiter, taking on human shape again, shamelessly rapes her.

In AD 400 the villa, a civilized microcosm of distant Rome, was burned down and gradually buried by the crumbling hill above as the countryside around it reverted to the Dark Ages.

Life is brought to the villa's low grey walls by exhibits in the viewing-galleries. Busts of flat-nosed Roman aristocrats with deep-set eyes; bronze ingots; tiles bearing imprint of kitten and dog; the bones of a goose that died in a pagan ceremony; a crushed lead coffin in which lies the skeleton of a man, left with food, gaming-board and thirty glass counters to while away his journey to another life: all have survived the ravages of time.

Little more than a No. 1 iron drive from Roman Britain, modern man (and woman) plays golf. An Iron Age settlement, too, looks down on Lullingstone Castle. The latter's handsome red-brick Tudor gate-house, sturdy, turreted and battlemented though it is, was surely never meant for war. Behind its mock fierceness, all is tranquillity. To the right lies an angler's paradise, a lake formed by damming the Darent; to the left, a seemingly medieval flint chapel but with trim bell-turret and classical porch. Sweeping lawns broken only here and there by equally impressive Cedars of Lebanon front the castle, no more in reality than a large Tudor mansion with simple and symmetrical Queen Anne additions.

But it is 'small' that is even more beautiful. The tiny chapel, white save for brick courses when the roof was raised, is full of interest. Ceilings of delicate plasterwork; stained-glass windows spanning the centuries (including an unhappy St Erasmus being disembowelled – by winch); and a splendid early Tudor rood-screen. Above all there are the magnificent and memorable tombs of the Peches and Harts, whose successors still own Lullingstone. The first Sir John Peche made his fortune as a member of the Grocers' Company: a second, at twenty one, breaking fourteen lances at the royal jousts, became Henry VII's Champion, later Sheriff of Kent and taker of the upstart apprentice Perkin Warbeck to the Tower.

Back again to the main road. Below Sparepenny Lane on the hillside above it, and with silver Darent below it, stands Eynsford Castle. Its almost circular curtain walls, of coursed flints thirty impressive feet high and seven feet thick, without grace of tower or turret; its too-neat turf and gravel within; and certainly its well, filled with tin cans, lack romance. Almost derelict, cobbled up from time to time, it sank to the ignominy of being the kennels for the Hart-Dyke hounds.

A mile on, Farningham lies amid orchards and soft fruit, yet is only seventeen miles from London. Once notorious for nearby Death Hill and traffic snarl-ups, it is now a peaceful backwater whose varied charms can be enjoyed at leisure. This thanks to a bypass and, to the north, a roundabout to end all roundabouts merging M20, A20 and A225 in a maelstrom of hurrying traffic.

Single-aisled but light and airy, the church of St Peter and St Paul sets the architectural ball rolling. Of split flints patched with red brick, its flat-topped tower was raised seven inches to culminate in majestic battlements and turret. Within, Anthony Rooper, with his three sons, in painted alabaster, faces his wife across a prie-dieu – her two daughters have not survived the ravages of time. A north window, rich in gold and blue and incorporating medieval glass, was designed by Charles Winston, a vicar's eighteen-year-old son; in the west one, Charles I kneels opposite Queen Elizabeth II! The octagonal font, carved with some panache, depicts the Seven Sacraments and Mass: bride and groom hold hands; a devil roughly seizes a penitent by the shoulder; a priest anoints a dying man . . .

A lingering idea that 'Bligh of the Bounty', after his epic – but involuntary – 3,600 mile open-boat journey, lived in Farningham was reinforced when I looked at Manor House itself. L-shaped, partly ivy-clad, of warm brick with white weather-board outbuildings, it lay behind tall and forbidding iron gates. 'Strictly Private' surely did not preclude a quick peek through their bars? It didn't – but a ravening monster of an alsatian did. Surely the reincarnation of bullying, blustering, hair-trigger-temper Bligh – or closely related to the Hound of the Baskervilles. It reared up on its hind legs and, with face none too far from mine, bayed for blood – vaingloriously supported by two shrill and demented Jack Russells. Further architectural detail, I decided, was a matter hardly worth pursuing.

An undignified retreat brought us to a local mason's tongue-in-cheek joke, a miniature folly: a triple-arched flotsam-barrier, of red brick with heavy flint rustication, and bold cut-waters spanning the river. A two-dimensional bridge so narrow that only a cat could cross it.

Ahead, tree-shaded lawns of the red brick, balconied and creepered Lion Hotel, a late eighteenth-century coaching-inn, slope gently down to the mirroring Darent. Beyond it, contemporary with the Lion, the White House, strikingly picked out in black, and striking too, with bay windows on one side and Venetian on two others.

Farningham plays its trump card last. Long lawns and flower-beds bright with marigolds and salvias lead the eye to an impressive white weather-boarded mill astride the Darent. The projecting hoist below the ridge of its mansard roof is flanked and underlined by three rows of

Farningham's unusual brick-and-flint folly catches the eye as surely as it catches Darent flotsam.

Farningham's trump card: majestic Mill, consort Mill House and, of course, *'Silver Darent' itself.*

symmetrically placed windows, and there are black, fanlighted doors at ground-level. Beside it stands the elegant mill-house with white portico, bay windows and dormers behind the parapet in front of its mansard roof. Expensive grey-brick chimney-stacks were deliberately built to the front; cheaper red brick at the sides. Grain store and cottages, white weather-board again, of course (for softwood was at that time pouring from Scandinavia through Deal into Kent), flank the miller's home.

For Horton Kirby the tear-away roundabout must be braved again; then, all will be tranquillity. Farningham Wood Nature Reserve on your left, down Button Street, with its 175 acres of mixed woodland climbing to a 400-foot heathery top, is well worth a detour. Walks and rides lead you past perfumed carpets of lily of the valley, which, according to the sixteenth-century herbalist Gerard, '. . . will renovate a weak memory'; hairy wood spurge with its unusual kidney-shaped bracts; long-lived, water-hoarding orpine with its large rose-red flower-heads; Solomon's seal whose clusters of white flowers have long been held to be a specific for black eyes.

Orange-brown gatekeeper butterflies live up to their names by belligerently patrolling their hedgerow territory. Aided by a ring of bird-deceiving 'eyes', ringlets make the most of their brief two-week life-span. Woodpeckers, tits and warblers are residents, and the rarer, heavy-billed chestnut hawfinch (*coccothraustes*) makes his presence heard with an explosive 'tik'.

On the outskirts of chimney-dominated Horton Kirby is Kent's most complete Elizabethan mansion, Franks Hall. Of warm red brick, stone-quoined and dressed, on a flint base, it has a lively gabled roof line – and a Victorian turret. Darent, tumbling over tiny weirs, flows through gardens that once employed twenty men. Rebuilt in 1591, it knew stark tragedy when its founder's grandson married four times – and each time saw his wife die within months of marriage. Fortunately, though once decaying and destitute, the house has been brought to life by a Big Business fairy godmother, Findlay Technical Publications. Its highlights? Ornate plaster ceilings and a frieze of caryatid-like female figures bought from the Earl of Anglesey's Staffordshire estate – for £2. Or, perhaps, a Moorish bathroom and dressing-room?

'Sutton for Mutton,' said the old jingle, but today Sutton-at-Hone smacks of industry rather than agriculture. All the more refreshing then to turn off the bustling A225 Dartford road and suddenly find the tranquillity of St John's Jerusalem, a Knight's Hospitallers' Commandery, set in a large garden, encircled by a willow-lined Darent and shaded by fine trees including cedar and copper beech.

It was converted into a graceful house after the Dissolution by Abraham Hill (who brought cider-making from Devon to Kent). Later it hastened the bankruptcy of Kent historian Edward Hasted, who spent five years in the King's Bench prison for debt when his love of the house outran his financial prudence. The thirteenth-century flint chapel, with lancets (converted for a time into a billiard room), is still preserved and, with its garden, is open to view on Wednesday afternoons, thanks to the generosity of writer and broadcaster Sir Stephen Tallent, who gave it to the National Trust. The fourteenth-century church is worth visiting – if not for the fact that it was nearly destroyed in 1615 by fire, caused by the discharge of a gun at a bird *in* the church, then for the monumental Jacobean alabaster tomb of Sir Thomas Smythe with its Corinthian columns and reliefs of an explorer's equipment. A Merchant Adventurer in the true sense of the term, Sir Thomas earned proud titles: 'Gouvernor of ye East Indies, Treasurer for the Virginia Plantations and Prime Undertaker for that Noble Designe – the Discoverie of the North-West Passage'. And yet, for all his journeyings from Amazon to Volga, in 1625 he died of plague – in Kent.

A pleasant finale, rivalling Shoreham's riverside walks, is the Valley Path, alongside Darent and its lakes, from Farningham to the centre of Dartford (six miles).

Index

NT = National Trust; EH = English Heritage

Abbot's Fireside, 124
à Becket, Thomas, 86, 87, 89, 91, 93,
    97, 194
Acrise Place, 124
Aldington, 114
All Hallows, 27–8
Allington Castle, 44, 135
Appledore, 107
Archbishops
    à Becket, 86–91
    Bourchier, 184
    Courtenay, 46
    Cranmer, 92, 184
    Ramsey, 92
    Warham, 114, 193
Arden, Richard, 65
Ashford, 60–1
Aspinall, John, 92
Augustine, St, 84, 107, 123, 128
Aylesford, 41–3

Barfreston, 98, 99
Barham, Richard, 75, 91, 106, 107
Bates, H.E., 59, 147
Bayham Abbey, 161, 164
Bedgebury
    Forest, 152
    Pinetum, 152–3
Bekesbourne, 92
Beltring Oasts, 158–9
Benenden, 154
Bethersden, 155–6
Betteshanger, 97
Bewl Reservoir, 164
Biddenden, 145–6
Bilsington, 116

Birchington, 79–80
    Quex House, 79
Birling, 139
Bishopsbourne, 123
Black Prince, 86, 167
Blake, William, 194
Bligh, William, of the Bounty, 197–9
Boleyn, Anne, 75, 115, 170, 172
Borstal, 40–1
    HM Borstal, 40
    Foord Almshouses, 40
Bough Beech Reservoir, 172
Boughton Aluph, 131
Boughton Malherbe, 57–8
    Church, 58
    Place, 58
Boughton Monchelsea, 54
    Church, 54
    Place, 54
    Quarry Cottages, 54
Bourne Park, 122
Boxley, 135
Brabourne, 126
Brands Hatch, 140
Brasted, 181
Brenchley, 159–60
Brenzett, 107–8
Bridge, 122
Broadstairs, 82–3
    Bleak House, 82
Brompton, 37–8
    RE's Museum, 37
    School of Military Engineering, 37–8
Brook, 126
Brookland, 108–9
Broome Park, 105

Burham, 41
Burnett, Frances H., 154

Cade, Jack, 60, 93, 107, 188
Canterbury Cathedral, 86–9
　Archbishop Langton's Tomb, 86
　Bell Harry Tower, 86
　Black Prince, 86
　Christ Church Gateway, 86
　Culmer, 'Blue Dick', 87, 89
　Ernulf's Crypt, 87
　Great Cloisters, 89
　Martyrdom, 86
　Norman Staircase, 90
　Warriors' Chapel, 86
Canterbury, City of, 89–92
　Beaney Institute, 91
　Castle, 91
　Chequers of the Hope, 91
　Dane John Gardens, 89
　House of Agnes, 92
　Poor Priests Hospital, 91
　Roper Vault, 92
　St Augustine's Abbey (EH), 89
　St Martins Church, 89
　Solomon the Mercer, 92
　Weavers, The, 91
　Westgate, 89
　Westgate Gardens, 89
Castle Coote, 69
Cement, 19
Chagall, Marc, 51
Chalk Village, 23
Challock, 129
Channel Tunnel, 13, 101, 104–5, 134
Charing, 133
Charlton Park, 123
Chart, Great, 60
Chart, Little, 59
Chartham, 127
Chartwell (NT), 179–80
Chatham, 36–7
　Dockyard, 36–7
　Fort Amherst, 36
　Great Lines, 37
　St Mary's Church, 36
　Sir John Hawkins Hospital, 36

Cherries, 64
Chevening, 182–3
Chiddingstone, 173–4
Chilham, 128, 133
Chitty-Chitty-Bang-Bang, 122
Church, Richard, 45, 46, 151
Churchill, Sir Winston, 9, 178, 179, 180,
　189
Cinque Ports, 99, 103
Cliftonville, 82
Coalfields, 94
Cobham, 135–6
　Church and Brasses, 136
　Hall, 135–6
　Leather Bottle, 136
Cobtree Hall, 43
Coldrum Stones (NT), 138
Combe Bank, 182
Conrad, Joseph, 123, 125
Cooling, 28–31
　Castle, 30, 31
　St James's Church, 28
Cowden, 169
Cranbrook, 147
Cricket, 46, 48, 57, 95, 118, 122, 125,
　129, 135, 155, 183
Crundale, 127

Darent, River, 121, 177, 193, 198, 200
Darent Valley, 193–200
Dartford, 15–16
　Cricket Ground, 16
　Royal Victoria & Bull, 15
　Wat Tyler Inn, 16
du Ruyter, 25
de Septvans, Sir Robert, 127
Deal, 94–6
　Castle (EH), 95–6
　St Leonard's Church, 95
Denton, 105
Detling, 135
Devil's Kneading Trough, 126
Dickens, Charles, 23, 28, 32, 35, 36, 37,
　44, 82, 83, 92, 134, 136
Dolphin Barge Museum, 63
Donne, John, 184
Dover, 99–101

Castle (EH), 100–1
Grand Shaft, 101
Harbour, 100
Maison Dieu, 99
Painted House, 99
Pharos, 101, 102
Russell Gardens, 100
St Edmund's Chapel, 99
Dover Patrol Memorial, 96
Dowde, 137
Dr Syn, 109
Drake, Francis, 62
Dungeness, 110–13
Lighthouses, 111, 112
Power Stations, 113
Dymchurch, 113

East Farleigh, 47–8
Bridge, 47
Church, 47
East Malling, 192
East Peckham, 51
Eastchurch, 75
Eastling, 129
Eastry, 97
Eastwell Park, 131, 132
Ebbsfleet, 84
Eden, Vale of, 166–76
Edenbridge, 170
Elham, 124
Elizabeth I, Queen, 25, 58, 59, 94, 106,
147, 162
Emmetts (NT), 181
Erasmus, 87, 114
Eynsford Castle (EH), 195–6

Farningham, 197
Faversham, 65–7
Abbey Street, 65
Church, 65
Creek, 67
Town Pump, 66–7
Finchcocks, 151
Fitzherbert, Mrs, 28
Flanders Kist, 76
Fleming, Ian, 92
Folkestone, 101–3

Harbour, 103
Old Town, 103
St Eanswythe's Church, 103
The Leas, 101
Fordwich, 92
Franks Hall, 200
Frindsbury, 32
Frith, W.P., 83

Gads Hill Place, 23
'Gamecock', 70
Gillingham, 39
Jezreel's Tower, 39
William Adams Memorial, 39
Glassenbury, 149
Godinton, 60
Godmersham, 131
Goodwin Sands, 95, 155
Gordon, General, 20, 38–9
Gort, Viscount, 70, 176
Goudhurst, 151
Grafty Green, 57
Graveney Church, 68
Gravesend, 20–3
New Tavern Fort, 22
Tilbury Ferry, 22
Tugs, 22
Windmill Hill, 23
'Gravy Boat', 68
Great Expectations, 29
Greatstone-on-Sea, 112
Greenhithe Merchant Navy College, 18
Greenwich Royal Naval College, 15
Groombridge, 167

Hadlow Folly, 51
Halstow, High, 28
Halstow, Lower, 63
Harrietsham, 134
Harris, Lord, 129
Harrys, Richard, 64
Harty Ferry, 65
Harty, Isle of, 76
Harvey, William, 102–3
Hastingleigh, 125
Hawkhurst, 153
Hawkinge Aerodrome, 105

Headcorn, 144–5
Hengist & Horsa, 42
Henry VIII, 64, 92, 95, 115, 125, 133,
    158, 162, 170, 174, 186, 193
Herne, 71
Herne Bay, 71
Hever Castle, 170–2
High Halden, 155
High Rocks, 166
Hilder, Rowland, 139
Hogarth, 73
Hole Park, 154
Hollingbourne, 134
Holy Maid of Kent, 114
Hoo Peninsula, 24–31
Hoo St Werburgh, 25
Hooker, Richard, 123
Hop, the, 158
Horsmonden, 160–1
Hothfield, 60
Howletts Zoo, 92
Hugin, 84
Hurricane, 1987, 13, 99
Hythe, 103

Ightham, 188–9
Ightham Mote (NT), 189–91
Iguanodon, 45, 120
Invicta, 69
Ironworks, 160, 162, 169
Isle of Grain
    BP Refinery, 24, 27
    Power Station, 27

James II, 67
Jumpitty-Gee-Gee Boy, Sir, 156

Kemsley, 140
Kent & East Sussex Railway, 155
Kilndown Church, 151–2
Kingsferry Bridge, 72
Kingsnorth Power Station, 25–6
Kitchener, Field-Marshal, Lord, 36,
    105
Kits Coty House (EH), 41
Knatts Valley, 140
Knole (NT), 147, 184–8

Korker's sausages, 154
Kossowski, Otto, 43

Lamberhurst, 161–2
Leeds Castle, 65
Leigh, 173
Lenham, 133
Leysdown, 76
Lindbergh, Colonel, 182
Little Hoppers Hospital, 158
Littlestone, 112
Loose, 53
Lords Warden of the Cinque Ports, 95,
    113
Lower Stoke, 27
Luddesdown, 137
Lugworms, 69
Lullingstone Castle, 196–7
Lullingstone Roman Villa (EH), 196
Lydd, 110
Lympne, 113
Lyttleton, Hon. Alfred, 119

Maidstone, 45–7
    All Saints Church, 46
    Archbishops' Stables, 45
    Crest, 44–5
    Mote Hall, 46
    Old Palace, 45
Manston, 85
Margate, 77, 80–2
    Bembon's Amusements, 80
    Caves, 80
    Grotto, 80
    Harbour, 82
    Tudor House, 81
Matfield, 159
Maugham, Somerset, 71
Medway, River, 40–52
Meopham, 136–7
Mereworth Castle and Church, 191–2
Mersham, 126
Milstead, 130–1
Milton Regis, 63
Minnises, The, 125
Minster (Sheppey), 74
Minster (Thanet), 85

More, Sir Thomas, 92
Mynn, Alfred, 135

Nelson, Admiral, Lord, 41, 74
Nettlestead, 48–9
New York, 129
Newman, John, 17, 46, 59, 104, 119, 173
Newnham, 129–30
Nobody, 54
North Downs, 121–42
North Downs Way, 101
North Foreland Lighthouse, 82
Northfleet, 19
    Associated Portland Cement, 19
    Rosherville Gardens, 19
    St Botolph's Church, 19
Northwood Hill Nature Reserve, 28

Oare, 64–5
Old Romney, 109
Ospringe Maison Dieu (EH), 64
Otford, 193
Otham, 54
Owl House Gardens, 161
Owletts (NT), 136
Oxney, Isle of, 119
Oysters, 63, 70

Paddock Wood, 159
Penshurst, 174–6
Pepys, Samuel, 34, 36, 73
Pilgrims, 87, 89
Pilgrims Way, 138
Plaxtol, 191
Pluckley, 58–9
PLUTO, 112
Pocahontas, 20
Port Lympne House and Safari Park, 114
Pugin, A.W.N., 83–4

Quebec House (NT), 178
Queenborough, 73

Ragstone, 54
Ramsgate, 83–4

Rano Ridibunda, 110
Ransley, George, 115, 170
Reader, Alfred, 48
Reculver (Regulbium), 78–9
Richborough Castle (EH), 93
Ridley, Bishop, 71
Riverhill House, 188
Rochester, 32–6
    Bridge, 35
    Castle (EH), 34–5
    Cathedral, 32–4
    Corn Exchange, 35
    Eastgate House, 35
    Guildhall, 35
    M2 Bridge, 35
    Royal Victoria & Bull, 35–6
    Watts Charity, 35
Rolls, Hon. Charles, 75, 100
Rolvenden, 154
Romans, 93, 94, 99, 101, 105, 113, 120, 122, 124, 166, 196
Romney, Hythe & Dymchurch Railway, 103, 122
Romney Marsh, 106, 120
Royal Military Canal, 103, 107
Royal St George's Golf Club, 94

Sackville-West, Vita, 147–8
St Augustine's Abbey (EH), 89, 153
St John Jerusalem (NT), 200
St Margaret at Cliffe and St Margaret's Bay, 97
St Mary-in-the-Marsh, 113
St Mary's Hoo, 28
Saltwood Castle, 104
Sandgate, 102
Sandwich, 93–4
Sarre, 85
Scotney Castle (NT), 163–4
Sea-bathing, 80
Sevenoaks, 183–4
Sevenoaks Weald, 182
Sharp, Dr Leonell, 58
Sheerness, 72–3
'Shelley, Miss', 186
Sheppey, Isle of, 72–6
Shoreham, 194–5

Shorne, 23
Sidney, Sir Philip, 174
Sissinghurst Castle (NT), 145–8
Sittingbourne Light Railway, 63–4
Slaughterhouse Point, 63
Smallhythe Place (NT), 118–19
Smarden, 143
Smugglers, 115
Snave, 107
Snodland, 139
Squeeryes Court, 177–9
Stansted, 138
Statham, Colonel, 53
Stone-in-Oxney, 119
Stone Lodge Farm Park, 16–17
Stone-next Dartford, 17
   St Mary's Church, 17
Stoneacre (NT), 54
Stour, River, 121, 124, 128, 131
Strood, 32
Sullivan, Arthur, 60
Sundridge, 181
Surrenden Dering, 59
Sutton Valence, 56–7
   Castle, 57
   Church, 57
   School, 56
Swale, 72
Swanscombe, 18
Swing, Captain, 125

Tenterden, 117, 118, 155
Terry, Ellen, 118–19
Teston, 48
Teynham, 64
Thanet, Isle of, 77–85
Throwley, 129
'Thunderer', the, 158
Thurnham, 135
Toke, Nicholas, 60
Tonbridge, 51–2
   Castle, 51
   School, 52
Tovil, 47
Toys Hill, 180
Trottiscliffe (Trosley), 138
Tudely, 51

Tullis, Julie, 166
Tunbridge Wells, 156–7
Tyler, Wat, 16, 91, 107

Ulcombe, 57
Union Mill, Cranbrook, 149–50
Upchurch, 62
Upnor Castle (EH), 25

Van Gogh, Vincent, 83
Vandals, 99, 112, 145
Victoria, Queen, 27, 83
Victory, 37

Wade, Virginia, 130
Waldershare, 99
Walmer Castle and Garden (EH), 96
Waltham, 125
Wantsum, 62
Warden Point, 75–6
Warehorne, 106–7
Wateringbury, 48
Weald, The, 143–65
Webb, Captain, 100
West Malling, 192
Westerham, 178
Westwell, 133
Whitstable, 69–70
'Who, Dr', 58
Who'd A Thought It Inn, 57
Wichling, 130
Wickhambreux, 92
Willes, John, 57
Wingham, 92–3
Wittersham, 119
Wolfe, General, 178
Woodchurch, 116
Woolwich Thames Barrier, 15
Wotton, Sir Henry, 58
Wrotham, 141
Wye, 127

Yalding, 49–50
Yellow Hands Girls, 67
Yevele, Henry, 46

Zborowski, Count Vorow, 120
Zeebrugge Disaster, 97